AT HOME IN THE WORLD

Zurich Lecture Series in Analytical Psychology

Murray Stein and Nancy Cater, Co-editors

SPRING JOURNAL BOOKS
NEW ORLEANS, LOUISIANA

ISAPZURICH

INTERNATIONAL SCHOOL OF
ANALYTICAL PSYCHOLOGY ZURICH

AT HOME
IN THE WORLD

*Sounds and Symmetries
of Belonging*

JOHN HILL

Spring Journal Books
New Orleans, Louisiana

Published by
Spring Journal, Inc.
627 Ursulines Street #7
New Orleans, Louisiana 70116
Tel.: (504) 524-5117
Website: www.springjournalandbooks.com

Cover photo: "Narrow Gate" © Andreasg/Dreamstime.com
Cover design: Ann Lowe, www.annlowe.com

Printed in Canada
Text printed on acid-free paper

ISBN 978-1-935528-00-5
Library of Congress Cataloging-in-Publication Data Pending

Contents

Editors' Foreword

The Zurich Lecture Series in Analytical Psychology was established in 2009 by the International School of Analytical Psychology Zurich (ISAPZURICH) and Spring Journal Books for the purpose of presenting, annually, a significant new work by a selected Jungian psychoanalyst or scholar who has previously offered innovative contributions to the field of analytical psychology by either:

- bringing analytical psychology into meaningful dialogue with other scientific, artistic, and academic disciplines;

- showing how analytical psychology can lead to a better understanding of contemporary global concerns relating to the environment, politics, religion; or

- expanding the concepts of analytical psychology as they are applied clinically.

For the Series, the selected lecturer delivers lectures over a two-day period in Zurich based on a previously unpublished book-length work, which is then published by Spring Journal Books.

We are pleased to publish *At Home in the World: Sounds and Symmetries of Belonging*, by John Hill, as the inaugural volume in the Series.

—Murray Stein and Nancy Cater
Editors, Zurich Lecture Series

Acknowledgments

No book can be created by one person alone, as implied by Aleksandr Solzhenitsyn in his preface to *The Gulag Archipelago*, which was a kind of monstrous abode that he grew to love. In the incubation period of writing this book, I found myself becoming a mouthpiece to many voices, visible and invisible. I would like first to thank the many clients whose anonymous voices can be heard throughout this work as they narrate their tales of homes lost or regained. I remain grateful to all those writers whom I have referenced and who have provided important building material in the framing of this book. A special thanks to Fritz Senn, Sabine Müller, and Ron Erward from the James Joyce Foundation of Zürich, who reawakened my love of contemporary Irish literature and poetry. John O'Donohue has been a source of invaluable inspiration. When he was alive, he would often insist that I write on this subject. His death in January 2009 was a shock to all. In moments of trial and despair, I have sought his help and the needed words fell from heaven.

I am grateful to all those colleagues and friends who provided input in unexpected, random encounters. In the course of writing this work, I have received much inspiration from my colleagues at ISAP (International School of Analytical Psychology, Zurich) and from the continual flow of ideas from the IAJS (International Association for Jungian Studies) discussion list. Many thanks to Mario Jacoby for his insights and his appreciation on the book's back cover. My friend Mark Patrick Hederman kept encouraging me to write; Laura Thayer, Mary Tomlinson, and Stan Fineman provided important insights; Stacy Wirth and Isabelle Meier helped with publication details; and Michael Hill furnished invaluable technical assistance. I remain indebted to Annemarie Hill for supplying a significant vignette, which greatly enhanced the quality of the work. Without the suggestions and careful editing work of Miriam Martineau Mason, Finn Hill, and Simon Mason the book would not have achieved the fluency it has today. I would like to acknowledge especially the untiring work of Sylvia Ruud, who did the final editing of the entire work. Her sensitivity to this subject, her invaluable suggestions, and her eye for detail brought this work to completion.

After my twenty years of pondering on the imponderable subject of home, Nancy Cater, after hearing a lecture I gave on the subject, said she would like to publish my book. Nancy lost her home in Hurricane Katrina, including all the photos from her childhood. Returning to the place she loved, she discovered everywhere signs of dead nature, dead people, dead homes. There are no words to describe such devastation, but I would hope that certain passages in this book might bring some relief to the pain of all those who have suffered a similar loss. In 2009, Nancy and Murray Stein announced the Zurich Lecture Series, launched by ISAPZURICH and Spring Journal Books, and invited me to present the inaugural lectures, eventually to be published by Spring. Now there was no escape. The wholehearted support of Nancy Cater, the helpful suggestions of Murray Stein, and a deadline for delivery did the trick, and so began the final phase of bringing this work to completion.

Finally, I would like to say that I coined the title of this book in an article, published in the *Journal of Analytical Psychology* in 1996, only to discover much later that it was the title of a chapter in Laurens van der Post's *Feather Fall*, published by Penguin in 1994. The subtitle is my own creation, which I contributed to Part I of *Intimacy: Venturing the Uncertainties of the Heart*, Jungian Odyssey Series, Vol. 1, published by Spring.

—John Hill

PART I

HOME: WOMB OF MANY STORIES

CHAPTER 1

Introduction

Dimmi che casa hai, e ti diro chi sei.
Tell me about your house, and I will tell you who you are.
—An Old Italian Saying

Are you at home anywhere? Do you need a home? Do you need to search for some person, some place, or something to which you can say: You are mine and I am yours? Have you ever asked what happens to you when you feel estranged from yourself or others? Do you feel you have been thrown into a world that sometimes makes or breaks you? Has the grounding anchor of home brought relief and safety, or has it become a place of captivity? Some experience a golden beginning, brought up in a secure, loving home. Others witness their early surroundings as a wasteland. Without a look or gesture of recognition, their depleted heart and mind retreat into a world of silence. Life becomes a matter of survival, or sometimes a matter of living the life of others without even knowing it. Regardless of whether one has had a good or bad beginning in life, the purpose of this book is to encourage those who are in search of home to continue the quest, for ultimately you are searching for the ground of your being.

The following chapters cannot do justice to all that can be said about home. I will, however, refer to material from diverse disciplines in order to understand the implications of an inexhaustible subject. My work can be considered a personal, philosophical, and psychological appraisal of home, its purpose being to remain focused on central questions: What does it mean to be at home in the world? How can we achieve this without denying the unexpected twists and turns of fortune, and ultimately the reality of death? Authentic reflection on home can only be grounded in personal experience. This book is not a pedagogical instrument of explanation; it simply bears witness to a life lived from the perspective of the loss and rediscovery of home. The thesis here presented approximates more to a work of art than a scientific paper. It can be likened to a "mosaic substratum," a term coined by a colleague who has written extensively on the subject, describing the complex relationship of home and identity.[1] Although emphasis will be on the inner dimensions of home, this book will explore the interweaving between the inner and outer home as encountered in the symbolic space between self and the world.

Home may be appreciated and understood as a narrative reality. There are personal narratives about the ways people have found or lost their home in the world. Then there are stories about actual houses —their history, architecture, and significance in the life of those who dwell in them. Finally there are the archetypal narratives of home, which have determined the identity of cultures and nations over generations. In this short introduction I will evoke images describing all three aspects of home: home expressing the ways individuals or groups attach to a place, person, or object; home as the transformation of the object house into a space of belonging; and home as attachment to a nation, culture, or ideal.

Regardless of whether we hear or see home in a myth, story, or work of art, its sounds and symmetries awaken perennial questions concerning who we are, where we have come from, and where we are going. We need to reflect on narratives about home, to understand more about the way home structures our identity. With the loss or gain of homes, we discover that our sense of self is continually changing. This book will explore the inner psychological dimensions of home, reflected in personal and collective narratives, as well as in the actual circumstances of our times. Many narratives reveal a remarkable creativity. They seem to tell us that despite loss, we can survive transitions and welcome new landscapes that will become our very own. As a dynamic principle, subject to the unpredictability of life's changing landscapes, the meaning of home cannot be understood solely as an outer or inner reality. We become conscious of it in a space between the outer and inner, the old and the new. As a symbol it mediates between outer reality and inner truth. We need objects to embody home; with their loss, home gains significance as a predisposition to create a new one. The longing to belong expresses a dimension of the soul, transcending the limited horizons of waking life.

HOME: A NARRATIVE REALITY

The biological origins of home are found in the animal's instinct to mark territory. When faced with a predator, animals will react with fear and defend their lairs, dens, or burrows. The emergence of the longing for home in humans can be traced to attachment and affiliation instincts, which later determine our feelings toward home through the ways we bond with people, places, and objects, all consolidating a sense of narrative identity and continuity.

Once over the threshold, the particular atmosphere of a home begins to tell tales about the life of its inhabitants. We learn about homes that are full of life, homes that are empty, homes of fear, homes of love, erotic homes, stuffy homes, homes that are chaotic, homes that are impeccable, homes expressing status, homes that are humble. The list is endless. Many are the personal narratives that bear testimony to the intimate significance of home, shedding much light on the formation of personal identity.

The following home narratives express nostalgia for the past, relief from the conflict of belonging to two places, a never-ending search, and a connection with soul. One woman remembered her childhood home as the only one worth living for. She grew up on a farm in the mountains, but now lives in the city. Her apartment is full of memorabilia of her first home. She always has to return to the mountains to recapture a sense of belonging. A woman from Slovenia had this to say about her two homes: "Slovenia is my country of origin and Switzerland the country where I work. When I live in one, I long for the other. When I travel, I am in a third space. In the space between Switzerland and Slovenia, I can feel home, because I am free from the conflicting question of belonging." A business executive described his dilemma about home as follows: "Home for me has been different airports, different countries. I never give up the hope that one day I can settle somewhere with someone." A woman from Eastern Europe visualized home as an odyssey: "I have lived in different countries and different homes and I could not settle in any one of them.

There was a time when I thought that without an outer home I had no place to belong. Maintaining connection with my soul is my true home. I can make a home out of any space where I feel settled, or out of any work that is meaningful and fulfilling."

Some people tell frightening tales about never having a home; others believe they are incapable of ever having one. Some will talk about traumatic experiences when leaving old homes; others express the unbearable pain of not being able to assimilate the new. Many tales reveal the need of home as a space of warmth and protection, particularly in the beginning of life. Intimacy nourishes the heart and furthers trust in human relationships. Family ties in homes can, however, be deceptive, especially for those in weaker positions. Once trust is abused, the heart is broken and a world falls apart. It is hard to imagine what went on in the minds of the wife and children of Josef Fritzl (arrested 26 April 2008) when they discovered that the missing daughter and sister and her children had been enslaved for twenty-four years in the cellar of their own house. Close relationships open the heart—if that heart connection is misused, different forms of splitting can ensue, usually having a devastating effect on any future attempts to develop intimacy with oneself and one's surroundings.

For most people, however, home is nourished from memories of intimate attachments to parents, caretakers, family, or loved ones. Eventually, you find traces of home in affiliation to a clan, community, nation, or landscape. The soul's need for home reveals a remarkable plasticity, even extending beyond a particular person, family, or nation. Some people, for example, find home in attachment to a favorite animal. For one woman, home was a stable. She had a closer connection with her horse than with her parents. There are also narratives in which home is neither place nor person but the way something is expressed. Home becomes a beautiful piece of music, a painting, an icon, a myth, a fairy tale, an embrace, a moment of deep emotional rapport. The well-known cabaret entertainer Georg Kreisler once claimed he could live well without having a home. Kreisler lived in several countries, but did not belong to any one of them. Home for Kreisler is the German language, music, and friends.[2] Some will say that home is not of this earth. Home is connection with the ancestors or with those loved ones who have gone on before us. Home as heaven; home as God.

Home can also be a particular landscape—an intimate memory of a mountain, sea, desert, or village. The following narrative describes the journey home of a young North American woman—a journey through a landscape imbued with archetypal myth and symbol, a journey that led her into a landscape of the heart in which self and other were scarcely distinguishable. She reconnected with her origins and the living universe responded.

> I went home recently and felt its significance for the first time. I never thought I would want to go back there, but as soon as I did and saw the landscape of my childhood home, I felt I never wanted to leave. As I drove through the open countryside, a moose blocked my way. She wouldn't move, and after some time it dawned on me this could be the welcome of the Earth Mother. When I arrived at our house, I climbed up a hill to my favorite place. From there I could "see" the rolling prairies, the buffaloes, and Indian tepees. This was my landscape and not the lush green woods and fields of Europe. I sat down and heard the wild geese flying south. I could have stayed there forever. When I was in Europe, and probably because of analysis, something changed in me. I have connected to the Earth Mother and am now capable of feeling at home—something I could never do before.

For some, home is an expanse—the body, an inner life, planet Earth, or a space in which to create. There are those who need an empty space in order to connect with something that they can call their own. Other home narratives are about being on the move. A woman once told me she had never stayed for more than a few years in one place. Already as a child, her encounters with the new, the foreign, or the alien were like a second home for her. She could not bear to stay too long in one place, and always felt curious to explore homes beyond the horizon. For another woman, home became her suitcase. She was the daughter of a diplomat, and the family constantly changed homes. Every time a move was imminent, she would pack her treasures in a little suitcase. She still takes that suitcase with her wherever she goes. Home may take on the significance of a place of exile, a pilgrimage, or being a nomad—a frame of mind so aptly expressed in the words of a Native American: "I can place my tepee anywhere in the world because my soul is at one with the earth."

Regardless of whether we find home in a cardboard box or in a palace, each home narrative reveals a unique human destiny. Memories of home release a life story. Some stories are less dramatic than others; few take home for granted. These few are more likely to be found in an ever-shrinking segment of the population, consisting of people who have never

moved, never changed their abode. There are also those who never see
beyond their accustomed home. When confronted with what they consider alien, their heart clams up. They become insecure and cannot
explore the riches that lie beyond their traditional environment. Home
can then become an ideology, a belief about keeping things the way they
have always been. Their devotion to fixed patterns prevents the heart
from being open to new experiences. The stranger, the migrant, and the
refugee are perceived as a threat, and everything is done to keep such people, especially if they are from another race or culture, out of their home
and out of their heart.

It would, of course, be absurd to suggest that all those who never leave
their native home are ensnared in some kind of ideological system. Some
are rather like old trees that have never been uprooted. Their innermost
being reflects their surroundings, as tales of their heart reveal the unfathomable richness of their environment. Cézanne renders this visible in
his painting of the gardener Vallier. He places him in a garden of magnificent form and color, all reflected in his face and clothes. Vallier's body
and clothes are scarcely distinguished from their surroundings. This way
of being is beautifully illustrated in Robin Flower's description of Thomas O'Crithin, the poet who lived on the Great Blasket, a rocky island off
the Irish coast. In his poem "Thomas," Flower speaks of the cultural
importance of the island, describing it as a last untouched egg of Neolithic
civilization.

> He had lived on the Island sixty years
> And those years and the Island lived in him,
> Graved on his flesh, in his eye dwelling,
> And moulding all his speech,
> That speech witty and beautiful
> And charged with the memory of so many dead.
> Lighting his pipe he turned,
> Looked at the bay and bent to me and said:
> "If you went all the coasts of Ireland round,
> It would go hard to you to find
> Anything else so beautiful anywhere;
> And often I am lonely,
> Looking at the Island and the gannets falling
> And to hear the sea-tide lonely in the caves.
> But sure 'tis an odd heart that is never lonely."[3]

As we can imagine, home narratives are not always happy narratives.

In today's world we increasingly hear tales of loss, abandonment, estrangement, exile, and mass-migration. The stories of the uprooted peoples of our fast-moving times have made home a key issue, and they force us to reflect anew on human destiny. Today we are likely to encounter dramatic tales among those who have suffered loss of home and are continually on the move. Indeed, home reveals a quest for identity. Once one is deprived of home, the search for home and its significance may become a lifelong one. Intimate emotional experiences, connected with the loss or gain of a particular home, throw us back upon ourselves, compelling us to reflect on the purpose and meaning of life. I am grateful to all those who shared with me tales about their search for home and especially to those clients and students whose tales of home achieved dramatic proportions. Their sufferings, endurance, and inspiration served as an indispensable source in my endeavors to do justice to this great theme of humanity. The despair and joy connected with peoples' real life narratives have helped to further my efforts in enquiry and research, and opened up the universal, cultural dimensions of the longing for home.

HOME: AN OBJECT TO POSSESS?

As an archetypal theme, the significance of home extends into all areas of human life: person, landscape, culture, nationhood, town, or a particular house. Most people consider home as something tangible, intimately connected with their everyday behavior. Home can be the actual abode we live in, be it a tent, trailer, house, apartment, or palace. The architectural design, size, interior décor, and comfort of a home reveal the different ways people eat, dress, work, and live. Homes convey information about customs, habits, and culture. On my travels I have seen many houses that made me wonder about the people who lived in them. I found it hard to imagine any kind of comfort in the turf huts of nineteenth-century Ireland, privacy in a yurt of Mongolia, or intimacy in the one bed shared by an extended family in the preserved historical houses of Tbilisi, Georgia.

Home, from a psychological viewpoint, represents the way we contain our life and define our relationship to the outside world. The actual interior of our homes in present-day Western culture is ideally a haven of memory, history, and grounding, an oasis of individual taste and culture. Jhumpa Lahiri describes the dweller in such a home: "She has the gift of accepting her life...she has never wished she were anyone other than herself, raised in any other place, in any other way." [4] We need personal space and time for rest and composure to recapture those parts of the soul that have been overwhelmed by all the pressure of the outside world. The need can be reflected in the kind of dwelling we choose, the way we arrange its space, or the type of furniture we possess. At home in one's own space, a person tends to ask: Does this place fit me? Is something missing? Do I feel relaxed, content, and at ease in the space I have made my home? The individual home, created as a shelter of containment and comfort, can prevent fragmentation of a life continually exposed to a world full of distractions.

The architecture, interiors, and decoration of homes have undergone radical changes in the course of history. The idea of home, known today as a place of domestic privacy, intimacy, and comfort of family life, has evolved over hundreds of years, in contrast to Witold Rybczynski's description of the homes in Medieval Europe as a venue for public affairs. Many of the houses consisted of one large room open to the rafters with "no specialized functions." [5] It was a place where many people would come together to work, eat, or sleep. There was practically no privacy and very little family life. The concept of childhood hardly existed. Children would usually be sent away to undergo an apprenticeship at the age of seven. In the seventeenth and eighteenth centuries, houses became transformed into homes, approximating the ones we know today. Their interiors emitted an atmosphere of tranquility, orderliness, and intimacy. Rooms were allotted specific functions, which allowed the inhabitants to be alone and pursue their individual interests—perhaps best expressed in the atmosphere of inwardness to be found in the portraits of that time. As schooling increased in significance, children were no longer sent away at an early age, thus securing the importance of family life. [6] Rybczynski is convinced that the change from the public feudal household to private family life signaled a transformation that "marked the emergence of something new in the human consciousness: the appearance of the internal world of the individual, of the self, and of the family." [7]

Humans have always needed a shelter to protect them from outside influences. Even if a family home erects a boundary between outer public life and an inner private life, a collective influence often enters "by the back door." This can be witnessed in the many standard styles of furnishings throughout the centuries, which do not reflect individual taste, but instead are a reflection of the fashion of a particular time. In addition, boundaries do not always work, especially when confronted with the compelling presence of electronic media and entertainment. Often one finds oneself flooded or fascinated by alien influences that prevent one from feeling at home in one's own house. The archetypal attachment to home lends itself to continual exploitation through the advertising and consumerism of our times. Just as the Medieval and Renaissance human used furniture not for comfort, but to consolidate his or her status in the world, we are still urged to arrange the innermost spaces of our home in terms of gaining one up on the neighbor.

Interior decoration is now offered as a collective style, sold with the exotic allure of "Arabian Nights," "Jungle Wonder," or "Hawaiian Dream," thriving on a short-lived fascination encountered in images of the tourist trade. One has the impression that something is missing when people model their home on some faraway land or some unreachable future. When a home becomes a mere product, dissociated from one's personal and collective history, it is probably in danger of losing its soul. What then happens to its inhabitants? Rybczynski believes that the need for domestic well-being is deeply rooted, and if that need is not "met in the present" people will look for security and "comfort in tradition," even if that tradition has to be invented.[8]

Many people do not have the privilege of owning their own house. Collective movements have nourished delusions of possessing a secure home. The recent U.S. financial crisis with worldwide implications evolved largely from the dream of owning your own home. Bankers resorted to all kind of means in order to exert pressure on people to buy a house. Credit was offered at ridiculous conditions to individuals who had no means of paying it back. The dream of your own home, often symbolizing a search for a haven of intimacy and peace, became a nightmare for many as the world economy plunged into a massive recession. A downward spiral commenced as more and more homeowners were unable to pay their mortgages and were forced to leave their homes. At this stage, no one knows where this will end. The tragedy might have been averted if those concerned had approached the archetypal longing for home with more care, concern, and psychological understanding.

HOME: AN ARCHETYPAL THEME

Home and homelessness have been cherished themes for novelists, poets, musicians, and artists. The twin themes give rise to grand narratives about the continual making and breaking of the heart. As we dwell on the significance of home, we discover that we are born not only into a particular family, but also into a particular culture. Our parents and teachers convey to us a set of cultural canons and beliefs that we may take for granted, but they often determine our most fundamental attitudes to life as we, for better or for worse, absorb the ideals of prophets, priests, philosophers, or political leaders. The biblical exile from the Garden of Eden, the search for the Promised Land, the Babylonian captivity, and the lamentations of Jeremiah—all bear witness to joy or grief over homes gained or lost. The wanderings of the homesick Odysseus, exiled from his beloved homeland by the winds of Poseidon, his lamentations for Penelope on the rocks of Malta, and his final return home represent yet another great story of humanity's quest for home. Epic tales, whether conceived by one man or written over generations, are narratives of endurance. The vision of a cherished homeland and the faith and courage of prophets, priests, and warriors in following this vision did much to shape the character of the Hebraic and Greek peoples, as Virgil's tale of the homeless Aeneas, the celebrated founder of Rome, later did for the Romans. The Hebraic "Never forget" is an example of the power of a cultural memory that has bonded a people over thousands of years.

Home has also been an important theme in religion, philosophy, anthropology, politics, sociology, and psychology. Great religious leaders—Buddha, Christ, Saint Francis of Assisi, Mother Teresa, and their followers—left the comforts of a secure shelter and devoted their lives to alleviating the sufferings of their homeless brothers and sisters. Philosophers, especially existentialist philosophers, describe humanity as being thrown into existence. A sense of alienation from one's environment has motivated humans to pose those fundamental questions: Who am I? Where have I come from? Where am I going? Anthropologists have thrown into relief the significance of ritual and sacred space in defining the clan membership and cultural identity of various indigenous peoples throughout the world. The anthropologist Victor Turner, observing the ritual practices of people celebrating together, "was primarily excited by group life itself, life as expressed in lived-through experiences of the participants. Here lay all of those contradictory features that gave humans the ability to laugh and cry together."[9]

Leaders of nations have waged wars in the name of "the homeland," not always in defense of their nation, but in pursuit of conquest, often ruthlessly destroying the homelands of those whom they subjugate. Politicians and sociologists have wrestled with the problems of population upheaval and mass migration. Today many millions are homeless and in search of a new home. Studies have shown that the process of finding home in a new cultural landscape involves a painful and complex passage of time and is often trans-generational.[10] As an archetypal theme, the hunger to belong embraces all aspects of life. You might have experienced home in positive or negative ways; inevitably it has formed and fashioned the fabric of your life.

THE SOUL'S LONGING TO BELONG

Those who own their house can enjoy the dream of transforming it into a home. Home, however, cannot be reduced to the house we possess. Regardless of whether we have had a nourishing or challenging beginning in life, or whether we actually possess a house or not, most of us will inevitably face the challenge of homes, lost or gained. Some people will have difficulty letting go of the old one; others will celebrate the opportunity to make new homes their very own. Transitions are often difficult. They are the moments when all seems lost, empty, uncontained. We are not created to remain in a void, yet in those liminal moments, when our very being seems to be unhoused, fundamental questions arise concerning the meaning of home. As we move through the stages of life, at the end we face ultimate questions. Do we belong anywhere, to anyone? Is the graveyard our ultimate abode? Is our final destiny simply to live on in the memories of others? Do we have a home in another world beyond life on earth?

In this book you will read about dreams, memories, and experiences that describe the inner dimensions of home, the main topic of this book, even as the inner home may be reflected in outer homes and vice versa. Despite loss, the soul weaves the threads of being at home in the world into a fabric of identity. The French philosopher Gaston Bachelard describes the space that is seized upon by the creative imagination as a transformation of abstract and indifferent space into inhabited space. He describes an archetypal house that "stretches from the earth to the sky," from the womb of the earth to the heights of the spirit, symbolizing an aspect of human existence that eclipses transiency.[11] As a poetic image and symbol prior to conscious thought, it transcends memories of the actual houses we have inhabited. In moments when memory and imagination unite and the past co-penetrates into the present, home becomes a multi-variant symbol of the intimate values of inside space. Through the metaphor of home we discover the structure and intentions of the human soul. Homes of stones and mortar become homes made of subtle elements, creating symbolic edifices, surpassing the house we actually possess.

I would like to illustrate such a process, one that happened to me several years ago. Sometimes the soul attaches itself to some object connected with the need of home, and won't let go of it until one understands its hidden purpose. I once saw an exquisite Kelim rug on a visit to Turkey. At the time, I did not want to buy a rug; my home was already cluttered, and I had no idea what I could do with it. However, as I looked closer, I became so enthralled with the rug that I started bargaining in the accustomed oriental manner. Finally we had reached a price that might still have been too high, but was reasonable for this object of beauty. I hesitated, and muttered doubts about its being too heavy to carry. The owner immediately dispelled them, promising to pack the rug in a light bag—all included in the price! I could no longer avoid making a decision. I ruminated back and forth until I finally decided not to buy it. I walked back to the boat about to depart for Greece, fully convinced I had made the right choice. On the long journey back, belief in my ability to make a reasonable decision began to fall apart. I could not let go of the image of the rug. I was obsessed with it. It became for me the most beautiful carpet in the world. Worse still, I was convinced this was my carpet; I had made an awful mistake by not buying it. I kept "seeing" its simple design: green patterns in the center and around its fringes on a background of light beige, all beautifully woven in intricate ways. The restlessness continued until the following morning. I knew I was in the grip of a complex.

I finally decided I would have to resolve this issue, and spent the rest of the day meditating on what to do. Why was this rug so important? Why was I convinced I should have bought it? Why could I not let go?—after all, it was only a rug. I then focused on what I remembered of the rug, and slowly realized that it was the colors and simple pattern that caught me on a deeper level. The light beige was the color of the Aegean Islands; the green was that of Ireland, my original homeland. I love these two places; my soul belongs to them in profound ways. I knew I could not let go of the rug until I understood what my soul was trying to say. In a kind of daze, a voice in me called out: "I am at home in these lands, in the rocks of the Aegean and the fields of Ireland. I love this carpet because it is me, your soul—your life that you must take with you wherever you go." After emerging from this reverie, the obsession to buy the carpet disappeared. The artist who had made this thing of beauty had also to let it go. The exquisite carpet became facets of soul, as originally in the mind and hands of the person who wove it. I knew too well that I could not possess the threads of my identity as I would possess a material object. The encounter with that magic carpet took but a few hours. Its significance will extend over a lifetime. I no longer need to possess more material objects in order to secure a sense of home. Letting go can be a way of opening up new horizons. In this last phase of my life, I hope to understand more about that magic event so that my life may express the beauty, colors, and patterns of the lovely Kelim rug.

A Space Between

In this book I do not claim that an inner home is the solution to all the problems connected with the sense of belonging. If your inner home is dissociated from the outer one, you risk losing connection with reality and may be in for some unpleasant surprises. There is a danger that your inner home becomes a rigid system, an ideology, which brooks no contradictions. You may fall a victim of that fatal error in believing you possess the one final truth.

One thing is clear: We are not made to live in isolation. It is impossible, however, to find one answer to deal with the world's complexity. Home cannot be exclusively reduced to either an inner or outer reality. Human life is a paradox, a strange mixture of many elements, none of them being complete in themselves. One of the main points of this book is that *the significance of home becomes conscious at the point of intersection of the inner and outer*. It is there that we catch a glimpse of its meaning, perhaps to lose it, but eventually to regain it on another level. Narratives of home are narratives of adventure, stories about winning and losing homes. We must avoid getting stuck, thinking that we have reached our final home. In my dilemma with the Kelim rug I encountered soul in the obsession to possess the rug. Only after I had begun to reflect and evaluate the ordeal could I make conscious the hidden intentions of my soul. It longed to belong to Ireland and the Aegean Isles, but does not possess them. It wants me to take those landscapes with me wherever I go. The subsequent associations were about the artist who had woven the rug, initiating solidarity with those who are creative and do not need to hold on to what they have made. From that experience I learned to distinguish the need to belong from the need to possess.

Author and poet John O'Donohue, writing about the hunger to belong, describes places of harsh judgment and condemnation where home becomes a mental prison of fixed certainties. In the following passage he describes Celtic spirituality as a way of freeing oneself from homes of rigid boundaries and certainties and of opening oneself to the interim regions of the world's hidden potentials.

> The world of Celtic spirituality never had such walls. It was not a world of clear boundaries: people and things were never placed in bleak isolation from each other....This means that the interim region between one person and another, between person and nature, was not empty....Such loneliness would have been alien to the Celts. They saw themselves as guests in a living, breathing universe. They had great respect for the tenuous regions between worlds and between times. The in-between world was also a world of in-between times: between sowing and reaping, pregnancy and birth, intention and action, the end of one season and the beginning of another.[12]

So rather than a stable state, being at home in the world embodies a process, a dialogue between self and world, the inner and outer, the subjective and objective. It manifests often in an interaction between an archetypal narrative expressing the need to belong, and the human capacity to reflect, evaluate, and discern the significance of that need applied to the actual circumstances of the times. The process requires inner work, listening to dreams and fantasies, and trust in the creative powers of the psyche. They not only reveal the records of past homes that have failed to satisfy the hunger to belong, but also provide creative solutions to bridge worlds, transforming barren wastelands into fertile landscapes.

THE ARCHITECTURE OF THIS BOOK

This book is divided into five parts, each with a number of chapters. Part one (chapters 1 and 2) began to take shape in my listening to the many tales about home and its loss. Impregnated by these stories, I soon lost the innocent belief that there could be one home where one lived happily ever after. Part two (chapters 3 and 4) is about making the world our own. Culture is born as we see ourselves reflected in our surroundings. We create narratives and rituals to transform experiences of the world into facets of self, symbolically re-creating the world in turn as a mirror of the soul's deepest longings. As we engage in the to-and-fro movement between I and the other, self and the world, we may call to mind the reciprocal relationship between mother and father tongues, a language of containment and a language of reflection. Part three (chapters 5, 6, and 7) describes the rich harvest accrued from working in a psychotherapeutic practice for nearly forty years. I am continually intrigued by how the psyche preserves and protects the hunger to belong, as witnessed in many tales of home and its loss, both personal and collective. Clients abandoned in early life, suffering from homelessness, test the analytic partner and container as they find themselves caught between the longing to be seen and the fear of rejection. Fantasies, dreams, and transference reveal the inhibiting power of fate, but also contain seeds of destiny to create new homes and sometimes a new identity.

Part four (chapters 8 and 9) describes home as an odyssey that is both a personal and collective endeavor in search of home. Here I attempt to unravel the complicated home heritages of my host and native countries, Switzerland and Ireland. Undertaking an odyssey in different countries, I discovered that home is not only about a house, but also about the evolution of nationhood. Home as a journey may entail the pains of homesickness, challenging one to relinquish the notion of identity as a fixed certainty, yet serving as a source of inspiration to link the multiple facets of one's being into a newly emerging whole. And finally, Part five (chapters 10, 11, and 12) concerns the plight of the many millions of people who do not have a secure home. People in transient spaces are often disorientated and risk losing a sense of self. One cannot stop migration; one can only channel it in better ways. Migration brings many benefits. Cultures do not develop in isolation, but in contact with other cultures. Individuals, organizations, and nations bear a responsibility in easing the pains of transition. Cultivating the art of hospitality, redefining cosmopolitan citizenship in nonexclusive ways, and helping people maintain a balance between the familiar and the strange are some of the ingredients essential to furthering a culture of exchange.

The book has taken on a life of its own as each section emerged. It began with murmurings in the womb, became enriched through the appropriation of diverse cultural traditions, was substantiated by the many tales from a psychoanalytic practice, was expanded by travels through time and space, and matured through a sense of responsibility for the less fortunate members of society. In writing this book I have gained consciousness of a theme that is perhaps of prime concern for the future of humankind. Home in both its real and symbolic dimensions makes human life on earth hang together in ways that can benefit all.

This work is also divided into twelve chapters. They are composed from many threads; threads from my own life, threads of others, old threads, new threads, threads from diverse cultures, and threads taken from the newly woven patterns of contemporary lifestyles.

Starting with my own home, you will see in chapter 2 that I have lived in many different dwelling places, visible and invisible. In this book I will use threads from my own life—not only because I have known them so well, but also because they fit into patterns that are not just my own. Abandonment, grief, homesickness, exile; home as family, friends, profession, community, or nation; home as a journey, dream, or connection with ancestors are threads that have initiated prolific communication with others who live beyond the threshold of their own home.

In chapter 3 I invite the reader to open mind and heart to the living universe. Having grown up by the sea, my attention has always been drawn to its horizon. Islands, ships, and strange cultures have stimulated the spirit of adventure. I delight in discovering new worlds, learning about their myths, history, and customs, wondering about how they began and how they fell apart. Home, understood in its wider symbolic dimensions, represents the way we connect with the world and recognize it as a source of fundamental forms that regulate and bestow meaning to our social and cultural practices. Home awakens the heart to love, protect, and take care of our planet, as witnessed in ancient hymns and rituals to ensure its survival.

In chapter 4 I try to understand the play between myth and reason, imagination and reflection, as well as the symmetry between the ideals of the Romantic and the values of the Enlightenment. Rootedness in myth and openness to the world as it is today further mastery of a communicative language that includes both mother and father tongues and encourages translation of one's home heritage into the contemporary environment.

Chapter 5 focuses on developmental psychology. It bears witness to devastating tales of abandonment and trauma, and the despairing cries of the inner child that express the need to be heard and seen again. Theoretical considerations will be concerned with foundational attitudes about home, which may determine a person's relational capacity for a lifetime. Continuing research in developmental psychology, attachment theory, and neuroscience with focus on early emotional processes has led to a new understanding of the human ability to adapt and make meaningful appraisals of self and environment.

In chapter 6, I will evaluate the significance of home as an instrument in therapy, and focus on its healing perspectives. The need to feel at home in the world can be encountered in the analytic space: in fantasies, dreams, transference, and relationship. Here lie the cues for the practitioner's response, which hopefully will meet the need of home in ways that repair and heal. This chapter is concerned with thoughts and feelings that have arisen from practice. As a Jungian analyst my entire professional life has been devoted to working with clients. I have witnessed their sufferings, anger, hate, despair, anxiety, shame, guilt, joy, love, and inspiration. Their narratives can be compared to a book of life. To them I owe gratitude. It has often been said that modern man is broken man. Many who come to therapy bear a history of broken homes. The purpose of therapy is not to provide a home for clients so that they will "live happily ever after." It can, however, help cultivate an attitude to life that survives loss and thus strengthens the soul's foundations, providing a basis for building new homes and sheltering a person's identity in a process of development.

In chapter 7, I will consider Jung's theory of individuation. I envision it in terms of moving through the stages of life without loss of identity. Here one encounters homes of fate and homes of destiny, homes of imprisonment that compel one to repeat destructive behavior and homes that provide a foundation on which to build a coherent life narrative. The enormous influence of mothers and fathers is both personal and collective. Often one's first home can be infused with mythological and religious determinates, and embodied in the voice, look, or attitude of a caretaker, shaping childhood and maintaining influence throughout a lifetime. I will also describe the many homes that Jung inhabited during his long life. I understand his notion of the transcendent function as the scaffolding that allows one to build a home that can be one's very own. If the foundations of being at home in the world and in oneself are secured, inner resources become available to celebrate life's changing landscapes.

In chapter 8, I outline some of the devastating effects of homesickness. It has long been known as the particular illness of the Swiss, associated with the loss of the subtle air and the pastoral life of an Alpine landscape. The notion of home, connected with an extended family, local village, or landscape, gradually changed in Europe, as attachment to home shifted from nature to nation. Home became a political reality, causing great wars and great human suffering. Today, homesickness is often associated with children and immigrants, revealing new dimensions of this age-old language of the heart. In this chapter I also describe experiences of home in Russia, the United States, and Turkey.

In chapter 9, I will focus on Irish myth and history. One myth, the *puella senilis*, the transformation of the old hag to young maiden, has had great influence in shaping the national identity of Ireland. It was instrumentalized in the struggle for freedom from British rule. Having served its purpose, the myth became transformed into a rigid instrument of religious and cultural suppression. Yet the call of the poets has not gone unheard. They have witnessed the changing circumstances of contemporary Irish life and have articulated the soul's need to create and weave new patterns from old threads.

In chapter 10, I investigate some of the political and sociological issues of integration. What does it mean to be at home in the "global village," a creation of contemporary corporate society? Many are the faces of today's homeless. Each story about the loss of home is unique. Can the contemporary urban environment provide an adequate home to nourish the souls of today's uprooted millions? How can one help nourish a new attitude to home, one of care for the less fortunate members of society who are excluded from the privileges most Westerners take for granted? Does contemporary homelessness imply loss of the ability to appropriate the world symbolically? Citizenship guarantees a basic security, without which it is nearly impossible to feel at home in the world. In this chapter I outline contemporary notions of cosmopolitan citizenship and their relevance to social integration. Cosmopolitan citizenship, understood psychologically, harbors a symbolic intention that signifies a process of connecting "polis" and "cosmos." Thus understood, it approximates Jung's understanding of the Self as a dynamic principle, stimulating processes of intercultural exchange and cross-fertilization.

Chapter 11 bears witness to the plight of the migrant population. There are many approaches to assessing the circumstances of today's immigrants. One view is conservative, emphasizing the limits of integration due to wide cultural divergence; the other, pragmatic and optimistic. One cannot expect immigrants to outwardly assimilate the social norms and practices of the host society and maintain their cultural heritage solely within the domestic sphere. The more optimistic view focuses on the life of immigrant children in today's global culture. Their identity can no longer be defined exclusively in terms of a particular village, family, or culture; it is to be understood as a process of formation rather than a state of being. Social workers and psychotherapists stress the slow process of integration, which takes place over several generations. Integration implies the ability to mourn what has been lost and to accept ambivalence. It also involves creating an identity that might not fit the new or the old, but is original, authentic, and sufficiently rooted to survive transitional processes. Change implies a process of self-awareness and self-transformation that balances two fundamental tendencies of the human psyche: the symbolic attachment to home and the ability to translate that attachment into the reality of another landscape. In the resocialization process, migrant populations are encouraged to take an active role in creating a new home in their host country. The task of a cosmopolitan society is to make transparent the common ground of values shared by most societies, despite representation in differing narratives. Narratives containing bonding memories of one's history of belonging must now be prepared to enter a culture of exchange.

The thesis in the final chapter of this book maintains that the experience of home transcends the divisions of inner and outer, subjective and objective, self and other. Home can be likened to a many-storied house. It has both a horizontal and a vertical axis, emerging into consciousness at their point of intersection, a midpoint between opposites. This approximates Jung's description of the Self. In memories of a good home we are drawn to people, objects, and events that we hope would never change, because they remind us of experiences where we felt whole, reflected in a world felt as whole. We tend to cherish, love, and care for those moments of homecoming, moments when our innermost being receives affirmation. Of course we all have to wrestle with the shadow, the desire for power, control, and possessions. Awareness and transformation of the shadow gives strength, confidence, and depth to our undertakings. Yet, even as such moments of homecoming are cherished, there lies beneath this affirmation a call to also let go, when our enterprises, achievements, and possessions no longer house the soul's aspirations. In order to enter new landscapes, they are to be transformed into facets of self, a self that seems to outlast the fleeting moments of time.

CHAPTER 2

My Own Home

An aged man is but a paltry thing,
A tattered coat upon a stick, unless
Soul clap its hands and sing, and louder sing
For every tatter in its mortal dress.[1]

—William Butler Yeats

CHILDHOOD

Home structures the story of our lives. Mine began in Ireland, in a cloud of unknowing. I was told that I cried so much in the first few months of my life that I had to be operated on for a ruptured hernia. The transition from home in the womb to a non-holding environment damaged my attachment potential, damage that it has taken a lifetime to repair. Some of my nightmares have kept alive memories of early abandonment. In my fourth year, I contracted tuberculosis, discovered accidentally while I was staying with relatives in England. Unable to walk, I created an imaginary home, inhabited by imaginary parents, during the two years I spent in hospital. I believe those imaginary homescapes and the regular visits by a faithful aunt helped me survive an ordeal that my mind could barely acknowledge.

Eventually I learned to walk again and returned to Ireland. I remained fragile, and was sent to a boarding school with only five pupils, run by a German baron and his wife. They were forced by the Nazis to leave their homeland, and created in Ireland a school inspired by Rudolf Steiner, by whom they had been befriended. It became my second home. I remember the affection and tenderness of that old couple who taught me to appreciate the beauty of nature. Still today, memories of the dark woods, winding rivers, and sparkling lakes, all alive with wondrous creatures, awaken in me marvel and wonder about the beautiful world that surrounds us. Attachment to the earth was further strengthened through our lessons on nature, often held under an old willow tree, and included writing about and painting all the wonders that impressed us. Now I can be thankful for those five years, in which the foundations of my appreciation of nature were formed. Some part of me belongs to nature forever.

My father died when I was eleven years old. I believed my father had gone to heaven. Whenever I was under stress, I prayed to him for help. Later, whenever an aunt, uncle, or close family friend passed on, I felt that something became added to my life. My mother belonged to a family that retained visible traces of its ancestry. Books, paintings, and a mausoleum were among the remaining vestiges of a long history. Perhaps those early experiences of loss, the visible signs of ancestry, and the continual exhortations of Catholic priests to believe in the existence of another world induced me to trust that I was just one link in a long chain of generations. From an early age I felt that my identity was embedded in a much larger landscape that contained who I was and wanted to be.

Surrounded by women in a fatherless household, I found home in my mother, my sister, and a housekeeper during my adolescent years. My mother loved fun and gaiety and she always advised me to be social and enjoy people, especially at parties and in sport. She hoped that I would become a banker or join the British army, and was unable to appreciate my decision to study philosophy. One day I tried to explain to her the meaning of "essence." She laughed and told her friends that the only essence she knew was the essence used in cakes. I knew my mother loved me, but she had no way of knowing who I was and especially what I was trying to become. Our housekeeper was different. She was a woman of the land, who had come to us before I was born and had devoted her whole life to our family. She provided the warmth and nurturance that my mother and sister could not. She communicated, in intimate ways, something of the ancient Irish heritage. She would tell us stories about the customs, superstitions, hardships, and dreams of times long ago, creating a world in which plant, animal, and human seemed to be woven in an invisible web of connections. Later, I came to understand this kind of relationship as an archetypal attachment to the Earth Mother, an attachment that heals the wounds of the heart. In my thirteenth year, I was sent to a much larger boarding school. I became conscious of homesickness as a painful and personal issue for the first time. I felt lost in the large, impersonal classrooms, refectories, and dormitories of that institution. My soul needed several weeks at the beginning of each term to befriend the new environment.

A HOME BEYOND THE HORIZON

There are moments when we feel a pressure to do something, and only later do we discover that our lifetime secrets are revealed in those acts. Three important events helped me find my professional home as a Jungian analyst. One afternoon, sitting alone in a classroom, my hand began to draw a spiral, radiating light. Underneath, I wrote: The Christian Communist Democratic Party. I informed my classmates that I had found my vocation. I was going to create a new political party, uniting opposites. Of course, they thought I was crazy. The headmaster was convinced that there was no place for the likes of me in the real world and that I had better become a monk. Many years later, I realized I had drawn a mandala, which C. G. Jung understood to be a symbol of the Self, that core part of our personality transcending the individual conscious ego and upon which health and stability depend.

The second event happened at university. Our professor of academic psychology described C. G. Jung as an abstruse mystic, who had lost his way in the mumbo jumbo of alchemy and whose Gnostic spirituality posed a greater threat to Catholicism than the atheism of Sigmund Freud. As a good Catholic, I attended Mass after that lecture. Suddenly an inexplicable energy seemed to speak to my soul, and I became convinced I would go to Zürich and study Jungian psychology. The incident helped me to become a rebel and listen to an inner voice—not an easy task, considering family expectations. Home became interiorized; perhaps this was typical of a young man's need to leave the parental home and create a home of his own. My mother was convinced that, as a member of an Anglo-Irish family, I would make a fine officer in the British army. She wished to see me in the colorful uniform of a prestigious regiment. But by then I knew that my heart was rooted in another soil and it was upon that ground I would build my house.

A final event sealed my conviction. I finished my course work for an M.A. in America. I had forgotten Zürich, and could not finish my studies in philosophy. The expectations of my mother had lost all meaning. I had no idea where I was going. Stuck in America, without money, the juices of life had run dry. Even if I had lost hope that one day I would study Jungian psychology, my dreams behaved otherwise. I remember a particular one from that time. Jung appeared in it. He wore a mighty turban. As I looked closer, I could see it contained all the stars of the heavens. Soon afterwards, friends invited me to stay at their house by the sea. Each morning I would stand before that great expanse, knowing that it touched every land in the world. Having grown up on the edge of the Irish Sea, the ocean was not unfamiliar to me. The ocean continually changes, and mirrors the mysterious origins of human nature. Its violent storms and reassuring tidal rhythms, its myriad shapes and colors celebrate life's intensity and diversity. Facing the ocean, I made a decision not only to undertake an adventure into unfamiliar territory, but also to respect the inner world of the unconscious as a matrix of unknown horizons. Only later did I realize that the soul's attachment to the ocean symbolized the deeper realms of the psyche, that which is not yet known but may one day become visible reality.

For months I would sit on the seashore and talk with the ocean: "Sea, you touch every land on the planet. You hold the secrets of my life. Show me your ways." Every morning I walked the docks of Norfolk, Virginia, approaching new ships for work, hoping the sea would take me to the next station of my life. I was lucky that some of those ships did not invite me on board; otherwise I probably would not be alive to tell this tale. Finally, an old cargo ship on its last voyage accepted me as a member of the Royal Merchant Navy of Norway, starting as a cabin boy, cleaning toilets. That was the definitive end to a future in a British regiment, but the beginning of a career and new life that required trust in oneself and perseverance in understanding the obscure messages of the human psyche. After an odyssey of five months through many lands, I found myself studying at the Jung Institute in Zürich.

That experience by the ocean forty years ago definitely shaped my attitude to the unconscious. Despite the skills of interpretation, I believe the unconscious remains something radically unknown and unpredictable. I am wary of all attempts to interpret this dimension of human existence in terms of fixed forms. The archetypal represents a species-specific potential, which acquires definite structure within a particular biological, cultural, social, and personal context. The source of that potential transcends any particular interpretation. The watery realm of the unconscious not only represents a challenge to essentialist interpretations; it provides a ground that allows space for a contrary viewpoint and encourages a process-oriented understanding of reality.

When faced with important decisions, I often dream of walking along a thin strip of sand between the ocean and mainland. Such moments, experienced in dream or reality, prevent me from getting stuck in the hundreds of routines that are continually imposed by our fast-moving times. That strip of beach represents a boundary between land and sea, between the plans and expectations of the waking self and the potentiality of that other life not yet lived. Here I learn to cast off patterns of daily life that have become fixed and rigid. I am aware that freedom is fragile and not unlimited in its scope of choice. Similar to the way the mighty ocean beckons one to be cautious, so freedom bears a responsibility. Sometimes I dream of the great rocks of Ireland's West coast, continually lashed by the Atlantic storms, yet standing firm against the violence of waves. The ocean can be dangerous. There are times when its luring appeal entices one to immerse oneself in oceanic experiences, which can harbor unrealistic illusions of beginning life all over again. The images and experiences of the sea have formed my attitude toward the unconscious. Timing is essential. There is a time to let go and a time to stand firm, a time to accept and a time to resist; equally in analysis there is a time to welcome the raw fantasies and affects of the unconscious and a time to sort them out, make interpretations, and link them to a particular context in meaningful ways. Process and structure are two sides of the one evolving life.[2]

Years later I finally understood what I was doing at that time. The utterly unworldly spirit of the undertaking reminded me of a quote from an Anglo-Saxon chronicle: "Three Irishmen came to King Alfred in a boat without any oars from Ireland, whence they had stolen away because they desired, for the love of God, to be in a state of pilgrimage—they reckoned not where."[3] There is a body of Celtic literature, known in Ireland as the Immrama, which tells about visits to otherworldly islands. Celtic hero or Christian saint would leave their accustomed homeland and set off on the high seas, sometimes without sail or rudder, guided solely by the winds and waves. They were in search of the Land of Delight or, as in later versions, a paradise promised by Christ. The lands they visited had little in common with the homeland they had forsaken. In and through the tidal movements of the ocean, the Celtic imagination sought to divine the will of "Dia Mor na nDul"—the Great God of the Elements. It surprised me that the analysts of the Jung Institute could give credence to this kind of behavior. Zürich was an odd place in those pioneer days of Jungian training; I remain grateful to the institute for being the first public body to accept the creature that I was.

Thirty-five years later, I am convinced that had I not followed those strange urges of my soul, I would have adapted to the expectations of others and become neurotic. I would never have found my professional home. The profession of psychoanalysis, Freudian or Jungian, is difficult, lonely, but immensely rewarding. For hours and hours one listens to the stories of clients. An analyst attempts to help his or her client to reconstruct those unlived, repressed parts of their personality, guided by the client's dream, fantasy, or emotional experience. This requires a capacity for intimate sharing without loss of boundaries. The work is a matter of the heart as well as the head; deep relatedness and intellectual reflection belong to the paradox of an analytical life. Over the years, I have looked over the hedge and learned from other schools, in particular from the Freudians. I have trained in psychodrama, a technique that provides a contained space to resolve conflicts of a forgotten past through embodiment and role-play. Speaking three languages, I have had the privilege of working with people from many different cultures. Belonging to an international organization, I enjoy dialogue with many colleagues coming from different professions and different nations. I openly acknowledge my professional roots as a Jungian analyst, but the boundaries of that home are continually being adjusted. I was fated to do this work, but I don't take that fate for granted. I continually have to measure fate in terms of reality, my own limitations, and the new discoveries in related disciplines. The challenges of patients and colleagues require maintenance of tolerance and flexibility. It all might have begun with the drawing of a radiant spiral. My life and work has, I believe, helped others find their own truths so that their lives might blossom in new and unexpected ways.

A Swiss Family

When I arrived in Switzerland, home became marriage, children, and profession. Despite financial stress in the first ten years of family life, I don't think I ever felt more secure and fulfilled than I did in sharing a home with a loving and loyal wife, partaking in the life and development of two wonderful boys. My family life was definitely matrilocal. My social life extended only to my wife's family and friends. Later, we lived in a beautiful wooden house in Einsiedeln, a small town with a massive basilica that houses the Black Madonna, and is situated near a picturesque lake nestled in the majestic Alpine landscape. For many hours I worked in the garden, transforming the rather plain Swiss garden into a landscape of rocks and boulders, embellished with colorful shrubs and flowers—little Ireland!

There were, however, times when I became homesick for my native land and culture. Each year, I revisited Ireland to reassure myself that my homeland would not disappear, but survive as part of my identity. Dreams of Ireland, Celtic myth, and modern Irish literature brought back the wealth of this background. They sustained my new life in Switzerland. As if to keep alive the memory of my original homeland, concrete sensory images would return again and again: the sound of the sea, the smell of turf, the lilt of Irish folk music. Conversely, today when I am away from Switzerland, I not only miss the music of the alphorn or the taste of Swiss pralines, but also the picturesque villages, the dark woods, and the majestic mountains of my adopted country. I must see, hear, or smell my home even when I am not physically in it. For the French philosopher Merleau-Ponty, the body was not an object among objects, but our way of belonging to the world.[4]

Another Kind of Home

Religion has provided another kind of home, sometimes permeating life with beauty and meaning, sometimes bringing awareness that one day I will be scattered as dust to the winds. It has provided consolation in difficult times, but also acted as a scourge when self-satisfaction bewitches me with indifference. I believe I was destined to meet in Switzerland a person who for the next thirty-five years would influence my religious affiliations. One prominent member of my wife's extended family was a woman with the gift of visions, who has been described as a down-to-earth mystic in the mold of Hildegard of Bingen. Often I sat near Joa Bolendas in various churches while she prayed and received messages from the heavens. The visions were essentially ecumenical. Joa Bolendas, a pastor's wife, was given the task of understanding aspects of Christianity—such as the significance of icons, Mary, the saints, the rosary, and the Mass—that were foreign to the traditional practices of her own Swiss Reformed church. Already in the early visions, a Johannine mysticism of divine light, life, and love, inherent in all being, illuminated the messages she received. The visions were not just creations of her intellect or imagination. She described the process of receiving visions as an infused state —accessing an energy—that enabled communication with a reality other than herself. Concomitantly, or sometimes shortly afterwards, she heard or saw the words and images that accompanied her infused state of being.

Reflecting on the difference between an illusion and a healing religious experience, C. G. Jung came to the conclusion that no one can know what these ultimate things are:

> We must therefore take them as we experience them. And if such experience helps to make life healthier, more beautiful, more complete and more satisfactory to yourself and to those you love, you may safely say: "This was the grace of God."[5]

Gebhard Frei, the well-known Catholic theologian who had the privilege of knowing both Carl Jung and Joa Bolendas, reached the same conclusion in his assessment of her private visionary journals in 1962. Following the criterion of John of the Cross, Frei found no evidence of disintegration of the personality. On the contrary, he was moved by this woman's love and active work for her family, parish, and fellow human beings. He was impressed by the courage and strength gained from her religious experiences in order to deal with the troubles, fears, and concerns of daily life; by her ability to accept sacrifice and suffering; by her prayerful attitude toward those who were near her, as well as toward important events in the community, the church, and the world. Regarding the content of these visions, he asked:

> How can this Protestant woman arrive at insights and convictions which at times contradict those assimilated in her youth, or, better said: which extend so thoroughly her image of

Christianity that they could not have come from her personal unconscious?[6]

Due to my Christian upbringing, this landscape was not unfamiliar. Nevertheless it took time before I could appreciate the influence of the visions on my own life and the lives of those who were close to me. A mysterious presence seems to permeate the revelations; at times I believed in them, doubted them, ignored them, or refused them. I think it was no accident that I was called into this family. I slowly understood that destiny demanded that I work with this extraordinary material. That endeavor is now partly completed in two books, which are published in an English edition of Joa Bolendas' visions. I would like to add that my affirmation of this material has not been without conflict. There was a long struggle with the language of the visions. Statements were unclear, and subject to all kinds of interpretation. Often I would ask Joa Bolendas for further elaboration, and another wording of the original statement proved to be a clearer description of what was witnessed in the vision itself. I struggled with the meaning of these visions; I had to meditate on the short, cryptic messages in order to appreciate their symbolic significance, and not assume that they would materialize in concrete form. The work of translation actually restrained me from becoming overwhelmed by the phenomena, and helped me to distinguish my work on the visions from my professional responsibilities as a Jungian analyst and psychotherapist.

It is not easy to preserve one's individuality in the presence of one who is directly wired into a world beyond the five senses. The fact that no cult was ever created around the person or her visions was helpful. Joa Bolendas and the messages she received exhorted people to think for themselves. It has been a privilege to be close to what one could describe as "revelation in the making." Concerning this matter, the author Robert Sardello wrote:

> Through a meditative reading of this work, sacred stories and persons, angels, saints and divine beings—realms that have for some, at least, been only a matter of belief—suddenly come near, almost near enough to touch.[7]

The strange and unexpected encounter with Joa Bolendas has helped me rebuild my religion in ways that are appropriate to the times we live in. It has taught me to appreciate a God who is still with humanity, who wishes that we develop our full potential and help others do likewise. I have come to appreciate Christianity as a life-affirming religion, a religion that must respect individual freedom, does not abuse power, and upholds the equality of men and women in all aspects of life. I have learned to pray, to respect the beliefs of others, to care for the well-being of the less fortunate, and to appreciate something of a home, where humankind might one day shine as the stars of heaven.

Exile

I assume most of us do not want to give up a secure life. I was no exception. I would have liked the gifts I received in the first half of life to last forever, but a mid-life crisis with all its ambiguities and uncertainties ravished me. Women were telling me a tale I could not understand— some part of myself was not alive, and they knew it. I eventually broke the home I had built and chose a solitary life, connected with a mature and free woman who lived in a land far away. This relationship was not about householding; its focus was on the recognition of a soul that animates body, heart and mind, and has a different agenda than the conscious self. The pain of separation from the old and the comings and goings of the new forced me to develop a fierce independence. I am grateful for all that happened during those years, yet my heart remains sorrowful for the pain I inflicted on people whom I have loved. I have learned to accept responsibility for who I am, accept my strengths and weaknesses, recognize the effects of traumatized, stillborn parts of myself and care for them and prevent them from hurting the lives of others.

After having experienced the trials of midlife, I am now entering the final stage of life. I feel more rooted and at home in myself than ever before. In the beginning, my life was invented by the expectations of an Anglo-Irish tradition at odds with a dormant inner self, which was connected with the unspoken ways of nature and nurtured by a housekeeper who embodied the mysteries of Mother Ireland. Later, different selves were added through a series of temporary identifications with strong personalities. I can accept the house that I have built, with its shine and its shadows. I have been able to translate, at least partially, the landscapes of Ireland into other homelands, particularly my adopted homelands, Switzerland and the Greek isle of Patmos, to which I return every year. My Irish soul delights in the sea, the barren rocks, and the little chapels of that holy island. I now have many loved ones—including my former wife, my children, dear friends, and professional colleagues—with whom I have shared the drama of life. It is only in these last years that I have learned to extend friendship in ways that are mutual and meaningful, and go beyond the confines of a matrilocal environment.

HOME: A MATTRESS OR A MAGIC CARPET

Home has become a function of consciousness, a consensual concept, and a way of constructing relationships to those near and far, to the city and to the cosmos. Home is a work of art that takes a lifetime to create. It began with my parents and later included my own family, my children, a mystic, and close personal and professional friends. Part of its story is contained in attachments to houses, gardens, animals, landscapes, schools, churches, ideas, music, and works of art. Home can also be understood as attachment to major attitudes that change during the course of one's life. The theologian Jürgen Moltmann once described the powerful forces that mold four stages of life as follows: trust, in childhood; longing, in youth; responsibility, in maturity; and wisdom, in old age.[8]

I have always been impressed by the Indian notion that a woman is never without a husband, imaged in the Gandharvas, supernatural lovers associated with nature and the stages of life.[9] One could also apply the Gandharva legend to male psychology. My heart seems to be saying that I have had four marriages: to mother, wife, soul, and death. I have felt at home in these marriages. The final one is still in the process of being built; it began soon after I reached midlife. It is the work of the spirit—a summing up, an acceptance of one's life narrative, for better or for worse, in order to face the final challenge. I hope that the shelters I have built for myself can in different ways provide shelter for others. I expect to take those shelters with me as I face the final question: Do we have a home that outlasts our short life on earth? Most of us will end our life on a mattress. That will be our final space on earth. I imagine the mattress could become a magic carpet that will carry me to unknown territory. Schopenhauer, in a remarkable statement, examined the fabric of that last space we call home:

> ...[L]ife may be compared to a piece of embroidery, of which, during the first half of his time, a man gets a sight of the right side, and during the second half, of the wrong. The wrong

side is not so pretty as the right, but it is more instructive; it shows the way in which the threads have been worked together.[10]

PART II

HOME: BIRTHPLACE OF CULTURE

CHAPTER 3

Preserving a Cultural Context

If we are, indeed, the highest of the brute creation, we should, at least, possess as much unconscious art as the lower brutes; and build nests which shall be, for ourselves, entirely convenient; and may, perhaps, in the eyes of superior beings, appear more beautiful than to our own.[1]

—John Ruskin

The purpose of this chapter is to describe the multifaceted significance of home, suggested by the word "home" and its symbolic extensions. Perhaps the significance of home first dawns upon us in those moments when our whole being becomes reflected in our surroundings. Through symbol and myth, we appropriate the objects of the world as facets of identity. Whenever they reflect what we consider to be truly our own, the incentive follows to make them our home, differentiating them from other objects that remain foreign. Such moments are moments of consciousness, moments when the world becomes alive, meaningful, and endowed with a cultural context—quite different from a world of facts, without symbol and without intrinsic significance. Home may be experienced on an individual and on a collective level. Many indigenous cultures of the past structured the universe reflecting the firm belief that they belonged to it and it belonged to them. While still in awe of the sacred and the mysteries of their surroundings, they ordered their place in the world according to cosmic principles. The gods, people, animals, and objects had their allotted place in an orderly cosmos sustained by myth and ritual, centered around a sacred axis, and having a bounded circumference that marked it from the world outside—a realm of chaos, of the enemy, or the alien.

The end of this chapter provides a bridge to the one that follows. When life structured by culture becomes fixed and rigid, the protests of the poet, philosopher, or architect will not go unheard. Conventions, tastes, and styles lose their significance. The old may then have to be destroyed for the new to be born. We may need to let go of the baggage of the past and place ourselves in a transitional space—a not belonging anywhere. Often the new provides an opportunity to reevaluate the past from a different perspective. If homes are not only to be places of comfort and security, but also of inspiration and meaning, those who dwell within them will welcome the winds of change.

Weaving the Threads of Containment

The word "home" has a multidimensional significance. Its etymology goes back to the Teutonic "haims," meaning "village," and possibly the Sanskrit *kshema*, implying "safety," or *kshi*, "to dwell." In Anglo-Saxon it became *ham*, meaning home or a dwelling, eventually to become *hoom, home, ham* in Middle English. In today's usage, many are the threads that make up the significance of "home." It may signify a center of rest and security, seat of domestic life, village, nation, region of origin, and place where one belongs. One can also feel at home in institutions or establishments that afford security and loyalty.

"Home" refers not only to a concrete place or abode; it has metaphorical extensions. In games it can mean a place free from attack, a goal, destination, or finishing point in a race, as in "home run," "home base," "home stretch." "Home" can denote an intended effect or future state: to strike home, to charge home, or to reach a final home, be it the grave or heaven. It can refer to a state of mind: to be at home implies to be at ease, to be welcomed, to be available to others, or to come home, implying some form of self-realization. Traditionally the word "home" was associated with some outer object, place, origin, or destination. Today, in our unsteady times, where loss of home has become almost a certainty, "home" has achieved a new inner significance. In the wider context, home implies a sense of identity, continuity, and containment; we discover a potential to select and use particular objects so that we can appropriate the world and history, space and time, as our own. Experiences of belonging and attachment, or of loss, deprivation, and alienation, reveal highly complex processes, involving transformation of one's personal, family, and collective culture.

As we move into the new millennium, a large sector of public opinion has altered its notion about homeland and nation. In my adopted country, Switzerland, the institute for national heritage protection is called *Heimatschutz*, literally translated as "home protection." *Heimat*, in German, has a wider significance than "home" in English, and implies something like "homeland heritage." In a discussion marking the hundredth anniversary of this venerable Swiss institution, it was suggested that the old-fashioned word *Heimat* be replaced by a more dynamic word, particularly because a populist, right-wing party has exploited the significance of *Heimat* as a major slogan to defend Swiss identity against foreign incursions. Opponents of such intolerant views argued that "home" today has a different significance than it did fifty years ago—it no longer can be interpreted as nostalgia for the past, a longing for a romantic agrarian landscape, or an expression of political conservatism. It was, however, agreed that the word *Heimat* should not be dismissed. It still maintains an inner symbolic significance. In contemporary culture, where mobility dominates, "home" has been reevaluated within an individual context, and is to be understood as a continuous process of encounter, assessment, and evaluation of the old in terms of the new—a process that each person experiences in a different way. Many national heritage foundations have taken these new perspectives into account, and have reformulated their policy as a process of protecting the local, familiar, and traditional within the wider context of contemporary cultural innovations. This way, they help create an environment that reflects a process-oriented conception of home that links heritage with innovation.

Home can also be described in terms of the people to whom one feels attached. Nevertheless, in such relationships you find that you may have appropriated emotions, thoughts, and bodily gestures that are not truly your own. You may find that your interior life is peopled by all kinds of unconscious figures that appear as an attachment to a specific person, but on deeper analysis you discover that that person represents values, which are collective and regulate the lives of many. Collective, cultural values are embodied in our primal caretakers and transmitted to us as children without our knowledge or consent. They regulate and confirm the identity of individuals, families, nations, or cultures over generations. On a deeper analysis you might discover that they possess a universal significance shared by humankind.

As children we appropriate cultural attitudes as normative, meaningful, and accept them as part of our identity. We tend to look at the world in the ways our parents do. As we mature, we begin to see things differently. We are less likely to uphold uncritically the cultural canons of the childhood home. Absorbing our surroundings, we learn to appropriate alternative ways of seeing the world. As we immerse ourselves in the wonders the world has to offer—nature, books, new friends, tastes, habits, and cultures—we learn that there are many ways of appreciating and interpreting this world. Our vision is heavily loaded with cultural constructs, and there follows a sifting-out process, a making conscious of complexes, a quest to discover what belongs to parents, family, culture, or God. Ultimately this is a search for consciousness, an attempt to understand who we are, where we come from, and where we are going.

If you are to find home in the world, you must first learn to look at the world—look at it long enough to assimilate its transforming mysteries. You may discover its secret intent in the people, events, and objects that surround you. You learn that it has a tale to tell, which is conveyed to you through symbol, myth, or narrative. You see parts of yourself that have hitherto remained hidden, but now become reflected in experiences that you encounter in the outside world. You may begin to understand why culture has been the most cherished accomplishment of humanity. Cultural accomplishments are not simply to be consumed, but appropriated in terms of what they mean for the human condition.

Home is a symbolic construction of the world, transmitted over generations. Through symbol we select aspects of the world, integrate them as our own, and appreciate them for their meaning and purpose. In a largely unconscious process, we also reject other aspects of our surroundings as being foreign, alien, or meaningless. Because home, whatever it may be, is so intrinsic to identity, we love it, take care of it, enjoy it, and defend it. The attachment to home can be powerful, even consuming. It activates complexes and bonding memories that first may appear in the context of a personal attachment, but on further analysis reveal themselves as cultural norms that have been unconsciously appropriated. They manifest in the way we decorate our houses, evaluate architectural design, perform social customs, and participate in secular or religious communities.

INHALING THE LIVING UNIVERSE

I grew up with the sea at my doorstep. The sea represented the end of the world as I knew it, but also the beginning of another. Home was thus not just *terra firma,* but also a place beyond the horizon. Home might have been family and house, but it also embodied a potential, a longing, and a hope to break out of confines that had become too narrow. In my youth I often sat on a mountain, looked out over the sea, and hoped my life one day would be different. Odysseus, a fellow wanderer, sat on the shores of Malta, his eyes moist from weeping, his life ebbing away in tears shed for his lost home. Perhaps it was my love of lands beyond the horizon or the spell of Calypso that made me write—and so began my work on the ever-shifting meanings of home in a world that is familiar yet strange, inviting or rejecting, offering shelter or exile.

I have always been attracted to islands, having spent my childhood on one. It is easier for me to feel at home on islands than in other landscapes. Islands are contained and encompassed by the sea. I have stayed many times on the islands of Malta. Inhaling the aroma of the wild herbs and spices, listening to the sounds of the sea, and inviting fresh Mediterranean winds to cool the body, I could embrace the message of these islands. Many civilizations have left their marks on them—Neolithic temples, a Roman villa, Arab farmhouses, and the palaces of the knights of St. John. History becomes visible and tangible in a small, contained space. The magnificent story of Malta, a miniature history of European civilization, awoke in me interest in home as a cultural reality, as well as those perennial questions concerning origins and the passing of time.

I have also traveled in many different lands. Whenever I feel at home in a place, I become aware of a psychic quality attached to it. I might go on to discover that the place possesses a long history, often reaching back into mythological times; to learn the significance of a site—why a rock, well, or tomb is located here and not elsewhere; to discover the remains of an old temple once used to worship the gods or goddesses of the land. My soul begins to delight in the sounds, smells, shapes, and colors of a landscape, its history, culture, and language. This is an experience of a whole world, a living in continuity with nature and culture, place and people, including the dead—for every country is a storehouse of the ancestral heritage. The origin of the English word "world" stems from the Anglo-Saxon *weorold*—from *wer* (man) and *eld* (an age)—the literal sense being "age of man" or "course of a man's life." An experience of "a world" comes from a person's whole lifetime. One purpose of this book is to encourage reflection on the affinity between two words with very different meanings: "home" and "world." The former implies a local, safe dwelling place, the latter an extension in space and time, as their etymology suggests. Human life is continually exposed to these poles of experience, and often we have no option but to discover who we are in those interim regions between the familiar and the strange.

The world envisioned as the course of a lifetime differs radically from the lifestyles of a newly forming global society, where space matters less as time is shortened.[2] How can we be at home in the world if time is shortened and space matters less? The world becomes real in terms of our narratives about inhabited spaces, as implied in the etymology of "world." The world gains significance if one can inhale it, hear it, and look at it in terms of a lived life. It is not a solitary "me" who perceives a world out there, but unconscious systems of deeper resonance that are formed over a lifetime. Humans create the world as an arena of meaning by bonding with their surroundings in a special context and a special time, selecting aspects of it that contain, nourish, and bring to blossom our very being. This is a symbolic act—moments when our being becomes housed. A symbolic appreciation of the world, however, requires intervals, rarely achieved if one is continually pressured by an expeditious agenda.

PERCEIVING A DEAD WORLD

What has happened to our culture that we no longer see the world imaginatively? Are we losing the silence and solitude so necessary to anchor humans in ways that embrace the complexity of identity and history? If the human psyche can no longer create a symbolic vision of its surroundings, the sense of selfhood diminishes. Our technological age continues to level nature to a collection of facts and figures, concentrating on its exploitation and usefulness. It is not the facts but the detached eye and ear—our very ways of perceiving our surroundings—that have reduced the symbol to sign, meaning to the level of the factual. In the Middle Ages, facts had little or no meaning. Today facts have become the determinants of truth and ultimate meaning. Through a self-imposed alienation from natural surroundings, we believe we can objectify and control the world as a body of facts, even creating a world of virtual facts for our gratification, forgetting the human soul that loves to contemplate each fact as a womb of inexhaustible possibility. As we lose resonance with our hearts and kinship with nature, we ourselves risk becoming a piece of information, a mere fact among facts.

In a world of factual information, we fail to appreciate the symbolic intentions of our surroundings. Through the electronic means of communication, men and women devote much of their lives to organizing and evaluating billions of facts. Living in a world of continual distraction, it is becoming increasingly difficult to maintain a sense of narrative continuity and integrity, and to see identity reflected in a larger cultural context. It seems crucial to protect oneself from these shallow influences of a lifestyle that prevents one from distinguishing superficial or pathogenic forms of attachment from those enduring attachments that mirror who we truly feel ourselves to be. As humans continue to exploit the world as mere matter, we are only slowly becoming aware of the dangerous consequences of treating our entire environment from a predominantly detached perspective.

Perhaps we cannot appreciate and love Planet Earth and her mysteries because we tend to see the world only in terms of its usefulness, productivity, and expediency. In an issue of the German magazine *Der Spiegel*,[3] two identical pictures of the same landscape seen through a car window caught my attention. In one picture prominent objects in the landscape were named: tree, field, hill, church steeple, road, sky. Over the picture was written: "Your eyes see a lot." On the opposite page the same picture was printed, but now objects invisible to the eyes were named: airport, golf links, congestion, the B244 (road), and your BMW agent. Over the second picture was written: "A BMW onboard computer sees more." The two images represent two different ways of seeing the world: one as a natural and cultural landscape, the other in terms of function and destination. Of course, humanity has always beheld the world from both perspectives. By identifying exclusively with a functional view of the world, we risk creating an artificial world that becomes increasingly alienated from a broader cultural heritage that once celebrated a profound indebtedness to the sustaining power and beauty of nature. Pursuing ever-distant goals at faster paces, we become condemned to live in an ever-diminishing present, a present that is incapable of reading the signs of the times. As the world becomes faster, we are hearing ever-louder calls of anguished souls who are concerned about the increasing superficiality of contemporary lifestyles. The protests of today's environmentalists echo the cries of an earth near exhaustion.

Susanne Langer describes a world that is no longer interpreted in ways that encompass the complexity of human nature. Language is reduced to a system of "familiar signs" and "abbreviated symbols." We are in danger of just "thinking with them," not "about them." Langer exhorts us to see the world in ways that allow for metaphysical space, the creation of symbolic form, and a world picture that captures a sense of the mystery, the unknown, the nonfactual.

> The tendency to demand ever more signs to replace sym-
> bols…makes our lives more and more factual, intellectually
> strenuous, wedded to the march of mundane events, and beset
> by disconcerting surprises….A life that does not incorporate
> some degree of ritual, of gesture and attitude, has no mental
> anchorage. It is prosaic to the point of total indifference,
> purely casual, devoid of that structure of intellect and feeling,
> which we call "personality."[4]

Despite the loss of connectedness with nature, we have no option but to contemplate and understand the world around us in ways that appreciate it as the abode that nourishes, sustains, and transforms our very being.

LOOKING AT THE WORLD FOR THE FIRST TIME

Looking at the world is more than just seeing the world, just as listening is more than hearing. Looking at and listening to the symmetries and sounds of belonging involve ingesting one's surroundings in those quiet moments of presence. The world becomes internalized in the eyes and ears of the beholder. The various systems of the mind absorb the objects and events of one's surroundings, which structure an understanding of world and self. The world is transformed into facets of self, and thus endowed with culture and meaning.

Attachment theorists inform us that in the mutual gaze and attunement between infant and caretaker a process of appraisal of good or bad experiences is activated. The contact through the mutual gaze, empathetic responses, and moment-to-moment matching of affective patterns creates attachment bonds, which enable the child to gain control of his or her affects and a positive sense of self. Young children first see themselves in the eyes of the other, and thus begin to create a symbolic construction of self and the world. The matching process is both emotional and cognitive, and allows children to evaluate early patterns of bonding with parents and others close to them. Allan Schore calls this "relational knowledge," which is retained in implicit memory systems throughout a lifetime.[5]

In those moments of deep bonding with one's surroundings—when mind, heart, and body are so connected with an object, event, or person—we see a whole world, and this signifies at the same time the emergence of a primitive self-awareness. Later we relive that experience in a favorite landscape, garden, story, piece of music, or close personal relationship. Childhood experiences with significant others may be positive or negative, fear-provoking or reassuring, creating moments when the child feels either accepted or rejected, connected or disconnected. These are the crucial instances of bonding with others, bonds that allow the true self either to blossom or to retreat into a world of silence. Once the child is capable of constructing symbolic representations of world and self, it can express these primal experiences in language. The influence of these experiences remains throughout a lifetime, often activating autonomous complexes, inner aspects of the personality that are only partially conscious, and, depending on the level of consciousness, compelling one to lead a life of healthy relationships or one of forced adaptation. The patterns of early bonding structure relationships and become the foundations of one's being at home in the world.

We need to look again at the world with another mind-set—perhaps in the way we saw it as a child. The eyes of a child may be innocent, yet the child is not uninformed. The child looks on the world with its whole being, and evaluates it in terms of mind, heart, and body. Perception of the world is not an internal reproduction of surroundings, but a re-creation and reappraisal of those surroundings in terms of an ongoing process of construction and reconstruction of identity. We rarely forget those deep, all-encompassing, yet vulnerable moments of receptivity when we are exposed to the mysteries and magnificence of our environment. Many will attempt to retain those experiences, reconstructing them according to their talents, skills, and profession. Not only the artists' paintings or the language of the philosopher or poet, but the expressions of anyone whose language resonates with the living world can bring to life the unfathomable interweaving of the human and environment.

Maurice Merleau-Ponty, addressing questions concerning the power of signification and the birth of meaning, wrote the following about the intertwining of the visible and invisible, the mute and the sonorous, in a language that reflects the enigmas of our natural environment.

> Language is a life, is our life and the life of the things….That the things have us and that it is not we who have the things….That it is being that speaks within us and not we who speak of being….Language is the very voice of the trees, the waves, and the forests.[6]

In a similar fashion, the Irish poet Seamus Heaney described the origins of poetry as looking at the world in new ways:

> Utterance is the basis of poetry. If you had no technical knowledge, you'd have difficulty writing good verse, turning the rhythms. But poetry is more than the shape of its verse, it's more than its line-turnings, and its pirouettings. It's a combination of some form of truth, wisdom, and a new way of seeing it, or saying it—as a refreshment of what you know. I believe that people can enter the kind of thing that poetry is without the slightest technical knowledge. I think of an old fellow down in Co. Donegal, beside the sea. He looked at the waves and said: "It's very shabby out there today." It's seeing the thing absolutely refreshed—the world, seen again.[7]

What happens to the imagination if we look at oil rigs in the sea, walled-in rivers, mutilated forests? We know that the creation of a symbolic language does not simply happen inside the head. It depends largely on the existence of an inspiring environment to stimulate and sustain it. In a world without the horizons of the sea, the meanderings of wild rivers, the bull oaks of yet-untamed forests, poetic imagination is severely impaired. The wild yearnings of the soul lose their source of sustenance. It is becoming increasingly difficult to envision the whole in the part, to construct symbolic narratives from the environment, and to find home in a world that no longer stimulates the longing to belong. David Abram, in his book *The Spell of the Sensuous,* connects the loss of the expressive power of symbolism with the destruction of the natural environment:

> As technological civilization diminishes the biotic diversity of the earth, language itself is diminished. As there are fewer and fewer songbirds in the air, due to the destruction of their forests and wetlands, human speech loses more and more of its

evocative power. For when we no longer hear the voices of warbler and wren, our own speaking can no longer be nourished by their cadences. As the splashing speech of the rivers is silenced by more and more dams, as we drive more and more of the land's wild voices into the oblivion of extinction, our own languages become increasingly impoverished and weightless, progressively emptied of their earthly resonance.[8]

SYMBOL: THE HOUSING OF SELF IN THE UNIVERSE

We live in a world that offers us two different ways of seeing it—one functional and the other symbolic. Functioning exclusively in linear time creates an ever-diminishing present; focusing on the level of self-awareness at a particular moment creates an expanding self-presence in the world. If you interpret the world exclusively from a functional vantage point, objects and events simply become a means to an end. The past disappears once a future goal is achieved. In a world of efficiency, the strategies and solutions you invent are designed to increase your productivity at an ever-faster pace. You are subject to an evaporating present between beginning and end, thought and action, heart and hand. There is hardly a moment to stop, to be conscious and gain presence of mind, to gain awareness of the underlying unity between start and finish, intention and goal. In order to see the world from a symbolic perspective, you have to pause, absorb your surroundings, and be connected to what is actually happening—see the events in terms of your deeper self. Perceiving the world as a symbolic representation of self, you begin to connect with those deeper aspects of your personality reflected in the events taking place around you. At such moments you may grasp the more complex dimensions of human existence and become conscious of an identity transcending the fleeting moments of time. A symbolic appraisal of the world harbors an entirely different perspective than an evaluation of it in linear time. It connects past, present, and future in terms of your life story, personal and collective, and enhances your unique presence in the world as a conscious human being. Martin Heidegger understood primordial time as a process of being conscious of your existence in the world. Time is not simply a succession of "nows." Seen in terms of being in the world, temporality creates "a whole," an "ecstatical unity" of "a future which makes present in the process of having been."[9]

Gustave Flaubert once wrote: "One has to look a long time before one sees anything." I experienced this once on a recent visit to the Greek island of Patmos, when I spent a long time witnessing a very ordinary event that happens every night: the arrival and departure of a ferryboat. That particular evening, something prevented me from going about my usual business. Pursuing an inner urge, I waited until the boat arrived. It first appeared as a spot on the horizon, assuming huge dimensions as it moved slowly into the harbor. Ships belong to the largest class of vehicles that humans have ever built. That evening, the boat appeared like a monstrous machine, linking this tiny island with the mainland and the rest of humanity. Its belly discharged and absorbed passengers and goods in the regular way, an event consisting of the usual mixture of Greek skill and chaos, together with an explosive flourish of shouting and yelling, whistling and honking, of man and machine. The people of the island depended on the boat in order to survive and make their living.

When the time came for its departure, I watched the ship heave its anchor, lift its ramp, and slowly move out from the harbor. Silence returned, and my vision of the world underwent an unexpected change. As the ship began to lose its shape and dissolve into the moonlit night, I could only make out an undefined body with a mass of bright lights, over which stood a huge funnel discharging clouds of black smoke. Associations flowed rather spontaneously and began to shape the world and myself accordingly. The slow and inevitable disappearance of lights and dark smoke evoked thoughts about the enormous power of modern technology, wrenching people from their homes, compelling them to vanish in the darkness of night. Thoughts about the history of this island and the fearful emigrations of old came to mind: mothers and fathers watching the slow disappearance of their sons and daughters, never to see them again. I remembered stories from my own homeland and could sympathize with the history of the islanders, aware of the plight of millions of emigrants who were forced to leave Ireland throughout the nineteenth and twentieth centuries. Ships are heralds of fortune and bearers of tragedy. I watched the Greek ship for a long time until it appeared to resemble one speck of light in the blackness of night. An image flickered across my mind for a brief moment, condensing past, present, and future: the ship became a vessel of death, a unifying symbol structuring self and the world, bringing the intense awareness that we all are travelers who have appeared from nowhere and will disappear beyond a horizon somewhere, sometime. We must look at the world for a long time in order to see it as an arena of multiple dimensions: the commotion of everyday life, tales of ancestry, and the vision of a moonlit sea, weaving before the eye a message of ultimate comings and goings.

SYMBOL AND THE CREATION OF A CULTURAL CONTEXT

Evolution tells us that attachment to environment is already evident in the animal behavior of marking territory. Reptiles acquire territory and are capable of defending it. Mammals are capable of a rich emotional attachment to their offspring. They maintain intense affiliation with their group and delight in play and all kinds of social activity.[10] When facing a predator, they react with fear or aggression, often in defense of their burrows, dens, or lairs. With the development of the human cortex and its capacity for language and thought, the earlier reptilian and mammalian attachments to the environment become transformed within a cultural context. Attachment in human relationships reflects profound symbolic processes, which create complex cultural representations of self and other. Symbols are not just images, thoughts, or words, but are born from human emotion, value, and meaning, which have evolved from various forms of attachment.

Through symbols, your curious mind connects you to the world that surrounds you in meaningful ways. Symbols are not innate, inherited packages of meaning, ready to pop out of some other reality, be it from a transcendent realm or some locality of the brain. Symbols are creations of the human mind that need the sustenance of meaningful surroundings in order to be stimulated. Symbols not only mediate environment in meaningful ways; they exist as points of intersection between the conscious and unconscious dimensions of the psyche and, in the case of dreams, between the waking and sleeping self. Symbols are not external to your identity; on the contrary, they are expressions of a healthy functioning mind. Linking the similar with the dissimilar, they reflect the natural ability of humans to create metaphor whether awake or asleep. Through symbol, you endow yourself and the surrounding world with meaning, and thus engage in an ongoing cultural process of de-constructing and re-constructing your identity.

The ability to create a symbolic construction of the world, pregnant with meaning, is evident in myth and ritual. The cultures of indigenous peoples are no longer considered the bizarre work of "savages," but as models of a highly sophisticated appreciation, conception, and organization of nature, family, and social structure. The French psychoanalyst Paul Ricoeur understands myth and ritual as expressing early humanity's ability to comprehend its being in the world first through action and only later in speculative ways:

> Myth will here be taken to mean what the history of religions now finds in it: not a false explanation by means of images and fables, but a traditional narration which relates to events that happened at the beginning of time and which has the purpose of providing grounds for the ritual actions of men of today and, in a greater manner, establishing all the forms of action and thought by which man understands himself in the world.[11]

Ricoeur contends that people first perceived the meaning of reality in terms of its functions. They used signs to denote the gifts of the sun, the moon, the trees, and the waters. The sun bestowed light and warmth on them. The moon guided their ways through the darkness of night. Trees provided shade and food, and in the waters they washed their bodies.

Long ago humans were conscious of what Ricoeur calls a process of "secondary intentionality."[12] Through this process, people perceived the objects of their environment as reflecting a meaning transcending their immediate usefulness, and inducing an awareness of selfhood as humans lived and moved in the world around them. The light of the sun was not just for sight and warmth; it became the center of the universe, on which all life depended. In the cycles of the moon, man and woman began to perceive the waxing and waning of the life energies. Earlier notions of life's movement were not represented as linear, but followed a cyclic pattern. In the life of the trees—the blossoms of spring, the fruits of summer, the golden leaves of autumn, and the barrenness of winter—humans perceived the stages of life: the joy and beauty of youth, the toils of midlife, the fruits of maturity, and a final radiance of life before death. The seasonal transformations of the tree became a symbol for the full cycle of human life. While washing one day, our ancestors perceived that we do not simply wash our bodies; we wash ourselves, our spirit, our innermost being. The movements of the sun and the moon, the life of the trees, and the flow of the waters revealed to early humanity the need to be centered, to suffer the cyclic patterns of life and death, to be cleansed, purified, and renewed. Like plants and animals, early humanity depended on nature for survival. Unlike the plant and the animal, humans became aware of a second self, an identity that could witness its own reflection in the movements of celestial bodies, the changing of the seasons, and the cleansing powers of the earth's waters. The task of transcending immediacy began —humans perceived that they were endowed with a sense of continuity and a consciousness extending beyond time's fleeting moments. Culture was in the making.

In order to maintain consciousness of self in a universe of meaning, rituals had to be developed. Clans, tribes, and nations developed rituals of worship for sun gods and sun kings in order to maintain a sacred nucleus upon which all life depended, the god or king representing the highest ideals of a people. There were rituals of agony and ecstasy, the mourning of the loss of life with the approach of winter, the celebration of its joyous return in spring. There were rituals of purification and renewal to prevent defilement from death, sickness, or sin. Symbolic representations and repeated ritual enactments endowed the universe with a continuity that kept alive a sense of the sacred, transcending the momentary concerns of everyday life. Humans began to become aware of their own transcendence, their capacity to create symbol and to place the reality of their being within a meaningful context. With the emergence of a cultural memory, regulating all aspects of life, the sense of self was extended both structurally and dynamically so as to embrace the living universe. Perhaps the words of the Nigerian writer Wole Soyinka[13] best describe the loss of this way of life: "The book religions transposed the mythic cosmos into non-terrestrial realms and thereby it loses the essence of the tangible, the immediate, the appeasable." Not just the surrounding universe, but the myths, legends, and stories connected to it preserve the national and cultural identity of a people. Eva Hoffman understands this kind of reality as an interior language and describes it as: "those images through which we assimilate the external world, through which we take it in, love it, make it our own."[14]

SACRED SPACE AND THE MYTHIC APPROPRIATION OF HOME

When God cried out to Moses, "Come no nearer, take off your sandals, for the place where you are standing is holy ground," ordinary, profane space was broken up, and sacred space became the point of departure for the creation of a symbolic construction of the world.[15] Mircea Eliade discovered that such encounters could initiate a foundational awareness of one's place in the world. For the people of archaic society, it was essential to have a fixed point of reference. It became the center of the world

and a means of orientation from which the vertical and horizontal ordering of an entire cosmos emanated. Diverse objects could represent this
center: a tree, rock, mountain, ceremonial house, pillar, or pole. Its power
could extend in different directions, representing the four directions of
the universe forming a totality of organized society, manifest in divisions
in the clan, tribe, or village layout. Often a ceremonial house stood at the
center of the village, its roof symbolizing the sky, its floor representing the
earth, and its four walls the four directions of the cosmos. To this day, in
Bali, the architecture of the village and of each house is modeled on a cosmological pattern.[16] The part of the building closer to the mountains is
connected to the abode of the gods, and the section closer to the sea is
nearer to the land of the dead. In a radio interview I heard that the Bali-
nese people, when traveling, continue to uphold their metaphysical system. Before sleeping, they place their head, considered as the superior part
of human nature, in the direction of the mountains and their feet towards
the sea, representing the underworld.

Different versions of mythic architecture, embodying the sacred center of the universe, are to be found all over the world. On a visit to Central
America, I was impressed by the triple function of the great Mayan pyramids, representing the vertical axis of existence. They reach to the heavens, touching the realm of the gods; they were used at one time in tribal
ceremonies for the living; and they also embody the underworld, housing
the realm of the dead. In many cultures, vertically oriented objects symbolizing the center of the universe touch all three realms of existence:
heaven, earth, and the underworld. The god, hero, shaman, or priest
would ascend or descend a sacred vertical axis, which linked the different
worlds. Sacred sites were not necessarily located in one fixed abode. The
Aboriginal people of Australia were nomads and, wherever they moved,
they took a sacred pole with them, recreating from day to day a home in
the world. A broken pole, however, meant "the end of the world."[17]

In early societies, the founding of a new world depended on genesis of
a sacred space, which anchored the center of the known world. Here the
deities contacted their people. The establishment of sacred space created a
sense of intimacy, belonging, and history, connecting people and objects
within a bounded cultural confine. Myths and annual rituals provided a
means of enacting the re-creation of the world, and thus ensured its continuity. In sacred space everything had to be accounted for; outside was the
profane world, without beginning or end, without a center, without

order, without meaning. Only "our world" existed; everything else was nonbeing, inhabited by enemies, foreigners, monsters, spirits, or demons.[18] The increasing alienation of contemporary humanity from their surroundings is equivalent to the loss of sacred space.[19] Many no longer have the space in which to encounter the gods, to orient themselves, to feel safe in the universe, and to invest kinship libido in the people, animals, or objects that are close to them. The house altar is now replaced by the television in modern homes. Already in the nineteenth century, Nietzsche, whose relationship to home remained ambivalent and radical, described the unending wanderings of an abstract, mythless man who nourishes himself from all other cultures, unchecked by any native myth, who has no fixed primordial site, who is exiled from the soil of his ancestors, who is eternally hungry for knowledge, but remains forever unsatisfied:

> The tremendous historical need of our unsatisfied modern culture, the assembling around one of countless other cultures, the consuming desire for knowledge—what does all this point to, if not to the loss of myth, the loss of the mythical home, the mythical maternal womb?[20]

Attachment to native soil and native myth and history is firmly entrenched in my own birth culture. The preservation of Ireland's cultural identity was always linked to the myths about the land. For the Celts, the earth was not just a material or biological reality. Nature, as the abode of the ancestors, was animated, and mirrored processes that were essentially psychic. A stone, inhabited by the spirit of a druid, had the power to anoint a king; a salmon gave knowledge of the future; offshore islands became the abode of the dead; caves permitted entrance to the underworld. The land of the ancestors has always been part of our being at home in the world. The ancient gods and goddesses, in the form of fairies or spirits, inhabited gnarled trees, standing stones, offshore islands, hilltops, or ruined forts. One Irish legend describes the formation of these psychic layers. Whenever new invaders conquered Ireland, the vanquished indigenous people went underground and became the fairy people of the other world. The land itself evolved into a storehouse of historical and cultural memory of the Irish people.

The survival of this way of thinking was recently demonstrated during the building of a new highway to Shannon airport. Irish people who cherished the old ways were furious with the project because it would have destroyed a "fairy tree." They managed to get its course altered, despite objections from the planners of the multimillion-dollar project. The highway now makes a curve around the small hawthorn tree. Sadly, some unknown person hacked the tree to pieces a few weeks after the highway was completed. Everyone believed that was the end of the matter. The next year, however, the tree made a miraculous recovery, regained its full strength, and still stands today as a resting place for the fairies of Munster on their way to meet the fairies of Galway. For all who cherish Irish folklore, destruction of fairy mounds, fairy wells, or fairy trees reduces the significance of history, roots, and cultural identity. Not simply the soil, but all the myths, legends, and stories connected with the land preserve the national and cultural identity of a people. The passionate language of the soul binds people to land and ancestral heritage in both destructive and creative ways. It has molded the history of my country. Ireland would never have been able to maintain its cultural identity and gain national independence from England without the influence of its mythic heritage, as we shall see in chapter 9.

Early mythic beliefs and ritual practices affirming the center and ordering of the universe still survive today. Rituals such as the blessing of a church, temple, or house symbolize "a new life, a new beginning."[21] In our secular world, not only religious events, but also intensely meaningful experiences, transcending the routine of everyday life, will have a similar significance. Such epiphanies can happen through a dream, a fortuitous encounter, falling in love, or unexpected coincidences. They become a symbolic space that regulates much of human behavior. Similarly to the older notion of sacred space, contemporary spaces of inspiration represent an ordering of the world upon which the entire meaning of life is projected. As Eliade writes:

> That is why settling somewhere—a building, a village, or merely a house—represents a serious decision, for the very existence of man is involved; he must, in short, create his own world and assume the responsibility of maintaining and renewing it. Habitations are not lightly changed, for it is not easy to abandon one's world. The house is not an object, a "machine to live by"….Since the habitation constitutes an *imago mundi*, it is symbolically situated at the centre of the world.[22]

TRANSITIONS

Sometimes you have to lose a home in order to gain another. This applies also to one's cultural heritage. Le Corbusier's conception of the "house as a machine," as simply an object to live in—a view shared by many of his avant-garde colleagues, but certainly not by Eliade—can only be appreciated within the historical context of architectural design. It represents a protest against all forms of revivalism. The clutter of the neo-Gothic, neo-Renaissance, or neo-Baroque design and ornamentation had to be stripped bare. People had to rid themselves of the baggage of period design if they were to be more content, more authentic, and more at home in the reality of the twentieth century. The break with the past, as witnessed in the works of Le Corbusier, Walter Gropius, or Mies van der Rohe, became more poignant in view of the oppressive, neoclassical fashion of a Europe engulfed by Fascism.[23] Tradition had lost its meaning, and cultural values were bereft of a sacred center; a rupture with the past became inevitable.

A break with the past, a separation from home, finds expression not only in architectural styles, but has also become a familiar pattern in modern life. Celebrating the "free spirit," Nietzsche was one of the first to advocate a radical severance from memories, which kept one bonded with "all that is time-honored and dignified."[24] Nietzsche chose solitude to be his final home—not a choice for everyone, but one that deserves respect for a man who, like Jung, avowed the central importance of individuality in a world of increasing collective standardization. The need for solitude can also be an important phase of life, when people feel they have to break with patterns that have imprisoned them in rigid habits of the past. Often an experience of the void, an empty space, or a radical change is necessary for a new beginning. Most people do not want to remain in void states. Likewise, many do not want their homes constructed with bare, white, undecorated walls, and floors of minimalist design. They start to rearrange furniture, hang pictures on the walls, place memorabilia on the shelves. Clare Cooper Marcus refers to this process as a "personalization of space" and notes that "even the prisoner, shut away by society because of a crime, is permitted to bring into prison certain effects that are personally meaningful (posters, pinups, family pictures)."[25] There is, however, the danger of filling in the void with pseudo-historical constructs, available in most furniture stores. Home décor, fueled by a cultural complex, can express a grandiose idea of a past that is unrelated to one's actual life situation.

Sometimes the creation of an uncluttered transitional space is necessary, so as to appreciate the past in new and innovative ways. Minimal design should not become an ideology or cult of originality, propagated by an intellectual elite as the fashion to follow. Rybczynski implies that the décor of the home can only evolve if minimalism is not seen as an end in itself, but as a fresh space to examine, evaluate, and translate what has gone before.[26]

Let us keep in mind that buildings speak to us, whether they are sparsely or lavishly furnished and designed. Quoting John Ruskin, Alain de Botton draws attention to a perennial nonfunctional purpose of buildings: "And we want them to speak to us—to speak to us of whatever we find important and need to be reminded of."[27] Buildings preserve our cultural heritage. Our rooms, apartments, houses, roads, bridges, towns—all have a tale to tell. They remind us of the tastes, customs, and beliefs of times present and times gone by. In contemplating a baroque palace, a medieval cathedral, or the pyramids of Egypt, you may discover states of the soul evoking pride, holiness, or fascination. You may wonder what these testimonies of the past may have to do with you. You may hear those edifices speaking to you, whether they be Spartan or decorative, beautiful or ugly, simple or stately. When some tourist guide or book informs you that profit, vanity, religious devotion, or a cosmological system has shaped these buildings, you may be curious to discover what cultural influence has shaped your own life. Have you simply taken over what has gone before, without making it your own? Have you stuck with the familiar and rejected the strange? Or has the wanderer in you embraced the unfamiliar, recognizing in it the forgotten longings of your soul? Are you ready to open the house that you have built, the life that you have led, to welcome the stranger, within or without? Have you stopped building your home, or have you extended it to embrace the mysteries of the world, seen and unseen? Echoing Blake's "Know all men, time's ruins build eternity's mansions," James Joyce, through the voice of "Stephenoumenos," invokes artistic imagination to impregnate and bring to new life the traditions of the past.[28] Can you resurrect the ghosts dwelling in your soul? Do you find space for them in your attitude to the world? Can you let the artist within you work on the dead forms of tradition, infusing them with new life and vitality, so that your deepest cultural convictions become a source of inspiration to help others create their own home in the world?

CHAPTER 4

Transient Spaces:
Between the Languages of
Containment and Reflection

No one experiences your life as you do; yours is a totally unique story of experiences and feelings. Yet no individual is sealed off or hermetically self-enclosed. Although each soul is individual and unique, by its very nature the soul hungers for relationship. Consequently, it is your soul that longs to belong—and it is our soul that makes all belonging possible.[1]

—John O'Donohue

TRANSLATING A HERITAGE OF CONTAINMENT

This chapter continues to elaborate on the mythic dimensions of home, and to outline its creative and destructive potential in influencing the lives of individuals, nations, and cultures. The tensions between the values of the Enlightenment and the romantic longing for home continue to haunt us—values not unconnected with Ernst Cassirer's distinction between the language of theory and a language of expressive symbolism. Cassirer is one of the few philosophers who has written extensively on this subject, his life work being an attempt to bridge mythical and theoretical interpretations of reality. Today we are still caught in the conflict between the two mind-sets: the detached intellect, which seeks objective knowledge, and the longings of the heart to belong to someone or somewhere. Once the two mind-sets are dissociated from one another, the intellect loses its substance and the heart its capacity to embrace the new.

We witness the destruction or weakening of a civilization in its inability to translate one cultural landscape in terms of another, often resulting in a devastating loss of home for a person or group. Imprisoned in the ensnaring power of mythic beliefs, the individual, community, or nation may be unable to integrate intrusions from other cultures. Through myth we make the world our home, but without the discriminating powers of the intellect, home may become a prison. Yet the intellect, when dissociated from the whole within or without, becomes a dangerous faculty. It has been instrumental in destroying the temple of nature and the values of indigenous civilizations, whose sacred rites and practices respected and honored nature's mysteries.

Consulting the works of Isaiah Berlin and Ernst Cassirer, I explore the facets of equilibrium between a romantic and classical *Weltanschauung*, and the contextual relationship of a mythical and theoretical approach to reality. I will end the chapter with an appreciation of "mother" and "father" tongues—one celebrating homecoming and the other encouraging translation of the old in terms of the new. Both tongues may be absorbed unconsciously. Lodged in the collective psyche as complexes or bonding memories that regulate the community life of a people, they may remain impervious to change. Unable to adapt to the circumstances of the time, they no longer provide an adequate home for human innovation and creativity. In a culture of exchange, reflection and communication must entail respect for the mythic home, but also encourage people to see beyond the confines of their traditional habitat.

THE MYTHIC HOME: BARRIER TO THE WINDS OF CHANGE OR CELEBRATION OF HOMECOMING

Let me begin with an appreciation of the mythic imagination. Since the beginning of time, mythic tales—narrated, sung, or danced—have awoken the soul of humankind. Myths have inspired humans to undertake heroic adventures, accept sacrifices, or lay the foundations of new civilizations. They have inspired men and women to extend their vision beyond the restraints and confinements of daily routine, perhaps to catch sight of those deeper structuring principles that bestow meaning and value to the dance of life. Myth captures the whole person. The sensuality, drama, and archetypal figures of the mythic narrative enthrall and possess the human mind. We become part of the myth, as the myth is part of us. To appreciate the reality of a myth, we must experience it with our body, soul, and spirit. Myth affiliates us with our roots. The mythic imagery restores a sense of belonging to our land, race, community, or family.

Myth contains a power that can be divine or demonic. It can possess the souls of individuals and nations. Once captured by the myth, you risk losing your humanity. The function of myth to extend consciousness is reversed, and the capacity to partake in human exchange and the realm of discourse is compromised. The horrors of Nazi Germany and modern terrorism bear witness to the destructive potential inherent in all mythic material. Twentieth-century European history provides examples of cultural regressions in which a repressed pre-Christian archetypal force erupted, creating a coercive bonding that systematically undermined the religious, political, and legal institutions of civilization. In the name of the "blond beast," the hunger to belong became abused, creating mythic distortions about racial superiority and seducing civilized nations to practice deeds of atrocity.

Jung's attitude toward a mythic home reveals an ambivalence in which he attempts to balance humanity's archaic heritage with the human ability to reflect, evaluate, and compare one mythic landscape with another. He describes the earth as being animated and having spirit. Such animistic beliefs, the source of mythic reflection, are not only to be found in the cultural traditions of an indigenous people, but also in the dreams, fantasies, or powerful affects of contemporary humanity. Following Jung, modern man and woman suffer the tension between the dark heritage of the earth, encoded in the unconscious, and the reflective capacity of consciousness, which can transform a cultural heritage in unlimited ways. In the following passage, Jung depicts the inhibiting capacities of ancestral heritage. Yet he admonishes humankind to be aware of the dangers of detachment, as in the pursuit of a purely rational interpretation of reality.

> The very fact that we still have our ancestral spirits, and that for us everything is steeped in history, keeps us in contact with our unconscious….Our contact with the unconscious chains us to the earth and makes it hard for us to move…..Nevertheless I would not speak ill of our relations to good Mother Earth….He who is rooted in the soil endures. Alienation

from the unconscious and from its historical conditions spells rootlessness. That is the danger that lies in wait for…every individual who, through one-sided allegiance to any kind of -ism, loses touch with the dark, maternal, earth ground of his being.[2]

For early humankind it was essential to re-create the world so that all aspects of existence could be accounted for, ordered, and embraced in a cultural system of meaning. Members of society acquired a sense of identity, continuity, and purpose that embraced the entire community. With the development of the scientific mind and its capacity to objectify, evaluate, and compare conflicting visions of reality, consciousness became detached from the world, even from the physical body, as witnessed in the philosophies of Descartes, Spinoza, Leibniz, or Kant. Dispassionate reflection, modernity's most powerful instrument, began to expose the limits of the ancient, inclusive belief systems. Being at home within an all-embracing mythic system not only prevented bridge building to other worlds, but also revealed an inherent vulnerability that led to flawed interpretations of reality and extreme cruelty within the system itself, often ending in its downfall. Despite bestowing a deep sense of being rooted in one's culture and natural surroundings, mythic homes were not always beautiful and secure; they could be ugly and abusive.

In a world of plural traditions and values, the human capacity to reflect, create concepts, and make a reasonable appraisal of experience not only gives fixed meaning to objects and events, but also facilitates translation of that meaning into the language of a different context. If a people are unable to maintain a circumspect attitude in face of the new, they are in danger of becoming victimized by the so-called more progressive nations. Yet history has taught us that the achievement of dispassionate reflection is not always stable and unfortunately tends to fall apart whenever a clash of cultures occurs; the people of progressive nations tend to regress and act on baser values, with the stronger exploiting the weaker.

The arrival of Cortez in the New World, or a Dutch plane landing on an Indonesian island in the 1930s, were projects undertaken with the intention of exploiting the Aztec empire in the former or for anthropological research in Sumatra in the latter. The symbolic vision of the world contained in the myths of the Aztecs of Mexico and the indigenous people of Indonesia led the native populations to interpret the invaders as a return of the ancestors, thus preventing insight about their true intent.

The consequent worship of the newcomers as gods was perfectly mean-ingful to the indigenous peoples and nonsense to the white invaders. The Europeans also became ensnared in an unconscious mythic system. In these encounters, the thin veneer of their civilization was stripped bare and replaced by an atavistic, all-inclusive belief in white superiority, an example of a racial myth permeated by an unconscious cultural complex. Convinced of their supremacy, the Europeans proceeded to destroy the Aztec empire and to rape Indonesian women.

An example of a breakdown in the translation of differing symbolic visions is the circumcision rites of females, still practiced widely in parts of Africa. In Dogon culture, the tradition goes back to a myth describing the union of the sky god with the earth mother. The termite mounds, consid-ered to be the clitorises of the earth goddess, prevent fruition and have to be cut away. Dogon women are considered to be hermaphrodite before the circumcision ritual, and only become real women when the remains of masculinity are removed. The painful and humiliating cutting of the clitoris is clearly acceptable in the Dogon vision of the world, but an example of extreme humiliation and cruelty from a Western point of view.[3]

Customs and beliefs of a society change slowly. It may take several hundred years before a cultural tradition can accept innovations, espe-cially when they are tied to religious belief. Norbert Elias describes the struggles of the upper classes in Medieval Europe concerning the use of the fork for eating:

> In the eleventh century a Venetian doge married a Greek prin-cess. In her Byzantine circle the fork was clearly in use. At any rate, we hear that she lifted food to her mouth "by means of little golden forks with two prongs." This gave rise in Venice to a dreadful scandal: This novelty was regarded as so excessive a sign of refinement that the dogaressa was severely rebuked by the ecclesiastics who called down divine wrath upon her.[4]

In this case, the Catholic Church, waging war on what it considered to be a vanity, forbade the use of the fork, and it took several hundred years before it could be used as an acceptable table utensil!

Contemporary Jungian analysts would probably interpret a collective belief, naively assumed to be true and motivating its adherents to resist all that does not fit their system, as an example of a cultural complex. Cul-tural complexes are highly emotional, function independently of the ego, and possess multilayered dimensions, their content being structured by archetypal, cultural, and personal elements. The authors Thomas Singer and Samuel Kimbles, applying Jung's theory of complexes to group psychology, have defined cultural complexes as tending "to be repetitive, autonomous, resist consciousness, and collect experience that confirms their historical point of view."[5] They also suggest that cultural complexes can manifest in the individual psyche as a collective inheritance, formed over generations. The Aztec reception of the Spaniards or the Catholic condemnation of the Byzantine fork describe how a cultural complex can fuel a mythic heritage, which then is projected onto the intruder in indiscriminate ways.

Distortions of myth will nevertheless not alter an essential function of myth, which is to preserve a psychic inheritance, reminding humans about their earliest experiences of dwelling on the earth. Myths generate affinities of kinship and, in view of the positive characteristics of bonding memories, create continuity in a group, encourage commitment to obligations, and satisfy the hunger to belong. Rollo May claims that a person without a myth is a person without a home.[6] Mythic imagery, in contrast to objective scientific knowledge, regulates through ritual enactment deep bonding with one's environment. Through the various types of myth, we become connected to our universe and our land (creation myth), our ancestors (ancestral myth), our race (heroic myth), our community (national myth), or our family (folktale). Myths express universal themes that structure human identity. Their sources are not only handed down in texts, but also reside as an archetypal disposition in the human psyche, which can erupt with an uncompromising and undifferentiated force. We must not forget that mythic narratives arise out of a local, racial, religious, or national collective memory. They are in our blood. Hitler understood this quality of myth when he wrote in *Mein Kampf,* "I think with my blood." Here lies the strength and danger of all myths and religious beliefs. There is not just one meaning to life but a plurality of meanings—a plurality of worlds, peoples, nations, families, and prophets, all with the potential conviction that their world, their home, is the only one worth living for. Hopefully the discriminating capacity of the ego will not be overwhelmed. The mind must not abandon its task of reflecting, evaluating, and interpreting the significance of the myth within the context of today's plural values.

HOME: A MATTER OF HEART AND MIND

Visions of home, expressed in myth, literature, and politics, have long been associated with nostalgia, sentimentalism, and romanticism. Love of nature, belief in mystery and magic, entry into a world beyond the senses, worship of otherworldly women, yearning for lost love or lost lands are well-known characteristics that belong to both the Celtic and Romantic vision of life. Having come from that cultural background, a critical audience may suspect that I am just furthering antiquated ideas of the unattainable by resurrecting the significance of home. Many condemn the longing for home as a Romantic ideal, nostalgia, or a flight from reality. Such judgments fail to honor an immensely valuable cultural heritage. They fail to do justice to the great artists of the Romantic period, whose visions grasped, represented, and transformed the elusive longings of the soul.

The clash between the canons of the Enlightenment and the great Romantic movement of the eighteenth and nineteenth centuries highlights a conflict between reason and imagination, science and religion, which is still with us today. Home, associated with Romanticism and revered as a source of human affection and attachment, represents a very different way of seeing the world than an attempt to capture its mysteries in the language of scientific objectivity. If contemporary humanity is to hear once again the poets' hymns to the universe, it cannot disown its Romantic heritage, which gives voice to the treasures of our beautiful planet.

A Romantic attitude, however, may not suffice to capture the complexities of modern lifestyles. Humanity cannot afford to ignore that other great cultural heritage, which might have started with Socratic discourse and reached its zenith in the Age of Enlightenment. We must learn to appreciate the historical antecedents of two very different languages, embodying two conflicting interpretations of reality, one of the heart, the other of the head; one expressed through bonds of affiliation, the other mediated through objective discrimination. If one of these languages is abrogated, the ability to continue translating an earlier mythic heritage in terms of a contemporary context risks impairment.

The Age of Enlightenment, while upholding the classical view of the world as being intelligible and knowable, added that reason alone, without revelation or dogma, was the only means of obtaining answers. The basic pattern of life was a jigsaw puzzle: find the laws and fit the pieces together. In the eighteenth century, the mechanical universe of Newton had replaced the sacred cosmos of antiquity. Applied to ethics and politics, the philosophers of the Enlightenment evaluated normative behavior as positive if one's actions were in accordance with reason. The identity of the human being evolved through the use of reason—an attitude that implied that natural man and woman were basically wrong and in need of correction. Reason is invested with a privileged position. It is the superior instrument through which humanity can discover, objectify, and change reality.

According to Isaiah Berlin, the Romantics, reacting to the Enlightenment, emphasized the mysteries of nature and human subjectivity as the source of goodness. Cults of the earth were to be honored. The movement affirmed the primitive, untutored, and youthful exuberance of natural man. Romanticism celebrated the noble savage, the longing for pastoral landscape, the mists of antiquity, revolutionary change, national identity, and unfulfilled love. Natural instinct, the forces of fate, as well as ritual and symbol were its means of expression. The Romantic chose exile rather than to identify with a society that was becoming increasingly subject to the rational order of an institutionalized world. Hence the themes of homesickness, the search for roots, and the longing to belong to the earth, a race, or a community, as expressed in the mystical vitalism of German romanticism, a tradition that influenced the work of C. G. Jung and lead him to draw some untimely conclusions concerning racial difference.

Berlin, while remaining critical of the Romantic movement, which eventually became a breeding ground for Fascism, outlines its positive contribution in the eighteenth and nineteenth centuries. It came into being at a time when the spirit of Enlightenment "tried to represent reality as having some kind of form which could be studied, written down, learnt, communicated to others, and in other respects treated in a scientific manner."[7] The poets protested. The fires of youth were not to be extinguished. The Romantics proclaimed that there is "no single solution" to the ills of humanity, and if a solution is imposed, it will manifest in despotic tyranny, subjugating all other visions that are not in accordance with its own. Berlin notes:

> The notion that there are many values, and that they are in-
> compatible; the whole notion of plurality, of inexhaustibility,
> of the imperfection of all human answers and arrangements;
> the notion that no single answer which claims to be perfect

and true, whether in art or in life, can in principle be perfect and true—all this we owe to the romantics.[8]

Berlin concludes that the inevitable incompatibility of ideas necessitates an attitude of tolerance, liberation, and appreciation of imperfection. This attitude stimulates the intellect to become flexible and search for a new kind of equilibrium and compromise so that the visions of fanatics do not triumph.

While Berlin emphasizes a compensatory relationship between the philosopher's belief in the supremacy of reason and the poet's appreciation of the forces of the earth, the philosopher and cultural anthropologist Ernst Cassirer outlines the slow evolution of mental activity in terms of a progressive differentiation of mental spaces: "expressive space," "representative space," and "significative space," each space determined by its specific language: the language of myth, of knowledge, and of disciplines related to logic and mathematics, respectively.[9] The process begins with a mythic appropriation of the world. Through mythic expression, the world of meaning comes into existence. For Cassirer, a myth-making process begins by noticing "something essential to the whole scheme of life" that then is distilled and raised above the immediate exigencies of the moment. It receives a "stamp of verbal meaning" and a substantiality that becomes fixed in consciousness. As with cultural memory, it yields a prospect and retrospect on human activities.

Cassirer describes the shadows that emerge once the mythical mindset dominates all other mental activity. As witnessed in the destruction of the Aztec empire, mythical language, fueled by bonding memories, can ensnare a people by "drawing a magic circle around them," an imprisoning influence that it is nearly impossible to break out of.

> This focusing of all forces on a single point is the prerequisite for all mythical thinking and mythical formulation. When…the entire self is given up to a single impression, is "possessed" by it…when external reality is not merely viewed and contemplated, but overcomes a man in sheer immediacy, with emotions of fear or hope, terror or wish fulfillment: then the spark jumps somehow across, the tension finds release, as the subjective excitement becomes objectified, and confronts the mind as a god or daemon.[10]

Standing before the unfathomable mysteries of nature, our ancestors attempted to appropriate the world through narrative, prayer, song, or dance. They created a link between the wonders that surrounded them and the language, customs, and traditions of their family, clan, or nation. Kinship was extended beyond the local and familiar to embrace the earth, the waters, and the skies. They were not the only ones at home in the cosmos. Conflict was inevitable. Some of our ancestors found ways of making peace with their opponents, celebrating through ritual a shared cosmos. Others chose a path of conquest. Unable to accept doubt, contradiction, or ambiguity, they could not translate one home heritage in terms of another.

The translation of one tradition in terms of another requires a process of reflection transcending the realm of immediacy. In Cassirer's philosophy, the transformation of the expressive space of myth into the space of representation and signification proceeds discursively.

> The aim of theoretical thinking is to deliver the contents of sensory or intuitive experience from the isolation in which they originally occur. It causes these contents to transcend their narrow limits, combines them with others, compares them, and concatenates them into a definite order, in an all-inclusive context….In this system there are no more isolated points; all its members are reciprocally related, refer to one another, illumine and explain each other….The theoretical significance which it receives lies in the fact that it is stamped with the character of this totality.[11]

The mythic language of the gods thereby loses its concrete identity and material restraints as language grows into a vehicle of thought, expressed in concept and judgment. Consciousness undergoes a further liberation from sentient existence and a "characteristic change of form," in which a rule of determination endows meaning to particular instances through confirmation of their universality and their "relational character."[12] Obviously, this process must remain flexible and allow for uncertainty when interpreting complex material.

With the above quotes, the reader might wonder if I am advocating the supremacy of rational thought over mythic imagination. On the contrary, this is not a question of opposition, but of context-bound relationship between the intellect and imagination. For Jung, the intellect becomes "demonic" only when it is dissociated from the total psyche and maintains a position of absolute power and authority.[13] When Jung translated his 1913-1916 visions of Philemon and Salome into the generalized symbolic form of "self" and "anima," the mythic vision underwent a transformation from the expressive symbolism to representative symbolism. Avoiding a cultic appropriation of the visions, Jung did not appraise them in terms of his unique personal experience but as a space of significance. The mythic vision, structuring Jung's identity and bearing a new understanding of the objective psyche, could now be communicated in a more generalized form and appreciated in relation to other identities, other psyches, and other homes.

The process was not reductive, replacing image with concept. Rather, a third intermediary space was introduced. Amplification consists of providing parallel material to dreams or visions with the intention of linking them with universal themes found in the narrative heritage of humankind. If used imaginatively, it elucidates the universal form of the image through poetic metaphorical comparisons, so that the vitality and meaning of the image extends beyond its immediate impact. The discriminating power of the intellect prevents the individual ego from being possessed by unconscious contents; imagination allows fantasy to spread her wings to adorn, refine, render transparent, or even tailor the original imagery. Amplification of a myth, dream, or vision initiates communication and discourse between self and other, opening up space for reflection, uncertainty, comparison, and choice—fundamental elements to identity formation.

BONDING MEMORIES AND CULTURAL COMPLEXES

To feel at home in a society is to share a common world of meaning. Such a world relies on a collective memory, forming a cultural identity often sustained by some mythic or religious belief system. The work of the Egyptologist Jan Assmann focuses on transgenerational cultural influences, which determine human behavior and thus also their sense of home. The identities of many cultures are formed, sustained, and articulated by a cultural memory, as in the biblical injunction: "Never forget."[14] Cultural memory can be oppressive, as in the case of Nietzsche's "bonding memory," which is constructed by humans to create coercive and cruel social systems that are consolidated by "sacrifices, torments, pledges, cults," and limit human freedom.[15] In contrast to Nietzsche, and closer to Jung's affirmation of the creative potential of the cultural unconscious, Assmann refuses to reduce bonding memories to a conventional straightjacket. On the contrary, he emphasizes its creative character. It commits people to fulfill obligations and maintain continuity in a group; it joins people together and satisfies the hunger to belong. Bonding memories have positive characteristics that prevent members of a community from being imprisoned in the nonreflective sphere of immediacy. Normative injunctions concerning loyalty and obligation to the group's beliefs encourage its members to maintain the values of a collective identity, despite adverse circumstances. Such trials can be experienced as moments of choice. They strengthen the continuity and consistency of the ego, even if a person functions within the context of a group consciousness.

In addition, let us not forget that an exclusively rational attitude to life can also create bonding memories and cultural complexes that confine people within a disembodied ideology, creating a disconnection between mind and life. The living universe becomes objectified and reduced to dead matter, fixed in a collective mental attitude that sanctions unlimited exploitation. Western culture has become increasingly influenced by theoretical and scientific systems of thought, which have relegated non-scientific belief to the realm of the insignificant. In the name of progress, people's homes, local communities, indigenous cultures, and even nature herself have suffered massive destruction. The philosopher Charles Taylor claims that with the advent of modernism, reason became dissociated from a self-revealing world in a meaningful cosmos.[16] The world of pure thought became an instrument for constructing rational systems of interpretation. Gaining supremacy over all other human faculties, it has determined human discourse concerning the nature of objective reality.[17] According to Taylor, the source of human identity was now seen to be in the mind, no longer in the world. The rational mind lost its attachment to the living universe. Human identity is associated with a disengaged subject, living in a world bereft of enchantment.

In today's global corporate society, the largely pervasive belief in profit and progress has emerged from a disembodied ideology that is unconnected with local custom and community. Convinced of its superiority and powered by bonding memories and cultural complexes that may be impervious to change, it has proceeded to destroy the homes of many and harm our natural environment. This is particularly tragic in the case of the endangered oral belief systems of indigenous peoples, the cadences of their voices emulating and celebrating the sounds and symmetries of nature. Ecopsychologist Andy Fisher points out that with the advance of written languages "our indebtedness to the natural world as the original site of all meaning is swept away."[18] In the meantime, the split between the human mind and the natural world is now fully implemented in the policies and operations of many multinational concerns. Their exploitation of the environment is destroying the last remnants of civilizations that appreciated and cultivated a soul-fulfilling kinship with the natural world.

One appalling example is the case of the Amugngme and Komoro people of West Papua. They regard the mountains as the head of a great mother and the rivers as the milk flowing from her breasts. Recently, a multinational mining concern quarried the mountains and polluted the rivers in search of gold and copper. For the people of the region, it meant their mother's head was decapitated and the milk from her breasts poisoned.[19] If this kind of activity continues, I fear some terrible price will have to be paid by later generations, not the least being a dehumanization of man and woman's relationship to Planet Earth.

Many today argue that the nonhuman world should also be granted rights: rights for animals, plants, water, etc. This would certainly be a first step in the direction of a "post-rational appreciation of unseen forces."[20] Granting rights to nature, however, lacks the eros, imagination, and artistic creativity evident in the earlier mythic appreciation of the natural environment. One is more likely to respect, love, and defend a mountain perceived as the site of the gods, a forest as the abode of the ancestors, and a river as the nourishing milk of a mother than to simply bestow on them the right not to be polluted. The former emerges from the heart's affection, the latter from a weighed conviction. As we enter a culture of exchange, the heart and head must learn to play together, if we are to save the last wilderness of our beautiful planet.

Archetypal Home: A Foundation for Multiple Dwelling Places

The significance of home has been continually undermined due to immature beliefs in the exclusive supremacy of either a purely mythical or a purely rational mind-set. Having sacrificed the animating powers of the mythic mind, the theoretical mind is in danger of losing its creative power. So that it does not become split off from the natural world, even threatening it with destruction, a new synthesis between expression and representation, between life and form, must be achieved. Cassirer locates this synthesis in artistic creativity in which "the mythic power of insight breaks forth again in its full intensity and objectifying power....The spirit lives in the word of language and in the mythical image without falling under the control of either."[21] Cassirer deplores any separation of life and spirit. Ideas arise out of the forms of life. In reality there is neither pure form nor pure life, neither lifeless form nor formless life. Life in all its fullness is a becoming of forms.[22]

Can Cassirer's neo-Kantian conclusion be applied to Jungian psychology? This would imply that there is no archetype without life, just as there is no life without the archetype; life in all its fullness is a becoming of archetypes. In Jungian psychology, the archetype is a source of creativity and manifests in life through symbolic expression. Applied to the theme of home, one might say there is no pure archetype of home, no "home-in-itself"; rather, homes are created out of a multitude of attachments, attitudes, complexes, and intentions, which evolve out of an archetypal disposition particular to all living beings. Home represents a creative capacity of the human being to invest dwelling places with symbolic meaning, motivating one to protect, appreciate, love, and take care of any place one should choose to inhabit. Home is not a self-contained innate idea. Having its source in an archetypal predisposition, home is also a creation of the waking mind that possesses the gift of imagination, operating in spaces between inner need and outer necessity. Perhaps this is the way we learn to sustain, understand, and give form to life in all its fullness. Such an attitude may prevent the world from becoming a dehumanized wasteland, exploited by one-sided beliefs in power and profit.

Cassirer sometimes tends to describe the relationship between mythical and theoretical thinking as one of inferiority and superiority. Susanne Langer, who developed Cassirer's ideas, has pointed out that theoretical knowledge would not be possible without mythical, intuitive thinking.[23] The relationship is not one of exclusion. There is no necessity to depreciate one over against the other. Mythic vision is an event, not a method. This process is not to be understood as a replacement of vital intuitions or mythic visions with dry, theoretical knowledge. The fabric of meaning involves both processes in a back-and-forth movement, as formulated by Langer:

> [W]e respond to every datum with a complex of mental functions. Our perception organizes it, giving it an individual definite Gestalt....Here is a crossing of two activities: for discursive symbolism is always general, and requires application to the concrete datum, whereas non-discursive symbol-

ism is specific, is the "given" itself, and invites us to read the more general out of the case. Hence the exciting back-and-forth of real mental life, of living by symbols.[24]

Here begins the work of translating mythic notions of home within the larger framework of differing representations of reality, which nourish a multitude of narratives of rootedness and belonging. The diverse representations of home are inevitably entangled with a person's identity, history, and cultural heritage. If one fails to translate one home in terms of another, attachment to it will remain undifferentiated, entrenched in rigid belief systems, and structured by bonding memories and cultural complexes that are resistant to change. Unconscious complexes, fueled by an archetypal disposition and layered with both personal and cultural affects, will then begin to shape fundamentalist notions of kinship, which may possess a group, convincing them of their own superiority. Home is not just about attachment to particular people or objects. Home attachments have a vast cultural significance with ramifications that affect family, social, political, legal, and religious affiliations. In the name of home, archetypal energies may be mobilized in order to influence people to erect barriers, splitting communities into friend and foe. Attachment to home may organize individual, social, and cultural life in a reductive, authoritarian way, depriving women and children of basic human rights, inciting racism, and even encouraging conquest of other homes by war, subjugation, or exploitation.

LANGUAGE: CELEBRATING A CULTURE OF REFLECTION AND COMMUNICATION

The careful weaving of mythic intuition and conceptual understanding can unveil the human capacity for self-transcendence, a capacity of the ego to translate one landscape into the framework of another. Considering visions of home, whether memories of lost ones or hopes for future ones, a process of translation will involve more than a dispassionate, rational approach. Within the framework of attachment, thoughts of home are never neutral. They usually appear in the form of cultural and personal complexes that can be creative or destructive. They invoke attraction or rejection, love or hate, trust or suspicion, hope or despair in accordance with one's personal attachment history. Home today may be understood as a synthesis of mythic ideas of one's identity and an all-encompassing process of translation, which may involve an entire lifetime.

In addition, being at home in the world is rarely a solitary affair; it encompasses a communal and social framework. It is no wonder that language is one of the greatest cultural achievements of humanity. In a culture of reflection and communication, great care must be taken to translate primal human affection and attachment, as encountered in a language of containment and the hunger to belong, in terms of an open-ended language, the meaning of which is not fixed, but evolves in a process of exploration. I quote Cassirer once more:

> Language…is not mere abstraction. The individual speech act does not hereby take place when the speaker merely reaches into a world of completely finished forms from which a selection has to be made, but which otherwise must be treated as given, like a minted coin. The speech act is never an act of mere assimilation; rather, it is…a creative act, an act of shaping and reshaping. It is a completely one-sided and insufficient conception of this act to regard it as though the subject was inhibited and constricted at every turn and with every step by a world of forms as something already present.[25]

In intercultural exchange, language can neither be exclusively mythic nor scientific, but a play between both. It not only includes communication of ideas, but also allows space for the nonverbal and the nonrational. Indeed, a dialogue cannot be structured by reason alone. It must embrace the heart and the voices of those unconscious complexes, both personal and cultural, whose language is often expressed in affect, fantasy, or dream. In the play between the mythic and the scientific, between desire and thought, image and idea, expression and signification, soul receives voice and form, becomes a presence in the world, reminding one of what a woman once said: "I know my soul is my true home. It can make a home out of any place where I have settled or any work that brings meaning and fulfillment." This may be the language of the consulting room, but it also can be the voice of communities, societies, and nations, when speaking about universal themes of great importance.

The use of scientific and technological languages has massively increased in our period of history. Living in a world of great diversity, humans have to acquire incredibly complex linguistic skills in order to survive in our fast-changing times. A "father-tongued" language—developed in school, specialized in university, and perfected in a profession—has become a powerful instrument that has enabled us to organize, control, and promote the vast complexity of contemporary civilization. Whereas a skilful use of language may lead to success in the outer world, we risk forgetting our first language, our "mother tongue." This is the language of mother and child, of lovers or close friends. It is a language of instinct and emotion, of musical sounds, polyphonic intonations, coupled with a myriad of facial expressions, and bodily gestures. It is a relational language through which we express our most intimate connectedness with another person. Being rooted in the unconscious, neurobiology confirms that its activity can be observed in the brain's right hemisphere, which develops in the first two years of life.[26] It is the language of depth and connectedness between self and other. Its sounds and intonations record the history of our early emotional encounters, our experiences of love, joy, hate, fear, guilt, or shame. In the mother tongue, we hear the sounds of a relational language through which we are most intimately exposed and vulnerable. It is not a written language, but one that is heard and sung, a rhythmic language of melody and emotional coloring, a language of soul utterances, a language that shows whether we are at home or not at home in ourselves or with another.

Language may determine the way we identify with or reject a particular cultural tradition. An increasing number of people no longer understand the fine subtleties of the scholastic language, and if so, often only in a fundamentalist way. Walter Ong, tracing the shift of language from orality to literacy and the consequent loss of a mother tongue, understands the scholastic appropriation of Learned Latin as profoundly influencing one's way of seeing the world. Learned Latin heralded the growth of modern science, but also led to detachment, isolation, and loss of empathy for the lived world around us.

> For well over a thousand years it was sex-linked, a language written and spoken only by males, learned outside the home in a tribal setting which was in effect a male puberty rite setting, complete with physical punishment and other kinds of deliberately imposed hardships. It had no direct connection with anyone's unconscious of the sort that mother tongues, learned in infancy, always have....Learned Latin was a striking exemplification of the power of writing for isolating discourse and of the unparalleled productivity of such isolation...making possible the exquisitely abstract world of medieval scholasticism and of the new mathematical modern science which followed on the scholastic experience.[27]

Ong describes a father-tongued language that has provided a basis for the enormous advance of modern science, but has become disconnected from its roots and its affinity with the unconscious, the subjective, and the biographical. The symbol-creating mind, nurtured from the child/parent relationship, tends to be more inclusive, and incorporate an appreciation of the emotional and the physical body. Inevitably, with the use of the mother tongue many levels of the unconscious are constellated, inhabited by complexes that are only partly conscious yet contain records of one's personal and collective heritage. Jung's attempt to come to terms with the scholastic interpretation of the Christian heritage in his *Answer to Job* expresses a critique of a rootless language that has lost its connection with the unconscious. In view of the affective and somatic power of complexes and bonding memories, expressing narratives of early childhood and accrued cultural influences in condensed form, language is not only about what is said, but how it is said. It is not just the word, but the voice; not simply the idea, but the image; not only the intellect, but the whole person who is at stake when in dialogue concerning matters of vital human interest.[28]

The process of integrating both father and mother tongues can extend over generations. A mind without soul, without mythic roots, without a mother tongue, can make quick connections, but it may fail to reach those deeper levels of the personality that bring lasting satisfaction and create lasting attachments. Many can make a reasonable and measured assessment of their place in the world, often involving a network of busy relationships, but continue to suffer from feelings of being disconnected on deeper levels. Today, you can become very attached to people in a virtual world, but if you live in a world of strictly virtual encounters, you may suffer the risk of dissociation from your emotions and your body. You may feel connected to the whole world, but not with any particular person. In extreme cases, people who are totally occupied with the virtual world often say that they are extremely lonely, and don't know anyone. This is like experiencing a permanent state of jetlag—like knowing you have arrived in another country, but your soul has been left behind.

A culture of dialogue is embodied within a linguistic framework. Through a sophisticated use of language, ideas are communicated, disputed, refined, or clarified. Language, functioning as a father tongue and used as a means of communication about issues in society, one's position in the world, or as a discourse of explanation and interpretation, cannot always guarantee authentic intersubjective exchange. Language conceals as much as it can reveal. With the use of language, complex defense systems may be erected, whether encountered in individual discussion or collective attitudes. Defense systems limit the level of communication. Psychoanalysts have learned to respect the defense systems in their capacity of acting as a protective function of a vulnerable self. You cannot pressure people to give up their defenses; it will only reinforce them. Many people live a life of fear and can only find security by living in bunkers.

A similar pattern is to be found in collective institutions. Some cultures have become fixated on a particular myth or religious belief, and defend their traditions with rigid explanatory systems. Cultures in denial tend to close off influences from other cultures and regress to a state of isolation, as happened in sixteenth-century Spain, in some recent attempts to erect communist utopias, and is witnessed in today's exploitation of the natural habitats of indigenous peoples. Communication on a level of rational explanation will rarely reach deeper levels of a nation's soul. A head without heart will fail to untangle the knots of intimacy—often a confused amalgam of earlier attachments, deep-seated collective memories and cultural complexes, infused with strong emotions, expressed through bodily gestures, and inspired by some unifying myth or ideology held to be sacrosanct.

The significance of home cannot be limited to some particular house or nation. Expressing a need to find shelter in the universe, its meaning can be extended to all levels of life, including death. Home is a way of becoming, more like a journey—a way of translating one's sense of identity in terms of other shelters beyond one specific cultural heritage. Homes do not simply contain, they provide a perspective to include a culture of communication. Language, as one of the great edifices of culture, can act as a shelter to a person's emerging identity. In listening and speaking, in facilitation and explanation, in allowing space for both the mother and father tongues, containment and reflection, a mastery of communicative language begins to blossom. Home as a narrative reality improvises a drama between the old and the new, as one home, culture, or nation becomes transparent in terms of another. A person whose foundations are rooted in myth and whose mind is open to the world of discourse and communication can relish life as a process of bridge building, connecting people and societies, cultures, and nations.

In summary, we need to hold on to our myths. If we lose them we lose

ourselves. This does not imply a dismissal of the values of the Enlightenment. Both pillars make up the edifice of our cultural memory. Wherever they intersect, consciousness blossoms. The mythic imagination—
whether manifest in the beliefs of earlier civilizations, the ideals of the
Romantic, or the dreams of an individual—may be incompatible with the
visions and dreams of others, but incompatibility does not mean exclusion. Here begins a process of exchange through which both parties learn
about the nature of the human encounter, a process that requires
patience, tolerance, flexibility, as well as recognition of boundaries and
difference.

WEAVING THREADS OF THREE WORLDS

Let us never forget that the process of bridge building can take place
within the individual human psyche. In linking the various identities one
has established in the course of a lifetime, one may discover that each
identity has its own personality, even its own language. Often one part of
the self does not know about the existence of the other. Connecting different levels of the psyche heralds transformation of the whole person and
prepares one to relate to others in more authentic ways.

A Czech woman once told me that she had to flee her country when
she was sixteen, due to the crushing of the Dubcek regime by the Soviet
Union in 1968. For many years she lived in England, and eventually settled in Switzerland. She worked in an important position in a multinational company based in Zürich. She shared her office with other
colleagues. After some time, she felt insecure, was convinced her colleagues did not like her, and even began to lose confidence in her work.

Gradually my client realized that her fears and insecurity came from
her childhood. Whenever she failed in schoolwork, her despotic parents
punished her. She was forced to learn everything verbatim. If she did not
succeed, she was beaten. She doubted her intelligence, lost all trust in herself, and eventually hated schoolwork. Once she had left her parental
home in England, she discovered that she was very talented and became
successful in whatever work she undertook. The old fears would return
only when she felt criticized by colleagues who were either more privileged or more popular than she was. Then a strange longing for home surfaced, despite the brutality of her parents.

One day she decided to work on the problem by impersonating various figures in a role-play. She set up a scene representing the office where

she was employed. It soon became clear that she had great difficulty creating a space of her own. She would let others invade her space by making them more important. In the drama, she could see how miserable, unhappy, and frightened she was, and could understand why none of her colleagues wanted to speak with her. As she began to create her own space, she felt better and explored ways to improve relationships with her colleagues. She repeatedly said to herself: "I must have space."

When I suggested that she say the same sentence in the three languages she knew—German, English, and Czech—she had no difficulty in saying it in the first two languages, but could not remember her own native Czech language, her mother tongue. Only then did she realize that she had learned to create her own space in England and Switzerland, but had still not redeemed an inner child who was not permitted to have a space of her own. By saying the sentence in her own native tongue over and over again, she connected with her psyche on a deeper level, eventually to hold all three worlds together. Her inner child, still imprisoned under the authoritarian yoke of her parents, could now gain its own space. Having rediscovered her mother tongue, she could understand that her strange longing for home represented not simply a longing for the past, but a need to create a new space to redeem the repressed emotions of childhood, imprisoned in the ambivalent relationship with her parents. Her longing for home revealed not only a search for a lost part of herself, but also opened up a space for relating with other people without succumbing to old inhibitions.

The integration of her forgotten childhood required further work, including a considerable amount of reflection and interpretative skills. Her analytical and professional competence, acquired in England and Switzerland, helped her to understand the ramifications of the forgotten childhood. A more personal and sophisticated "father tongue" replaced the inadequate one thrust upon her by insensitive parents. She began to link the two languages. As the threads of a forgotten identity were woven into the tapestry of her current reality, her work and private life took on new meaning.

PART III

HOME: TEMENOS OF THE SOUL'S LINEAGE

CHAPTER 5

Developmental Perspectives

I alternate between thinking of the planet as home—dear and familiar stone hearth and garden—and as a hard land of exile in which we are all sojourners.[1]

—Annie Dillard

ABANDONMENT

The well-guarded secrets of devastated homes resist consciousness. You may not even be aware that you have such secrets. They may not only express moments of despair, but also hopes, wishes, and expectations for another home, other parents, or other siblings. Children are at one with their surroundings. They absorb the atmosphere of an unloving or abusive environment. Nature provides them with one weapon to survive—the abused parts of their identity retreat from the world and are no longer accessible to consciousness. Traces of forgotten, repressed, or lost identities manifest in symptom, affect, fantasy, or dream, revealing old wounds, portending new opportunities. Forty years of clinical experience have taught me never to ignore the narratives of childhood. It is a period when one is most vulnerable, when one assimilates the environment for better or for worse. Therapy is like a filter, which develops an ear to listen to the sufferings of the inner child and provides a context to help differentiate the creative from the destructive.

Having received my diploma in Jungian psychology as a young man, I was content to do analysis in the classical manner, concentrating mostly on dreams, watching for signs of potential development, and helping people adapt to the changing circumstances of life. All this presupposed that the conscious personality of my clients functioned sufficiently well enough to understand and resolve conflict within themselves or in their relationship with the outer world. Several years passed before I recognized the narratives of devastation referring back to early damage accrued in home life. My interpretative skills at that time did not sufficiently equip me to work with such material. Later, I realized I had not yet unearthed my own deficiencies. I was not aware to what an extent I had suffered abandonment in my own life. Unanalyzed fragments of my psyche passively succumbed to the expectations of others. I began to read literature on trauma, early personality development, and attachment theory. Gradually, I gained more confidence in my capacity to understand the psyche in imaginative ways. Finally, by doing further analysis and supervision, I could voice those parts of myself that I had preferred not to know about. Less overwhelmed by the devastating narratives of others, I learned to probe their defenses, listen to their tales of horror, and help them gain access to the silenced segments of their personality. I also learned to respond in ways that their deeper self needed to hear. This was no longer a matter of only interpreting their dreams and life narratives, but also included what is known as "mother tongue," a language that expresses a relational knowledge that touches those areas of our being where we are intimately connected with others.

Individual narratives concerning home and its meaning certainly have been the focus of psychotherapy. Practitioners encounter deep and moving home narratives in the symptoms, sufferings, hopes, and aspirations of their clients. Non-empathetic parents and early abandonment can damage the ability to attach to anybody or anything whatsoever. On the other hand, compulsions to stick with the familiar at all costs have been interpreted as a defense against coming to terms with life's inevitable changes. Dreams and transference can help people find roots, create new and meaningful relationships, and initiate authentic understanding of what it means to be at home in self and the world. Home is a foundational experience. The therapist cannot provide home as a material replica of childhood, but home's meaning or lack of meaning can find reappraisal within the context of analysis.

To appreciate what it means to have a home or to lose a home depends greatly on one's childhood. If one is lucky, home begins in a family. The family is a containing structure that offers protection and safety for a growing child. It is a place of security, intimacy, and love, which makes available the deepest kind of bonding between self and environment. If the primary caregivers are consistent and reliable, the child can develop an identity that is stable, continuous, and a felt reality. With this foundation secured, home becomes a function of consciousness that can survive change and enable one to connect with a larger social framework in authentic and original ways. According to Renos Papadopoulos, it is a "key construct, which interconnects three overlapping realms—the intrapsychic, the interpersonal and the socio-political."[2] Unfortunately, family homes are not as secure as they appear. Tales of unhappy homes may not express the devastating effects encountered in narratives told by victims of war, hunger, or natural disaster. Indeed, many homes outwardly epitomize ideals of success and happiness, commanding the respect or envy of neighbors, while neglect and abandonment prevail inside.

In the past, abandonment has been associated with the plight of orphans, widows, refugees, and those who suffered misfortune. Today, abandonment has been reevaluated and interpreted as an inner state of mind. The ability to feel at home in the world and thereby participate in the storehouse of cultural experiences may be severely impaired in childhood. Apart from the continual loss of objects of attachment—so characteristic of our fast moving times, and often achieving tragic social dimensions—the more fundamental concern for the psychologist is the loss of the ability to attach to any object or person whatsoever. Abandonment has become an important feature in understanding the formation of personality disorders. Alice Miller[3] and Kathrin Asper[4] stress the inability to feel as one of the most devastating aspects of abandonment. In such cases, therapy becomes a search for lost feelings, which often appear symbolically in dreams and fantasy as a dead or frozen person. Both authors outline the fatal sequence of events that leads to the formation of this disorder. The process begins with some form of emotional abandonment, followed by an outer adaptation to the needs of the parents, which in turn creates low self-esteem, prevents an unfolding of autonomy, and blocks expression of authentic feelings. In addition to these features, the authors outline other important ones that relate directly to our theme: self-alienation, loss of roots, lack of a sense of belonging, little consciousness of personal biography, and the adopting of a social conformity that inhibits the discovery of one's own personal truth—a truth that Miller regards as the main weapon against mental illness.

Many who have suffered early abandonment experience childhood as being forced to live in a home that they feel is not truly their own. Behind a facade of outer adaptation lurks an abyss of emptiness, depression, and rage. Resistance to any form of intimate connection prevails. This kind of resistance plays an important role in psychotherapy, particularly when the client begins to form an attachment to the therapist, which in turn activates memories of loss and abandonment. Clients feel torn apart by a longing to be loved and by the denial of that longing, which is perceived as dangerous. Defensive attitudes are usually tied up with attempts to maintain a provisional identity that is fragile, inflexible, vulnerable, and in need of adequate boundaries. Personal identity developed in such circumstances may lack roots and history. It is often "up in the air," as manifest in what Jungians call "puer psychology" or "animus possession"—in idealism, nostalgia, longings for paradise, or in an intellectualism that is not grounded in personal experience. In this frame of mind, one might outwardly know who one is, where one comes from, or where one is going. But, more often, it leads to isolation; only in great pain can one accept the companionship of another.

A woman in midlife once described the horrors of her childhood, while lying on the couch. She was often left alone, and did not know how to play. In school, she would stand in the playground not knowing what to do. She was often bored. When she would ask for a present, she was always given what she did not want. Nobody seemed to listen to her or take her seriously. She had her own room, but her mother would constantly fill it with things that did not belong to her. She remembered calling for help when she was five years old and feeling very sick. Nobody appeared—there was just a door, closed shut—and so she stopped talking for several months. Her mother tried to insist that she talk, but she was scared—scared of being noticed. She simply wanted to disappear. As a child, she believed that she belonged to another family and that one day they would rescue her.

Once, as an adult, she asked her father about her childhood. He said: "When you were born, you were a burden." This statement confirmed that she really was unwanted—a feeling that accompanied her throughout her life. She felt she was born into a hostile world. Nobody seemed to listen to her, and she felt she was not worth anything to anybody. Even her husband never seemed to take her seriously, and thus the marriage went from one crisis to the next. Immersed in a difficult relationship, she relived the horrors of her childhood once again. Although outwardly she had a home, inwardly she had none. She was afraid of the past and the future. She only clung to the present, but that was temporary and passing in nature.

Children who have suffered abandonment will attempt to establish some kind of provisional identity that functions as a survival strategy to avoid further damage to a vulnerable identity. Often, at night, when the dreaming mind is free from the constraints of the external world, we get a clue about the significance of complicated protective systems that consist of a mixture of human ingenuity and gifts of nature. One young woman who suffered from early abandonment in childhood had a dream in which she was competing with a man whom she regarded as being rather macho and unsympathetic towards women. In the dream, she was losing the competition, and in sheer rage threw something at her opponent. As is usual with dreams, the therapist and the dreamer at first had no clue as to what the dream could mean. After connecting the dream with earlier memories, the dreamer came to the conclusion that her dream was telling her to establish boundaries and fight for equality with men. The interpretation brought no relief. She then decided to induce a state of relaxation, and almost immediately the image of throwing something at an opponent entered consciousness. She remembered an incident during childhood, when in a state of fury she threw dice at her cousin after losing a game. The dream and memory became cues that unleashed a trail of associations revealing deeper structures of her personality. The following narrative testifies to the child's incredible capacity to build up a protective system in order to maintain a sense of identity, belonging, and continuity, especially when the home environment failed to mirror a true sense of self:

> My whole identity was caught up in winning or losing a game.
> Recently, I have had feelings of being left out. If I am not invited, I
> feel jealous and left out. I keep measuring my success or failure on
> this scale. As a child, I did not feel at home anywhere—not even in
> myself. But if I won a game, I had a right to exist and I felt I
> belonged to someplace or somebody. I usually felt so awful about
> myself; but winning a game, I felt a sense of myself. My identity was
> built on winning. I would always measure each situation to see if I fit-

ted in—if I had the right clothes or if I said the right thing. You know I was abandoned and could not bond with my mother. I never have had a home; I have had to make it myself.

ATTACHMENT

Abandonment understood as a structural deficit of the personality that severely limits attachment possibilities can be considered as a more radical and obscure variation of the homelessness encountered in our times. As early as 1949, John Bowlby indicated how interrelated the two phenomena are. Employed by the World Health Organization to study the needs of countless homeless children after World War II, he brought forth evidence confirming the adverse influences of inadequate maternal care on a child's early personality development. Later, influenced by Konrad Lorenz, Bowlby formulated his attachment theory, which is based on the principles of the ethological tradition (the observation of behavior patterns in primates living in their natural environments) for the study of human parenting. He concluded that the primary bonding between mother and child could be elaborated in terms of attachment. Attachment can be observed in the infant's early recognition of the mother, in its proximity-seeking and clinging behavior patterns, and the efficacy of attachment as a protective survival strategy that allows for better coping with the world, especially when a "person is frightened, fatigued or sick."[5] From his observation of animal and human behavior, food and sexuality are secondary derivatives. I understand an awareness of being at home in the world to be a further, perhaps specifically human, development of the original attachment instinct shared with other primates.

Anthony Stevens, who worked with Bowlby, has described his research at the Institute of Child Health in Athens. He discovered that the institutionalized children did not attach themselves to any available nurse, but specifically to one nurse whom they preferred above all others. Stevens not only described the observable behavior patterns, but also appreciated their inner workings. He would ask each nurse what motivated her and the infant to become attached to one another. The answer of the Greek women was always the same: *Agape*, meaning love. For Stevens, love develops out of the same social, emotional, and sensual experiences that sustain attachment, causing the latter to become stronger and more exclusive. It cannot be interpreted as a "mere behavioral sequence," but as a relationship to the mother "as a person, an indispensible 'other,' with recognizable features and personality characteristics which are uniquely precious to [the child]."[6]

Many Freudians (Balint, Stern, Lichtenberg) have moved away from the idea that psychological existence begins in a state of solitary primary narcissism, in which the infant experiences an oceanic feeling of omnipotence and self-satisfaction. In contrast to this view, infant research confirms that right from the start of life there is evidence of a perceptive-motor-affective dialogue between mother and child.[7] This is usually referred to as the primary relationship between mother and infant. Daniel Stern, reminding us that continuity is the crucial ingredient, similar to Winnicott's sense of "going on being,"[8] believes that the roots of making experiences one's own are already evident in the third month of infant life. The infant's sense of core self can be identified in four "self-invariants"—as witnessed in the gaining of an integrated sense of self as a distinct and coherent body, in control over actions, in ownership of affectivity, and in an awareness of continuity. Stern indicates that self-continuity is already demonstrable in the motor memory, and later, after the seventh month, in recognition of a context (room, crib, personnel) and affective events (mother's smile). Already, in the preverbal stage, the child is in a process of developing a sense of belonging and a sense of its own history. Specific images, sounds, smells, or gestures, a common feature of home memories, mark the quality of early attachment or abandonment.

Winnicott describes the earliest patterns of relating in terms of a holding environment. "Holding" is not just physical relationship, but an expression of the total environmental provision.[9] The child's whole being is oriented to the holding environment. The "good enough" mother has to be reliable, available, and possess an ability to empathize with the psychological reality of her child. If this is successful, the child can mature to form healthy object relations. Winnicott's "transitional object" manifests when the infant attempts to possess objects of the environment, somewhere between the fourth and twelfth month.[10] The object acts as a bridge between the inner world of fantasy and the outer world of culture, and manifests as a double reality in that it is both given to the child—as a teddy, a blanket, or sucking object—but is also created by the child into something else (beloved person). According to Winnicott, it represents the child's first expression of a symbolic construction of the world, which enables a gradual and cautious separation from the mother. The child acquires more autonomy and freedom from the omnipotence/impotence split, omnipotence being a form of bondage to the grandiose self and impotence to the idealized other. The creation of a transitional object allows the child to accept paradox and create a world of meaning that cuts across the barriers of space and time, creating an identity, surviving fragmentation.

> Playing and cultural experiences are things that we do value in a special way; these link the past, the present, and the future; they take up time and space. They demand and get our concentrated attention, deliberate but without too much of the deliberateness of trying.[11]

In 1968, Michael Balint described insecure states of mind that influence one's attitude to home. His description of "Basic Faults" outlines features of a non-containing environment. Basic faults refer back to disturbances in the primary relationship with the mother in which some form of emotional abandonment takes place. They cannot be analyzed when the ego is not mature enough to cope with new material. Balint replaced the Freudian notion of primary narcissism with the notion of primary love. He believed that primary narcissism was used to explain the source of id-libido, but that, when compared with the notion of secondary narcissism, it is of little clinical value.

> According to my theory, the individual is born in a state of intense relatedness to his environment, both biologically and libidinally. Prior to birth, self and environment are harmoniously "mixed up," in fact, there are as yet no objects, only limitless substances or expanses....Wherever the developing relationship to a part of the environment or to an object is in painful contrast to the earlier undisturbed harmony, libido may be withdrawn to the ego, which starts or accelerates developing...in an attempt to regain the previous feeling of "oneness" of the first stages. This part of the libido would be definitely narcissistic, but secondary to the original environment cathexis.[12]

Balint describes two forms of secondary narcissism that influence one's inability to form mature attitudes to home. Ocnaphil and Philobat are terms used to describe contrasting expressions of anxiety due to lack of a secure childhood environment. The Ocnaphil will cleave to places and persons. Fear of separation induces clinging, passive, or timid behavior patterns. The thought of a change of place or relationship terrifies those who suffer from this structural deficit. Symbolic constructions of home will tend to remain conservative and fixed. The Philobat suffers from the same basic problem, but is defensive and denies the wish for security. Individuals with this disorder tend to develop shallow relations with people or places. They will break off relationship once they feel threatened or when they sense rejection. Ocnaphilic and Philobatic personalities bear resemblance to the well-known dog-type and cat-type types of homesickness. The former tends to bond with persons, the latter with physical environment.[13] According to Balint, both types are driven by fear. Little is required to activate these early deficits, especially when things go wrong for those transiting between different homes, cultures, or nations. They invariably complicate successful integration. Once activated, symbolic constructions of home tend to be unrealistic or unstable.

According to Allan Schore, experiences of early relationships occur on nonconscious, affective levels. In the first two years of life, the child downloads information from interactions with the mother. The mind learns to adapt, appraise, and process situations in early relationships. The contact through the mutual gaze, empathetic and attuned responses, and moment-to-moment matching of each others' behavior patterns create empathetic bonding, which enables the child to gain control of his or her feelings, and a positive sense of self. This matching process is emotional and cognitive, and allows the child to make appraisals of early intersubjective patterns. Schore calls this "relational knowledge," which is retained in implicit memory systems. According to attachment theory, the unconscious is now seen as a "cohesive, active mental structure that continuously appraises life's experiences and responds according to its scheme of interpretation."[14] Parents with mature psychological organization serve as "self-objects" that perform critical regulatory functions for the infant, whose affective life still possesses an immature, incomplete psychological organization.[15] Emotional knowledge of early relationships, stored in implicit memory, is preverbal and reactivated later in the adult through facial expression, tone of voice, touch, and body gestures that correspond to the original experiences with primary caretakers.[16] At eighteen months, these structures have achieved maturity and correspond to what infant observers term "the reflective self" or the "reflective function."[17] The young mind, prior to the development of linguistic skills, can now take into account the mental states of self and others. If the interactive processes of attunement, mis-attunement, and re-attunement are not successful, the child's affective development will be disturbed. It will become increasingly hard for him or her to adapt, appraise, or create meaningful relationships with the environment. Mis-attunements and failed processes of adaptation and appraisal, with a corresponding loss of sense of self, will be stored in implicit memory and determine later relationship patterns. The ability to bond with others will be impaired.

The more the primary relationship is disturbed, the more likely that one will encounter a psychological condition of abandonment. Structural deficits may impair a feeling of home, impede the creation of mature and lasting attachments, and prevent development of a flexible attitude to the changing circumstances of life. Abandonment can be experienced as traumatic, depending on the intensity of earlier and later events, and is often linked with the formation of a personality disorder. Homesickness or experiences of homelessness do not necessarily imply trauma or a psychological state of abandonment. Homesickness and homelessness differ from early abandonment in that they presuppose ego development and the capacity to form enduring attachments with others.

CHILDHOOD AND INDIVIDUATION

Margaret Mahler remarks that, in the fourth and last subphase of the child's "separation-individuation process," there arises more or less at the same time a consolidation of lifelong individuality and the internalized image of the mother: personality formation and object constancy.[18] The process begins approximately in the fifth month and ends in the third year. In the first phase, the child learns to differentiate itself from the mother. Having practiced a sense of separateness, the child initiates a "rapprochement subphase," during which it tolerates contradictory self-images of being dependent and independent. It reassures itself by adopting a pattern of separation-reunion with the mother. The child learns instinctively how to survive loss, indicating a precursory stage of coping with later homesickness. Finally, having achieved linguistic skills and the use of personal pronouns in its third year of life, the child can appropriate objects. It becomes aware of people, places, or objects as belonging to it. A coherent identity is secured. The sense of home now becomes internalized, symbolized, and objectified. Hence, memories of specific objects and repeated events emerge, evoking feelings of belonging, security, and containment.

Should this stage of the child's individuation fail, however, there arises the danger of autistic withdrawal or symbiotic identification. An unsuccessful maturation process complicates later transitional phases. When the adult is faced with separation from an old home and the trials of accepting the new, regression may ensue. Conflicts of the present become confluent with earlier experiences of an insecure and unpredictable world. An otherwise coherent identity, held together by and reliant on a collective, local, and relatively stable environment, begins to fragment. Isolation, withdrawal, or nostalgic idealization is likely to emerge, should adaptation to a new home prove to be disappointing.

This reminds me of the story of a young woman who suffered from an inexplicable depression. She was an outgoing, jovial person, but, once depressed, withdrew and could not stand contact with others. It happened whenever there was a change in her life, as when a relationship ended, which usually meant a change in living quarters. Only after she told me a repeated childhood dream about "the other mother," did we begin to talk more intensely about her adoption. She had been separated from her biological mother of Latin origin as an infant, and was quite happy with her Swiss foster parents. She was convinced the bouts of depression had nothing to do with her adoption. Unfortunately, there was no hope of making contact with her biological parents, despite repeated attempts to do so. Her depressions receded when she recognized and valued a darker, passionate, "wordless identity," which, prior to therapy, had been denied in her external life. Her sense of self could no longer be uniquely "Swiss," but included the temperament of a repressed Latin culture. She could not take her identity for granted, but had actively to create it. Her life narrative gained continuity through acknowledgment of "the breaks in consistency." Accepting this paradox, she could recognize not only a "likeness," but also a radical "difference" in the way she related to her foster family.[19]

If the child has implicitly retained memories of a holding, life-affirming environment, and if it continues to experience a world that is relatively stable and consistent, peopled with good enough caretakers, then he or she will be capable of internalizing a deep and lasting sense of belonging. The child will bond with people and places in such ways that it feels at home with them. His or her life achieves a continuity that includes experiences of the objective world, but also presupposes a subjective capacity to create a symbolic construction of it. A child in its post-Oedipal phase of development still lives in a world of fantasy. It does not only want to hear about the objective world, but also about its hidden magic, which awaits discovery in the womb of that same world. The fantasies express not only the child's perception of the world, but also his or her deepest longings, hopes, joys, or fears, which emerge from intense interaction with the environment. In this phase, the child invests kinship energy in the people, animals, and objects of its surroundings. According to James Hillman, such a personified world is not just a "what" but a "who."[20]

Children in the post-Oedipal period of their development love fairy-tales and myths. In fairy tales, the universe and everything in it becomes alive. "Mother Holle" is a story about a deprived young girl, Gold Marie, whose wicked stepmother treats her like a slave. Her life is one of drudgery. She falls into a magic well and enters the realm of the Great Mother. In that other world, nature is alive, nourishing, and beautiful. The bread in the oven and the apples on the tree speak to her, pleading with her to take care of them. The girl works hard for Mother Holle and even assists her in making snow fall on the earth. After a while, she feels homesick and longs to return to her family. Mother Holle leads her back to the upper world. As a reward for her good work, she is covered in gold. All ends well for the heroine—not so for her lazy half sister, Black Marie, who is covered in black pitch.[21]

"Mother Holle" is a tale about bridging diverse worlds. The story could be about any child who has suffered neglect and deprivation. It is a message of hope and healing. Deep within the child's psyche is another world—a world of older gods and goddesses, once cherished in long-forgotten times. Despite neglect in her family home, the story of Gold Marie introduces us to alternative home, Mother Nature. Here the flowers blossom, meadows are fertile, the trees are abundant, and bread is plentiful. The heroine treats the beautiful temple of nature with care and attention. The relationship to nature is one between mother and daughter. It is a relationship of love and service.

Do we treat nature in the same way today? I hardly think so. Abundant are the tales of its exploitation. David Tacey calls the present environmental crisis a "crisis of human consciousness, a failure to view the physical world and its elements as sacred. Only the sacred is treated with respect; the profane is taken for granted."[22] "Mother Holle" suggests that humans need to listen to those older mythologies, cherishing the sacredness of all living beings and caring for them in more loving ways. The tale also reminds us that we cannot remain in a temple of long-forgotten times. Like Gold Marie, we must return to the civilized world. Perhaps we can bring back treasures of the imagination to adorn our world with new colors and new sounds. The narrative of "Mother Holle" suggests that if we don't take care of our environment, our lives may blacken and our environment become barren. We may fall victims to despair or resignation, as witnessed in the fate of Black Marie.

Still living in a world of fantasy, children explore ways to establish kinship with the nonhuman environment. They make it come alive by looking, listening, and transforming nature's hidden shapes and sounds. They not only create princes, fairies, goblins, or ogres; they pour out their aching heart to the trees, embrace domestic animals with their unloved bodies, or build a secret shelter in a loft or garden to protect and contain their vulnerable souls. If their imagination has not been strangled, they weave all kinds of narratives around pet animals, rivers, lakes, stones, and caves. Their new friends are their new home.

One of the great home stories, lived and written by Jungian analyst Alice Howell, is *The Beejum Book*. I once visited Alice in her lovely rambling house in the Berkshires of New England. There she introduced me to Beejumstan. Alice, who calls herself "Teak" in the story, learns about Beejumstan from Lonesome, a black and white rabbit with one drooping ear. On the way to Beejumstan, the human world gradually becomes populated by magical animals—a zebra gentleman, a mouse lady, and a giraffe who talks about investments. The train that took her to this strange and wonderful country could go underwater or up in the air, and Teak could see colorful fishes of the "deep blue-green world" or talk with the birds of the sky. Once in Beejumstan, she gets to know the two principal tribes: the Elbedridges, whose "mushroom apartments grow on trees," and the Bunnywidgets, who live "close to the ground under things like ferns."

Alice told me why she needed to create Beejumstan. When she was five years old, her father's company required that he work abroad. From five to twelve, Alice lived in no less than thirty-six countries. As an only child, she was lonely. Her parents, whom she loved dearly, would often disappear for long periods. Her life was constantly interrupted by separations and reunions. In an appendix to the *Beejum Book*, Alice writes:

> I had also learned a great deal about exile. Painful partings
> from parents, from childhood friends, and from places cher-
> ished. But hidden in the pain was also a gift, one "invented"
> by my mother, for on realizing my growing distress and anxi-

ety, she hit upon the idea of an imaginary land where every night we might all meet together, no matter how distant we were from one another.[23]

Gold Marie and Teak could transform the sounds and symmetries of belonging into a second home, allowing them to interact with it in ways not possible in the parental home. Such playful attitude has deep significance not only for the child, but also for the adult. Harold Searles cautions us to avoid being possessed by "the processes and products of technology," in order not to forget our "basic kinship" with the nonhuman world.[24] Finding home in nature may be the foundation of a more creative, caring, and loving attitude to Planet Earth. Have we suppressed that post-Oedipal child who once played in the trees, on the banks of a river, or in mysterious dark caves? Have we lost respect for the animals, our brothers and sisters from a time long ago? Have we forgotten nature, our friend, our second home? In the post-Oedipal stage of a child's development, we witness the foundation of an attitude sensitized to ecological issues, as outlined in Thomas Moore's *The Re-Enchantment of Everyday Life*.

> The way to an ecological way of life is to treat our houses as homes, our communities as homes, and nature as home. It is the intimacy in each relationship that serves the welfare of the other; at root, ecology is an erotic attitude of closeness, relatedness, and care. We have made it into a rational/activist project and lost sight of its heart.[25]

Once the post-Oedipal phase of development has been secured, the child builds on those foundations and gains a sense of home in the world that possesses precise ethnological contours. This is evident in the period of latency, from the fifth to the tenth year, when there is a shift in the child's interest from the realm of fantasy to the objective world. The child identifies with people and objects outside the family home, making them an integral part of its own social and moral standards. As the ethnopsychoanalyst Mario Erdheim points out:

> In the latent period, the child internalizes a relationship to objects that is specific to his ethnic heritage; what is determined in this period is the way one moves and behaves, what trend of taste to follow, what kind of food is disgusting and which children to play with and which not. Authority outside the family decides what is permitted or forbidden.[26]

Erdheim understands the present manifestations of divisive nationalism and racism as an inability of the adolescent to put into perspective and gain critical distance on an ethnic identity defined by family and society during the latent stage of a child's development.

Erdheim is depicting children of conventional families. Of course, no one theory does justice to the complexity of child development. Conflicts in this period of maturation often prove decisive in the formation of one's attitude to society. The renowned Palestinian intellectual Edward Said experienced childhood as one subject to parents who continually enforced a conventional code of behavior on their children. Said grew up feeling lost, insecure, and confused. He saw his early life as a struggle between created identities imposed on him by his parents, and a sense of a deeper self, largely dormant and rarely accessible except in moments of struggle or seclusion.[27] His biography remains a moving account of a man who lived in a secure family home, but where something was missing: a home of origins, nationhood, and people. His parents repressed the loss of Palestine by adopting a Western standard of life, thus preventing their son from having access to a deeper cultural identity connected with his nation and people.

Said's lifelong struggle was to make conscious a repressed home lingering in the shadows of his soul. Not so with Eva Hoffman. As a Jew growing up in postwar Poland, exposed to a broad cultural context, she looks back at this particular period of her life. She describes her relationship to people and places in ways that are very different from Erdheim's examples—a relationship that is created by her true self, not by outer authority. For Hoffman, the more creative, comprehensive, and tolerant the family and cultural home is, the greater the grief at its loss. A removal of any significant part of home surroundings signals a loss of identity. She recalls that when she was thirteen years old and just about to leave Poland, she said farewell to her music teacher, Pani Witeszczak. The teacher asked her what she would miss most. Eva's answer:

> "You. Everything." Pani Witeszczak strokes my hair to let me know that she understands, and from then on I don't talk much, because I can't stop myself from crying. It turns out that this is the person and the room I can least bear to leave; after all, it's here I've felt most intimately understood; it's here I've felt most intensely all my hopes for the future; it's here

that I've acquired perhaps the only ideal I'll ever really understand.[28]

Mahler and other psychologists remind us that, in the course of the
child's development, the role of the father is as important as that of the
mother. In the past, the responsibility of the father was to convey to his
children as much of the cultural values of his homeland as possible. The
industrial revolution took the father away from the home. He became
available to his children only in limited ways. What can a modern father
give to his children as they move away from the family and begin their
own life and their own profession? Can he help them to establish a rooted
relationship to the greater world in a convincing way? Has his absence
been one of the causes of a withdrawal of interest in social matters, with
the consequence that many seek meaning in the private sphere only? Has
the father's abdication of his role influenced his offspring to create a world
that has become increasingly impersonal? Having to constantly battle
with the outside world, a father's soul may remain hidden and well
defended. If he is not afraid to acknowledge the presence of his soul in
family, community, or nation, he can provide inspiration to invest kinship libido in today's world, so that we may once again call it home.

CHAPTER 6

Homecoming:
A Metaphor in Therapy

…Yet the wanderer too doesn't bring from mountain to valley
a handful of earth; of for all untellable earth,
but only a word he has won…

Praise this world to the Angel, not the untellable:
you can't impress him with the splendour you've felt; in the
    cosmos
where he more feelingly feels you're only a novice. So show
    him
some simple thing, refashioned age after age,
till it lives in our hands and eyes as part of ourselves.[1]

—Rainer Maria Rilke

PROFESSING SOUL

My profession is about the encounter, understanding, and healing of soul. The work may begin in silence, begin with the
untellable earth, the raw material of the unconscious, the
"prima materia" of the alchemists, the unexplored sufferings of the many
who seek therapy for their souls in need. Often analysis is just a matter of
listening; sometimes this kind of listening can last for many months, even
years. During this time both analyst and client seek to find an adequate
context, a setting, a vessel to hold and contain the soul's wounds. It is not

we, the therapists, who heal. We provide the setting only. We make sure there are enough elements in the field of healing, so that the soul's life regenerates on its own. This is the way I work, the form I seek, the "making tellable the untellable." Analysts are not chemists, who attempt to insert the correct drugs so that the soul's demons—its manias, fears, or depressions—are pacified, hopefully to bring relief from suffering to those not able to maintain a social life or sustain a livelihood. The chemist tends to treat disorders of the mind in an impersonal, abstract, and quantitative manner. Their work, however, is necessary for severe cases of mental illness and, coupled with psychotherapy, can bring decisive change in a patient's life. Alchemists must continually ask themselves if they have overlooked the possibility that the mental disorder contains a hidden message, perhaps the soul's hidden agenda? If the demons are simply eliminated, their tales may never be told. Their stories not only inform us about another world, but reveal the trials of life encountered in this world. As alchemists, we try to place ourselves, together with our clients, in the vessel of the raw materials, in the fantasies and images that give us clues about the soul's demons, perhaps even the soul's history. We try to stay with them long enough so that they yield their secrets, allow themselves to be transformed in ways in which soul becomes narrative, our very own story, perhaps a tale to tell the Angel.

What do I mean by the word "soul," here understood as the equivalent of "psyche"? Aristotle understood psyche as the inner life principle of every living being. In his philosophy, soul was not identified with the rational mind, as in modern philosophy. Psyche regulates and bestows form in an increasingly complex manner to all living beings in accord with their species. Referring to the active, organizing life principle in humans, Aristotle's definition of the psyche approximates to a contemporary definition of the unconscious as a "cohesive, active, mental structure that continuously appraises life's experiences."[2] Psyche, according to Aristotle, organizes our mental and emotional life, acts as a dynamic system of transformation of personal and collective experiences, and generates the imagination, both sacred and profane. Psyche, in this sense, includes consciousness and the unconscious as a dynamic, interactive, self-organizing process.

The human soul is directly perceived in the ability to feel—"feeling" understood in the broadest possible sense of the word. A. N. Whitehead defines feeling as "connection," or in his own language, "'vectors'; for they feel what is there and transform it into what is here."[3] We feel things whenever we are connected with them, as in our bodily awareness of physical pain, in emotional experiences of love and hate, or in moments of spiritual consciousness when we gain insight or inspiration. Feeling in this sense is not only emotional. It is also cognitive and represents a continuous system of appraisal of one's environment. Whenever you feel connected with something, the various systems of the mind absorb objects and events of your surroundings, which then structure an understanding of world and self.

Appreciation of the soul as the animating principle of mind and body avoids the duality of Cartesian philosophy. "For Aristotle, the soul is not a substance imprisoned in the body; rather, the soul is the particular plan, shape, and capacities of a body."[4] As ensouled beings, we are alive to ourselves and to all that surrounds us. One of the most extraordinary qualities of ensouled bodies is their ability to regenerate themselves in different ways according to the level of evolutionary development. Thus, healing as regeneration is a fundamental property of ensouled beings. A psychologist does not heal the soul, but he or she can provide a helpful, balanced, and nourishing environment, so that this mystery may happen. This is a fundamental tenet of a psychotherapy that includes work with the unconscious. If healing does happen, it is unexpected and comes as a surprise to both therapist and client.

NARRATIVES FROM THE CONSULTING ROOM

Psychotherapists encounter deeply moving home narratives in the symptoms, sufferings, hopes, and aspirations of their clients. Non-empathetic parents or early abandonment create an atmosphere of fear that damages a child's ability to form attachments to anybody or anything. The same fear can, however, activate a compulsion to stick with the familiar at all costs, acting as a defense against coming to terms with the changing circumstances of life. Analysis can help people find roots, create new meaningful relationships, and initiate authentic understanding of what it means to be at home in one's self and the world. Home is a foundational experience. The therapist cannot provide home as a material substitute for what was missing in the client's childhood, but he or she can provide a context in which the meaning of childhood experiences can be reappraised.

Psychotherapy can provide a setting in which the hidden tragedies of the heart, transpired in soulless homes, are received by an empathetic listener. One listens to scenes of unacknowledged violence and abuse that have devastated people's lives. Often the narratives do not hang together and are told in a confused or fragmented way, articulated with fear, anger, despair, guilt, or shame. If analysts attempt to intervene, they may find themselves shut out by a protective system that was erected to protect a core self that has long retreated into a world of silence. The damage done in childhood may have long-term effects. Images or dreams may reveal what it feels like to live in such a home. Some have experienced home as a dungeon, a dwelling place without windows or doors, or a tower in an isolated or frozen landscape. Images of not having skin, being turned to stone, or being buried alive give visual form to the inner torment of those who fear their uncontained identity is continually threatened. Some feel so alone that they are afraid they will go mad. It is not easy for an analyst to enter such an abode. But once the analyst recognizes an invitation to enter, he or she can embody an empathetic presence of a supportive witness, crucial to the healing process. Within the new therapeutic alliance, the analyst can create a context in which the significance of home may be reevaluated.

As an invited guest, the analyst must learn to appreciate the hospitality of the host's inner home. He or she may not always be acquainted with the customs of that home. The analyst may feel awkward, ill at ease, or even misunderstand the purpose of the visit. One analysand required that I always speak in a low voice. Another wanted to play games, but insisted that he would have to win. The rules of this inner shelter might appear odd and irrational, but on careful analysis one discovers that there are very serious reasons for their creation.

The following narrative reveals the soul's capacity to build up and maintain a protective system in order to preserve a sense of identity, belonging, and continuity, especially when the original home environment failed to do so:

> As I did not have a real home, I always had to create it. When I move
> from one place to another, it is always a traumatic experience. It is
> then that I need to have things planned. It is my way of keeping the
> container, otherwise my world would fall apart.

This young woman went on to talk about a Freudian analysis done a few years previously but conducted in a rather rigid and amateur manner. The analysis consisted of a purely reductive approach to the psyche. Hour after hour she was asked to go back into her past and relive the pain and suffering of her abandoned self. The therapist believed that a recovery of early memories would bring relief. At first she concurred, but gradually experienced the constant repetition of the past as a violation and, in the end, instead of relief, experienced abandonment in a new way.

Once our work started, it was obvious that the analyst had to provide a containing environment for the abandoned parts of her personality. The analyst's aim was not to lay bare the facts of early childhood, but to allow life to unfold. He had to work with the early material of her life because it impeded the client's development. Towards the end of our work, she went on to say:

> All you have to do is to provide a home and then life will evolve. You don't have to force it, you respect resistance, and you respect my self. It is ultimately the self that enables life to unfold and it is the protect-ing circle of analysis and your trust in the self within each person that brings healing. Because you have trusted in the healing qualities of my life, you have helped me understand that the life force transcends the bare facts of the past. Life is not to be reduced to the concrete, nor is it a repetition of what has gone before. Life in all its fullness is a felt experience and also a deeply spiritual reality because it brings healing and gives hope that I may become a whole person.

The statement describes in a beautiful and authentic way a Jungian understanding of human development. Yet we must ask: What does it mean to provide a home so that life will unfold? What is the protecting circle of analysis? How do we trust in the healing qualities of the soul? How can we understand life as transcending the facts of the past and as a spiritual reality that brings healing, hope, and wholeness? From a Jungian point of view, there are of course innumerable responses that attempt to approach such questions. In the following sections, I describe how I make use of the metaphor of providing a home, especially in working with dreams and transference.

An analyst encounters the need for home in many ways in therapy, particularly when clients reveal the deficiencies of their childhood home. If the ego is strong enough, children can survive a loss of home, adapt to a new environment, and start life all over again. Frequently, feelings of homelessness arise from a disturbed relationship to the parents. Despite abandonment, all kinds of longings, fantasies, or attachments to objects disclose the child's need for home. One woman, who remembered her parents as being cold and distant, would spend most of her free time in the barn or the forests, feeling more at home with the cows, horses, trees, and open skies than with her mother and father. Another woman, who felt no love from her parents, believed she belonged to another family who one day would come and take her away. A man, who as a child felt unloved, would take every opportunity to stay with the neighbors, wishing they could be his real family. A childhood fantasy of another woman, who was brought up in the city and had a disturbed relationship with her parents, placed her real home in the pastoral landscape of a distant past. Another woman, rejected by her cold father and alcoholic mother, substituted the beautiful house and garden of her childhood for her unavailable parents. These fantasies of childhood are important and should be appreciated with care. They are not to be understood as a way of escaping from reality, but reveal the soul's archetypal need for home, despite the impaired relationship with the parents. They can be part of a lifelong quest, defining identity and purpose in life. The twelve-year-old C. G. Jung was convinced that he really belonged to another century. He later attributed this childhood fantasy to the reality of personality Number Two, indicating an identity transcending the one experienced with his parents.[5]

In the first hour of therapy, the therapist may recognize an epiphany of homecoming when a client comes into the office, looks around, and wonders if he or she can feel comfortable in the room. One of my clients needed to do just that, for the first few sessions. She had to interiorize everything about my office, so that she could connect with it, and ultimately with the analyst. Later in therapy, the first signs of attachment can manifest in the client's concern about any changes in the office or the therapist's attire. I remember one client being rather upset when I wore a tie. She felt my whole identity had changed and I was no longer the same person whom she could trust. I had become a "bank manager," someone who was just out to get her money, like most of the men she knew. It is important that the therapist probes such reactions and approaches the "bank manager" in a nondefensive way, in order to help the client understand why such a figure should be constellated. Negative projections cannot be discarded; even a "bank manager" may need to participate in the containing space of analysis. The reliability and continuity of the containing and holding function of place and person are essential. They become the vessel through which the client's soul enters into a felt relationship with the therapist. Analysis can be compared to a sacred space, which provides the context for a symbolic reconstruction of the world so that the client can relate to his or her surroundings in meaningful ways.

To be at home somewhere with someone is a process continually subject to change. The role of aggression needs to be carefully evaluated in terms of its potentially disruptive influence on home life, even if Hestia, goddess of the hearth, was the only Greek divinity who never partook in warfare. But preserving a home at all costs may stifle a person's future development. A middle-aged male client once informed me of an irrational fear he had whenever he anticipated a change in his family. As soon as his children reached puberty, they rebelled against family life and began to break away from parental influence. He could not understand why he was overwhelmed by rage. He tried to prevent their departure from home by ignoring their friends and partners, or withdrawing affection and even financial support. He was horrified to realize how quickly he had become totally self-absorbed and disconnected from his children. In analysis, he began to work through the guilt that plagued him about his destructive behavior. The guilt became alleviated once he could establish the source of his strange conduct, which could be traced back to his childhood home. When he was three years old, his parents forced him to live with his grandparents. He spent many years with the elderly couple. Whenever he was disobedient, they threatened to give him away to strangers. As a child, the man lived in terror of losing his home. Later in life, he enjoyed a successful marriage, had children, and was very content with the intimacy and security of his new home. Once the increasing autonomy of his children signaled a change in family unity, the terror of losing his home surfaced again. The early trauma was now transferred to the adult home. In analysis, he became able to separate the anxiety he had as a child from the anxiety of losing his children. The defensive structures connected with home receded. The underlying aggression, once understood, brought to consciousness a psychological understanding of home as providing space not only for intimacy but also an esteem for differences. He could begin to establish a new relationship to his children, one that respected their autonomy and freedom.

THE DREAMING MIND, OUR SHELTER OF THE NIGHT

Speculation about the origin of dreams has always been a matter of intense discussion. Freud believed that dreams are created by means of ingenious distortions of painful encounters with reality. Jung understood

dreams to be the outcome of a creative activity of the unconscious, involving both personal and collective material. One approach understands
dreams to be a distortion of a language once known, the other as an
expression of a yet unknown language. Whatever school one belongs to,
most psychoanalysts who work with dreams hardly dispute the fact that
dreams arise largely out of imaginative processes not in control of the ego.
The psychoanalyst Charles Rycroft rejects all attempts to explain dreams
as the outcome of largely mechanical processes. Such explanations ignore
"the person or agent" who creates the dream.[6] Dreams are best understood as communications between the waking and sleeping parts of the
self.[7] Dreams are not external to identity; on the contrary, they are part of
a universal normal functioning in every individual. They reflect a natural
human ability to create metaphor that is analogous to artistic abili-
ties—the only difference being that this function continues in sleep.

The dreaming mind is active at all times. It frequently selects material
from the building blocks of our waking life to which we have scarcely
given attention. The day residues, which make up the largest percentage
of dream content, are reassembled in narrative form, together with other
material, mostly from long-term memory.[8] Our dreaming mind reveals
hidden connections. It brings to awareness fragments of ourselves that we
hardly register or don't want to recognize. It is intimately connected with
implicit and explicit memories of early childhood, which influence later
adult behavior. Similar to memory, dreams cut across time, condensing
the past as if it happens in the present or future. Dreams are a composite
of the familiar and the strange. Our dreaming self features images of our
identity where we feel strangers to ourselves. We are convinced that it is
we who are active in dreams, but when waking up we are often relieved to
know it was only a dream. Dream narrative reflects self-images and
images of the other, free from constraints of the external world. Although
we alone invent our dreams, we do so involuntarily. We cannot control
our dreams nor can we force recall. They allow us to play with our life
experiences, as the mind's fertile ingenuity extends beyond the mere
recording of actual events. During sleep, the dreaming mind brings
together people, objects, and events that were previously disconnected.
They permit us a second existence, another home, in which the familiar
and the strange achieve equilibrium. Dreams challenge us by continually
reworking the various dimensions of identity, continuity, and attach-

ment, reminding us that our nocturnal shelter is very different from our abode of the day.

Recent memory research confirms that many parallel and identical functions of the mind appear both in memory and dreams. The building up of a coherent life narrative context requires a combination of long-term memory, imagination, dream, and reflection. Until recently, most people understood memory as a process in which you retrieve experiences of the past that have been stored in the brain as photographs of original experiences. The strength of associations was considered the "royal road" that enabled one to recall those experiences.

Research tells us a very different story about what is now known as implicit, nonconscious memory, which underlies much of our behavior. According to Daniel Schacter, memory is not simply composed of various pieces of objective information stored in one part of the brain and waiting to be reactivated like a computer retrieval system. Memory does not exist as replicas of past events, but as records of how we experienced those events. Long-term memory consists of an elaborate encoding process of converting daytime events into a matrix of meaning. On the one hand, preexistent knowledge influences how we encode and store memories, and how we construct the nature, texture, and quality of the recalled events. On the other hand, cues from the present, whether they be individual or cultural, shape and mold the recalled events of the past. Cues provide the necessary stimuli that combine with engrams (stored knowledge) to yield an ever-changing entity: "the recollected experience of the rememberer."[9]

Memory is now understood as a subjective phenomenon. Memory is the story of our lives. It is a process of construction and reconstruction of one's identity. It does not function from "a unitary faculty," but from a variety of processes. "Specific parts of the brain contribute to different memory processes."[10] Similar to the containing function of home, memory holds together the meaning, sense, and emotions activated in one's perceptions of the present, past, and future. The past is constructed not only from cues operating in the present, but also from intentions for the future. Memory is continually changing as our life narrative evolves. As we become more conscious, recollections of our childhood home change. We appreciate it from a different perspective in youth, midlife, and old age.

As with dreams, long-term memory is creative, and structures knowledge of self and the world. Memory and dreams are like filigree of the one mind, expressing the threaded patterns of human identity and continuity. Both appear as particle and wave, as having fixed content that may be condensed or dissolved into a new context. Both rely on imagery and depend on cues from the external world. Both are creative in the way they transform events experienced in the external world into facets of self. Personal, cultural, and archetypal influences in memory and dream reveal a trans-generational process of identity formation, transcending ego-consciousness and approximating to Jung's notion of the Self.

A study of memory and dreams shows how the human mind operates. It is not a computer, a machine compiling millions of facts and combinations of facts. It is now generally accepted that human intelligence is not just a question of solving mathematical or logical problems. It is an embodied emotional intelligence, which is intrinsically connected with behavior and survival. It emerges in interaction with environment, constructing narratives that inspire an ongoing process of identity formation that is meaningful and continuous.

From recent studies, we discover our dreaming and remembering mind is largely unconscious. It is continually occupied, day and night, in processing our waking life in order to achieve equilibrium between the familiar and the novel. Seen as a whole, the human mind sustains two modes of existence. The one, known through dream and long-term memory, functions differently from the one that has learned to adjust to the cultural and social environment. Particularly in dreaming, a segment of the mind maintains an enigmatic autonomy that can be at odds with the mind's adaptation to the external world. Despite apparent discontinuity, the human mind continually attempts to reconfigure the two modes of existence, day consciousness and night consciousness, into a narrative whole. We may discover that these symbolic narratives are open-ended, connected with the external world and forever creating an alternative world. Paul Ricoeur has reviewed the open-ended function of narrative with regard to the unity of life and human identity.

> And this, I now think, is what we mean by the identity of someone; this too is discordant concordance. Sometimes discordance prevails; other times concordance does....The open-endedness places us in a situation where we can bring ourselves together narratively only by superimposing in some way a configuration with a beginning, a middle, and an end-

ing. But at the same time we are always in a process of revising
the text, the narrative of our lives.[11]

I have described the dreaming mind as the guardian of human identity, continuity, and transformation. It is now time to describe this mind
in practice. The symbolic realm of dreams is not simply made up of
images, but also of sounds and silence; after all, the dreaming mind
already begins to develop in the mother's womb—a world of sounds, not
images.[12] When I first started to work on my personal dreams, I had no
idea about interpretation. I would sit with my dream in silence, allowing
it to gain presence, eventually to become aware of energy inherent in the
dream narrative. I could not say I understood the dream, but I felt better
afterwards, more complete and more rooted in myself. That was forty
years ago. I still practice this approach with my own dreams and those of
my clients. In approaching the dream, one should not begin with a conceptual interpretation. In order to grasp narrative, one has to create a containing framework to make present its pre-symbolic intentions,
particularly its affect, energy, and motivational drive. Narratives, like
symbols, are intentional; they always contain an excess of meaning
beyond the actual image or plot.

A STONE OF CHOICE

I am often amazed at how the dreaming mind transforms experiences
of the outer world into facets of identity. As an example, I would like to
present a dream of my own that I had a few years ago. Work on the dream
brought awareness of the ingenious activity in nighttime consciousness.

> An unknown woman brings shrubs and plants them in the center of
> the garden of my childhood home. I don't think they should be in
> the center, and plant them in another part of the garden. The woman
> objects and I change their positions again. She still does not like them
> there, because it is not what she decided. I then make an arrangement
> of stones in the garden. One arrangement has a phallic shape. The
> woman asks me to remove it.

As usual, I awoke not knowing what the dream could mean. Gradually, three relevant associations came to mind, each part of a puzzle representing a lifelong struggle to achieve autonomy and independence. The
woman is unknown, but reminds me of a woman of my childhood who
bullied me. Thoughts of a powerful female colleague came also to mind. I
"knew" the dream was activated by an impending power struggle. If the

stone penis is removed, could it mean that I would capitulate before the powerful colleague?

Suddenly, a memory of the day before the dream came to mind. I had driven past a stonemason's exhibition of headstones full of beautiful sculptures. Whereas most of my attention was focused on driving in a busy street, for a fraction of a second another part of my mind was drawn to one large standing stone. The mason had chiseled on the stone: "Bush destroys the people's rights and freedom." Focused in keeping my car on the road, I had completely forgotten about the event.

The above associations show how the dreaming mind works. It shifts waking experiences, selects hidden feelings of apparently insignificant events, and weaves them into a new narrative form expressing an important segment of one's life. The dreaming mind connected the insignificant event with other experiences, structures, and intentions of a lifetime that are embedded in my psyche, and that were now activated by an impending power struggle. All this, without my awareness. Only on later reflection did I become aware of the mind's capacity to recast daytime events into a nighttime narrative. Reflecting on the dream, I experienced the mind free from the external world. Objects of the external world became transformed into facets of self. I understood that the dreaming mind had selected a memory of the stonemason's standing stone and transformed that memory into meaning. The standing stone became the necessity of securing my own position in the impending power struggle, the dream gently persuading me that this, too, could and should be part of my identity.

The day residue in the dream brought me back to waking life and encouraged me to explore its interiority, its secrets, its depth, which in the rush of life are quickly cast aside. In this process, day residues become alive as facets of psyche perceiving the world out there. Waking consciousness is for the most part directed, and often excludes nondirected mental activity, which perceives the world differently. Day residues draw our attention to our dreaming in waking life, not just to our waking life in dreams. They are Janus-faced. Our attention is looking in and out at the same time, twilight moments when waking and dreaming consciousness seem to be identical. At that point of intersection, a process of appropriating the world and making it one's own commences.

As I gradually understood the meaning of the dream, an archetypal intent unexpectedly came to mind. The dream not only encouraged me to take a firm position in an impending struggle with a powerful woman, but also awoke memories of a deeper cultural heritage that has always been part of my cultural identity. Standing stones, otherwise known as menhirs, have been traced to a warrior cult. Defeated warriors in Celtic Ireland tied themselves to them in order to die standing upright. In Corsica, standing stones have warrior faces. The stone of Fail in Ireland is known as the stone of choice. If a candidate for the kingship passes by, it will give a shout of recognition. As with *"le cri de Merlin,"* the cry decides the choice of the next king.

The dream linked the diverse identities of my life into a narrative whole. Memories of childhood, fear of women, and conflict in my professional life were now woven into a new pattern, inviting a reappraisal of those events in terms of taking a firm standpoint. The foundations of that standpoint reach deep into history. A psychological lineage is remembered that transcends the personal and initiates transformation of old patterns of avoidance that have compromised the warrior heritage. In such moments the mind, which creates dreams, becomes a trusted shelter, and, acting like an archetypal womb, gives birth to new chapters in one's life narrative. As we open the doors to dreams and implicit memory, we might discover that we are entering the womb of the mind, the birthplace of our longing to belong.

DREAMS OF FORGOTTEN HOMES

Dreams can help us find new and authentic ways of being at home in the world, often by presenting us with messages from fragments of ourselves that feel unfamiliar, forgotten, or disconnected. I remember the case of a middle-aged man who could not understand why he felt increasingly alienated from life. He would dream again and again of frozen landscapes. Associations led back to the first three years of his life, when he lived on a farm and remembered feeling at one with the mountains, fields, and animals of his Alpine home. The farm was sold, but his dreams did not want him to forget the powerful sights, smells, and sounds of the earlier agrarian environment. The task of analysis was to bring back to life the frozen parts of his existence in order to gain a sense of home in the world once more. Many changes occurred—an important one being his decision to relinquish a prestigious career as a banker. He eventually chose another profession that brought him into direct contact with people.

Gradually, the alienation from life lifted, and the images of frozen land-scapes were succeeded by dreams of fertile pastures.

Dreams betray an incredible capacity to represent intimate feelings of loss and attachment in condensed imagery. I witnessed this process in the dream of a woman in midlife. The dream presented an image of two pillars; the first one was shaky and leaning, the second strong and upright. The dreamer awoke in terror. The dream happened on the first night she was not at home and was staying with her partner in a place far away. She was considering moving to her partner's new house. Strangely, the first associations that came to the dreamer were connected with her ex-husband. She was afraid something terrible could have happened to him, felt impelled to telephone him, return to him, and, to her surprise, even be his wife again. As the fear increased, she could find no peace until she finally phoned to see if he was all right. Nothing was wrong. He felt dis-turbed by the call, and she felt stupid. She now had absolutely no idea about what the dream could mean. She was shocked that she could still be so dependent on her husband; even old feelings of guilt returned. She could not understand why she was still attached to him in this way. She had moved away from him several years before. It was an impossible rela-tionship—he allowed her little freedom and could not relate to her. Since the separation, she had blossomed; her confidence increased, and she became a successful artist.

In working with dreams, it is important to be aware that an implicit, unconscious level of communication is taking place that is more con-nected with the mother tongue and may manifest in unexpected fantasies or thoughts. This was the case with the image of the two pillars. As the dreamer spoke, something in the intonation of her voice gave me an indi-cation that I was not talking to an adult, but with a six-year-old child who felt frightened and wanted to go home. I asked if anything had happened to her when she was six. She hesitated, and slowly remembered leaving the family home, which was situated by a river in the countryside. Her heart could find no security in the new home on a busy street in a big city. She was homesick. As she got older, she adapted to city life, but the loss of that childhood home was never healed. She realized that one of the reasons she had married her husband was because of the lovely house he owned, situ-ated on a lakeshore. It took several weeks to realize all this. She felt the despair of the homesick child begin to lift as she relived the pain of the forced adaptation to city life. She could surrender the last vestiges of attachment and security connected to the lovely lakeside house of her ex-husband. This was the story of the dream's first pillar. She also realized that the second pillar was telling her a different story. She could become a pillar of strength, ready to explore and support a new home and a new life.

In both cases, the motif of home did not mean that the dreamers had to go back to their original home to find roots and a sense of belonging, but rather they had to understand the significance of home in their actual life situation. In a state of alienation from their environment, the dreamers felt the need to understand assimilation psychologically and thus connect the inner and the outer home in meaningful ways. Once the soul becomes attached to a person, place, or object, one will not forget such experiences, because they nourish, strengthen, and endow one's existence with substance and structure. Such memories encourage people to extend the horizon of consciousness beyond accustomed habits, perhaps one day to discover new, meaningful ways of bonding with their surroundings.

One can only be full of gratitude whenever the soul, understood as the storehouse of one's attachment history, keeps reminding us that the search for home is a continuous process. Once, a training candidate told me about a dream she had just before seeing her first client:

> I am on a ship, full of refugees who had to leave their home behind. I
> was going from person to person, assuring them with soothing words.
> I told them: I know you have left everything behind, but you are
> heading to some new place and you are safe. My job on the boat was
> to soothe and accompany them.

The candidate's training analyst remarked that the dream was a wonderful image of analysis. Often analysis starts with some kind of loss. There will be periods where both analyst and client do not know where they are going. In such transitory spaces, the empathetic support of the analyst is crucial. The dream reassured the candidate that she need not fear; she had the basic qualifications to be a good analyst.

RELATIONSHIP AND TRANSFERENCE: HOMES REVISITED IN THE ANALYTIC SETTING

Having been raised in the classical school of Jungian psychology, I felt quite at home in working with dreams. Relationship and transference in analysis was far more complex and challenging. That relationship is basic to human existence and is crucial for identity formation is now recognized by the social sciences, infant research, and many Jungian analysts.[13] Throughout life, one is exposed to the reality of another person. Existentially, an I-Thou relationship in analysis is similar to a relationship outside of analysis; it differs only in its purpose and function. In analysis, clients present problems and expect the analyst to accompany them, understand them, and if possible provide a context that will bring healing and renewal. Clients will not only solicit help from the analyst—often, their deeper self will provide guidelines and offer creative solutions to their problems. The analyst is not just a person who interprets problems, but also one who supports, facilitates, and learns from the creative potential of a client. Many times, clients have better insight into their process than the analyst. In the analytical relationship, the analyst is in a position of power, but that power is limited in that it bears a professional responsibility to respect the dignity, integrity, and freedom of the client.

Images alone do not necessarily address key psychological issues or cross the great divide between Thou and I, but images offer both client and analyst a means of communicating and opening doors to start a dialogue about what needs to be explored in the image. Often clients will talk about images they see in their minds, but afterwards remark that nothing happened, nothing changed. Images, as in dreams, may conceal or reveal; one may feel connected to or disconnected from them. In the process of healing, the therapist has to find ways of entering the client's soul through the image. Like a shaman or hero of fairytales, he dons the cloak of invisibility and, as a presence among presences, descends with the client into the underworld of their battered soul. There he may witness tragedies of the past: abuse, abandonment, or betrayal. In such moments, rage can emerge. It may have such a powerful effect on the analyst that he or she can lose structure, identity, and boundaries. Here the community of analysts, as in supervision, is essential. If the analyst holds his position, he may become a guide, parent, or playmate—assigned roles that are in constant need of adjustment according to the shifting needs of the clients as they relive the past through memory, dream, or personal encounter.

The analyst and client form a tandem in which both poles of the duet are registered and enacted. Through a finely tuned sensitivity, the analyst adjusts his or her responses to the client's soul in need, and attempts to provide what was never before given. In that process, an unfinished chapter in the client's life may be continued or a new chapter opened. One client's afflicted soul, imaged in the flight of a wild bird, cried out hour after hour: "Am I welcome? Do you hear my story? I was never welcomed and had to live a life of pretence. I flew away from the earth and from my body. My soul was never born, and now I am looking for a home on earth." And the analyst, recalling to mind the tale of the bewitched children of Lir who were turned into swans by their evil stepmother, would reply to this wild bird, hour after hour: "Welcome, dear bird of the wilderness, I have heard your story. There is a home waiting for you here on earth." In this narrative space, analyst and client initiate a mutual entry into an intense and genuinely felt symmetry of image-to-image, soul-to-soul matching. Narrative spaces, together with the continuous holding structure of the analytic setting, provide the basis for care and soul healing.

In the practice of psychoanalysis, the primary focus is on the relationship between analyst and client, a relationship that includes conscious and unconscious transactions. The relationship is asymmetrical, focus being on the client's life and only on that part of the analyst's life directly connected with the client's process. Symbolic material from the unconscious, as in dream or fantasy, illustrates how the client's unconscious is monitoring the analytic process. Transference is one aspect of the analytic process that concerns those transactions, the sources of which are stored in the unconscious. The child who is exposed to unbearable traumatic events, repeated disappointments, or hopeful expectations in early relationships had to suppress them for his or her protection. In transference, however, they surface again in the adult to become reexperienced in the person of the analyst.

Often in the deep constellations of transference and countertransference, the client finds opportunities to relive much of the past. Clients who have experienced loss of home or abandonment have the possibility of repairing and restoring what has been lost, when entering into the deep mutual bonding of transference. Conflicts arising in analyses revolve around the issue of the analyst's accepting or rejecting the abandoned child in the adult client. The inner child rarely measures up to the rules and regulations of the adult world, particularly those norms that resemble the destructive ones of childhood. Having once been abandoned, the inner child feels doubly let down when the analyst goes away on holiday, or when a process gaining in momentum is suddenly interrupted because the hour is over, or when the analyst gives more attention to his or her "other" family than to the "adopted" child in analysis. The analyst must realize that he cannot indulge in the fantasy of providing a home for all those who need one. But he must also recognize that the anger and rage that the client feels towards the analyst, when he or she fails to meet the client's needs, has its place. The analyst must remain tolerant, for behind such rage the earlier disappointments are being relived. Once the connection between the analytic constellation and the pain of the past reaches consciousness, the client can relive the despair of abandonment, this time aware that the analytic partner, as witness, serves to provide a context of containment, connectedness, and continuity, so that the analytic sessions do not turn into mere repetition of earlier traumatic events.

Three Levels of Transference

I have experienced three levels of transference that affect the analytical relationship and its symbolizing capacity in different ways: projection, projective identification, and interactive transference.

In the case of projection, the relationship is usually one-way, nonreciprocal, and often antagonistic or idealistic. The analyst becomes a carrier of an earlier relationship, usually some parental figure. The analyst has to accept and eventually interpret the projection in a related and connected way, until clients are ready to assimilate it within the context of their own life.

In the case of projective identification, the symbolizing capacity is impaired and unresolved conflicts are reactivated in highly concretized ways. Unwanted fragments of the client's personality are projected onto the analyst, who is experienced as being identical with the content of the projection. Subject to the intensity of the projection, the analyst finds his personality becoming molded in alien ways. Boundary issues become crucial. The powerful impact of the projection triggers the analyst's defenses, and he may react unconsciously. When the projection is activated, interpretation can be misplaced. Once a client came into my office and started the hour by saying: "You look tired, I don't expect anything good to happen in this session." I replied by saying: "Well, let us see how it develops". He replied: "You have just said the wrong thing, I am wasting my time. I might as well leave right now." A silence followed, lasting a few minutes. Then I said: "Let us try to find out what has gone wrong." The client: "When you were silent I could feel your anger." At that moment I wanted to protest by saying I was not angry, but realized this would have been a defensive reaction on my part. Under the onslaught of the projection, my own complexes were activated. Instead of simply reacting, I had to sit through the tempest that had been stirred up in my own psyche while attempting to detect the source of the projection in the client. Once the storm subsided, the client could hear my voice, a voice that was not reacting with a counterattack. He had expected me to attack him; that was the pattern of earlier relationships. Gradually, he could appreciate my efforts to simply get to the source of the rage. He could eventually talk about the cruelty he suffered in childhood. Boundaries were reestablished as the projection receded.

The process in interactive transference is one of a pairing or matching between the analytic partners. Within this framework, the adequate and related responses of the analyst are ways of caring for the abandoned child in the client. They provide a symbolic home for the inner child of the client, so that it may mature and develop. The analyst may find he is becoming a mother or father to this child. It may be necessary to spend hours mirroring the responses of the child, as any mother would mirror her physical child, or to explain things to the child, setting limits or providing reliable structure, as a father would do for his real child. When the inner child suddenly turns into a young woman or a young man, the analyst has to find ways of confirming the newly discovered identity without abusing it. In other words, within the interactive space of analysis, imaginative, mutual, and deeply involved kinship narratives take place. They convey to the client what it means to be familiar in the presence of another, reconstructing the image of self in and through a relationship with the analyst. This is not just a matter of replacing the non-empathetic parent. Empathy does not just enact an ideal parent-child context; it serves primarily as a means of registering, understanding, and communicating the meaning of such experiences to the adult client.[14]

On several occasions, I have discovered that overemphasis on the symbolic dimension of the analytic relationship can impair interaction between analyst and client, lending it an unreal character. Relationship in analysis is a mutual and existentially real encounter with the other. I cannot say I am only a symbolic or mythic father. I am also one of flesh and blood, related in healing and tangible ways to the problematic childhood of a client. If the client has never had a real father, then, within the analytical container, the analyst will become the real father for that inner child. Once, a client resented my description of our relationship as one between a symbolic father and daughter. She felt insulted, and protested, saying that the relationship was not something ephemeral, but intensely real for her, a foundation upon which to build her future life. I felt challenged to the core. It took a while before I could realize how some-times I use words lightly and do not sufficiently consider the impact they may have on another person. Timing is crucial. Here, the word "sym-bolic" was used in an interpretative way, which put me outside of the actual relationship still in the process of unfolding. The language of inti-macy, enacted in close relationships and otherwise known as mother tongue, is very different from the specialized language of the professional.

Interactive transferences constitute a new relationship in which pro-spective and creative aspects of the unconscious are constellated in both analytical partners. A mutual and innovative process begins, which stems from deeper levels of both the client's and analyst's personality. The client delegates roles to the analyst in the hope of creating a relationship that is authentic, existentially real, and was never before available—a clinical phenomenon that the psychoanalyst Heinrich Racker called total trans-ference.[15] The responses of the analyst might be very different from the original attitude of the parents or siblings. As in projective identification, clients expect the analyst to react in the same way as their primary caretak-ers, but when they hear a different voice, one amplifying and discriminat-ing the original text, a connection is made and a change is likely to occur. As we have seen, cues can transform memory so that clients relive the past in ways that were previously not possible. They recover a lost freedom, sacrificed to those people and events that hindered ego development. They begin to see previous events and relationships from a fresh narrative perspective.

A Skin Relationship

In cases of early wounding, work on the foundational levels of a per-son's ability to attach and communicate requires patience, flexibility, and sensitivity to a psychological space developing between analyst and client. In this "in-between" space, both analytic partners are monitoring the pos-sibility or impossibility of contact. Often, clients caught in a phase of early development are full of fear, cannot trust anyone, do not have secure boundaries, cannot defend themselves, and are unable to form lasting relationships. Working with children, Winnicott discovered that on this level there is no distinction between the outer and inner space; the outer space becomes an inner one, and vice versa:

> Certain aspects of a child's play are shown to be "inside" expe-riences; that is to say, there has been a wholesale projection of

a constellation from the child's inner psychic reality so that the room and the table and the toys are subjective objects, and the child and the analyst are both there in this sample of the child's inner world.[16]

Winnicott later termed this stage of maturation a "potential space," which becomes a third space between dependency and separation.[17] Separating from the mother is achieved by transforming the "space between" to a "potential space," which the baby structures with play and the creation of transitional objects that embody inner and outer reality. Likewise the French psychoanalyst Didier Houzel termed the space between inside and outside in the adult as a "psychic skin," which he described as:

[A]ny structure that performs a boundary function between an inside and an outside and thereby allows the elements contained within it to be included in one and the same whole. The concepts of container, psychic skin, skin ego and psychic envelope are in my view equivalent.[18]

Once the adult regresses to this level of their being, analyst and client are plunged into a realm of invisible connections. Every look, sound, word, gesture, or movement has to be carefully evaluated. When an authentic contact is established, the wordless, unheard, and unseen child in the adult enters a space between self and other. As we shall see, it is a bounded, protected space, often symbolized by skin. Skin embodies a boundary between the inner and outer, similar to the way a home represents the threshold between the private and public spheres of activity. If this boundary area is respected, trust and contact is established. The inner child extends its existence to the outer world and allows itself to be seen and heard by another, eventually to shake off old dependencies and to achieve autonomy despite boundary violations of the past.

Barbara, a woman in midlife, would experience an amorphous fear on the way to analysis. As soon as she sat in front of me, the fear would intensify. If she turned her chair away so as not to face me, the fear would disappear, and she then felt connected with herself. As soon as she looked at me, she again became disconnected. She wanted to face me, but could not. She wished to know if there was any way out of this dilemma. We commenced the following dialogue:

Analyst: Let's try to gauge this process. Feel free to turn the chair around or turn it halfway around or leave it as it is where you already face me. You can close your eyes or you can leave them open.

Barbara: Okay. I am afraid, afraid of the hole inside of me, afraid of emptiness.

Analyst: But you are also afraid of the outside, afraid of coming out. The outside is dark and devouring, like the way you described the violent attacks of your mother. *(As I was speaking, I closed my eyes in order to feel the energy that was activated between us.)*

Barbara: I see you with your eyes closed; that means you are vulnerable. That scares me.

Analyst: Yes, I also feel vulnerable.

Barbara: But that is me, too. I am vulnerable. I have no boundaries. Whatever happens outside, I become it. I live my surroundings. That is why I have to hold on to my last skin. I can't give it up.

Analyst: Yes. When you dare to come out, you feel you might be annihilated. *(We had talked about feelings of being annihilated in a previous session.)*

Barbara: What you just said is very difficult. I can feel myself avoiding it. *(Barbara looks at me, and we experience a moment of intense eye contact.)*

Analyst: We just met.

Barbara: Yes. It was scary. For one second I came out, but now I am in again.

Analyst: That is all right. We are just exploring the space between us.

Barbara: It is like taking off my skin. *(Barbara remembers one of her first dreams, in which whales had no skin.)*

In the next session, Barbara told me that for the first time she did not feel afraid on the way to analysis. This was a crucial moment in therapy. Some part of her wanted to run away, but another part knew she was now working on the first year of her life, perhaps even on intrauterine experiences. She felt most vulnerable. Any noise, any distraction would terrify her and force her to disconnect. She then felt sad, alone, and empty. She knew those feelings went back to being an unwanted child, as well as to the violent, cruel attacks that she had suffered during childhood. She felt that the tiny, frightened infant in her might begin to trust me. It was her only hope to change a pattern of fear, disconnection, and withdrawal.

Two weeks later Barbara started the session:

When I look at you I still disconnect. If I turn the chair around I can connect with myself. If I look at you, I can't find peace. I am nerv-

ous. I have to control everything. I start to think and can't turn my
head off.

Barbara then turned her chair around with her back to me and waited
until she felt at peace. She then turned the chair around again and faced
me. She looked at me, shut her eyes, and said she could still hold on to the
feeling of peace. Now she needed to hear me say: "Don't fear. No one will
hurt you. Don't be afraid." I repeated these words gently and slowly. Barbara felt relief. Something new had happened. A hidden part of her could
reach out to another person and explore an affinity that did not annihilate
her, an experience she had not known before.

In the follow-up discussion, Barbara was aware that in the above
exchange a repetition of her early childhood had transpired. Barbara held
on to her last skin to protect her core identity. She grew up in a world
where annihilation was a constant threat. On the way to analysis, she was
overtaken by an inexplicable anxiety. In the transference, I had become a
figure who could destroy her. I also felt vulnerable, exposed, and unsure
about what I was getting into. I had to trust that my psyche would
respond appropriately to Barbara's dilemma. I knew I had to provide a
setting so that Barbara could be conscious of her protective defense system and reevaluate it in the context of the analytic relationship. Instead of
it controlling her, she began to explore a space between self and other that
allowed her more options and choices. Barbara herself could decide when
to be present and when to withdraw in the presence of another.

HOMES OF ANGER

Sometimes an analyst has to encounter a lot of rage before clients feel
safe enough to create their own space in the analytic relationship. Analysis
provides an opportunity not only to relive the past, but also to make
transparent wishes, hopes, or expectations that were never allowed
expression. Rage may be a protection or an expression of self-assertion,
depending on what was permitted in the parental home. Daphne, a
thirty-five-year-old woman, would become enraged with me whenever I
was too solicitous in trying to find out why she felt so much despair and
sadness. When she would come to her session and begin to cry, I would
ask what was the matter and tried to find out the reason why she was so
upset. She felt enraged by my questions, but did not know where the rage
came from. She also experienced intense guilt. After all, the analyst was
caring for her, and she interpreted her rage as a proof that she was a failure

and that I would be disappointed in her and not want to continue the work. She thought she should be a mature, adult person and overcome those dark feelings.

It gradually became clear to her that this rage was only indirectly connected with me. It revealed a memory—her rage against her mother. The mother rarely permitted her daughter to have her own feelings. She constantly invaded her child's space and would make inappropriate comments whenever the child expressed strong emotions. Daphne remembered that when she was upset, her mother would say: "Everybody will think I am a bad mother if you look sad." So Daphne felt guilty and had to hide her feelings. She was not even allowed to own her sadness. A similar situation emerged in analysis. As soon as I showed concern and enquired about her feelings, she felt threatened and invaded. At this stage of the analysis, she needed space to feel her emotional life as belonging to her. Any interference on my behalf was unnecessary; I had to be present as a silent witness. Daphne was in the process of creating a space in which she could appropriate her feelings as her very own. She was giving shape to a new chapter in her life by investing soul energy in those invisible fertile spaces between self and other.

The place of aggression in the analytical container was even more obvious in the case of a young woman who dreamt that I, as therapist, was not at all interested in her, but spent my time "looking at films and talking to others." This young woman had never experienced real home life, and was brought up by a series of foster parents. There was little time to establish a close connection with those caretakers, for she would soon be moved on to others. She grew up with an exaggerated deference for people's roles; she possessed little understanding of what it meant to have had good enough parents. In therapy, she could see me only in the role of analyst—someone who did his job but was not personally engaged in the process.

Gradually, she became aware that something was wrong, and knew a change would have to take place. As I began to state my commitment to her as a person and not just as "a client," she went through a period of turmoil. At first she could not believe anybody should be interested in her as a person, and thought I was just pretending. Both her fear of rejection and a longing to be accepted as someone who counted determined many of our sessions. Alternately she would feel accepted and at home in the analysis, and then enraged with me as someone who was just playing a role and had no interest in her whatsoever. I felt it was important neither to interrupt this process of turmoil, nor to become defensive and insist that I cared for her. The longing for intimacy and understanding had to be balanced by the need to allow anger and protest, reinforcing attachment on the one hand and autonomy on the other. Being at home in analysis did not get her stuck in the parent-child constellation, but gave this woman the opportunity to eventually terminate analysis and establish another home outside of it.

AT HOME IN ANALYSIS?

Analysis as home is a difficult, ambiguous, and controversial idea, especially in view of the fact that one day it will have to end. Clearly, a home in analysis is not an option for everyone. Indeed, it might be only for the few whose early development has been so impaired that they have been unable to form lasting attachments or to know what a good enough home can be. Home in analysis is like the navigating of a ship in uncharted waters. On the one hand, the analyst provides a context in which the good parent or caregiver offers a new perspective on home as a place of safety and containment; on the other hand, this approach will trigger the client's memories of the old home, releasing outbursts of mistrust, terror, rage, or guilt. As the analyst attempts to provide a more secure base for authentic attachment, he may well be verbally attacked for destroying the client's hope for security. If clients have not had the experience of having a home or having intimate and lasting relationships outside of therapy, it is understandable that they will seek those qualities inside therapy and inside the therapist. The heart begins to open once the therapist is seen as the one who provides protection, care, and understanding—something the client never received, but always wished for. Obviously, a lot of energy is transferred onto the analyst once the therapist becomes the good father, mother, sibling, or fellow human—or when the room, ritual, or setting of therapy becomes the home the client had always longed for.

When home enters therapy, a new level of relationship begins, creating a new narrative of childhood. I have noticed sometimes that the inner child of the client could only speak to me when I became the mother or father whom the client would visit in an imaginary landscape. In this situation, the client may be terrified that any look, gesture, or sound of voice on my behalf could destroy the budding, yet-vulnerable relationship. In such moments, overwhelming memories of the abusive parent are activated and transferred onto me, the therapist. All this may be unavoidable, and at times it feels like embarking on a rollercoaster. At the appropriate moment, I try to consolidate the rich narrative context we have built up over the years, and contrast it with the earlier behavior of the non-empathetic parent. I remind the client of the various times I approached the devastating moments when pain was inflicted, and how, as an understanding parent, I tried to meet the broken fragments of childhood and adolescence. In the course of analysis a new landscape is created, peopled with figures with whom the newly emerging identity of the client can communicate. Healing conversations may take place in an imaginary home—a beautiful house, a protected space, full of people who provide support and understanding.

At home in analysis may activate a kinship bonding that transcends the analytic context and may even outlast it. The origins of kinship established in analysis are difficult to decipher. Not only do they emerge from personal biography; they also have a collective, cultural significance. Possibly they are a modern way of enacting the kinship bonding practiced in indigenous societies. Diane Bell, in her book *Daughters of the Dreaming,* describes the waiting period needed before she could begin her research on the tribal secrets of Australian Aboriginal woman. Only after she had been incorporated into the so-called skin relationships—as mother to A., daughter to B., aunt to C., cousin to D.—could the women talk about their tribal mysteries. They would communicate their deepest secrets once a kinship was established that was both symbolic and real.[19] One may ask if an analyst's attempt to relate with the client in the context of transference represents a modern version of the Stone Age pattern of relating? We discover again and again in analysis that people are ready to speak about their deepest secrets only after some form of authentic attachment has been established.

Perhaps it is too simple to draw a parallel between the patterns of relating in analysis and those of non-sanguine kinship, as encountered in the Aboriginal traditions of Australia. It is, however, possible that the same archetypal source is activated in both cultures. Transference in analysis and the customs of the indigenous people of Australia may point to a fundamental need of the human soul. Deep secrets, individual or tribal, are communicated within a framework of kinship. Skin in both cases symbolizes a sensitive boundary between the inner and outer, I and

Thou. Only if there is mutual rapport of mind and heart can a relationship of intimacy take root. In kinship pairing, the soul blossoms and is ready to undo the knots of mistrust, eventually to yield her secrets. Jung understood this archetypal source of transference when he wrote:

> To the extent that transference is a projection and nothing more, it divides quite as much as it connects. But experience teaches us that there is one connection in transference that does not break off with the severance of projection. That is because there is an extremely important instinctive factor behind it: the kinship libido.[20]

Not all the varieties of relationship in analysis are based on a parent-child model. Publications on mutual transferences indicate that a working through of difficult asymmetrical connections between analyst and client may lead to experiences of a common meaningful world, implying equality, kinship, and a sense of belonging to one another that transcends the actual analytic setting. Acknowledging common cultural interests may be particularly significant for the ending of analysis.[21] Sometimes an extremely painful process begins when the client leaves the home, which analyst and client have constructed, and which has provided shelter over a long period of time. Nevertheless it can happen that the recognition of shared human interests, which transcend the work done in analysis, will provide a foundation to survive loss and act as a support for the building of another home outside analysis.

In my work as an analyst, I have experienced many different ways of terminating analysis. When analysis has been a home, ending therapy can be extraordinarily difficult. Disappointment, mistrust, betrayal can complicate a good ending—the client has experienced the analyst as a father, mother, friend, helper, or simply a fellow human, and in the end the client feels this had no substance. There is no one solution to the problems that arise in such a situation. Obviously, an abrupt end should be avoided. Occasionally an ending has to be negotiated over a long period of time. It may happen that the relationship after analysis consists of discussions about how the years in therapy have changed one's life, what one has learned from analysis, or what could have been done better. Subsequent meetings may have the purpose of giving assurance to the client that the relationship established in analysis was authentic.

Although each ending of analysis is unique, I will conclude this chapter with a dream of a client who suffered from various anxieties that inhibited her from living a full life. The dream illustrates an ending of a long analysis that assured both analytic partners that the task had been completed, and that she was ready to enjoy a newfound freedom.

> I find myself in a green landscape. On a hilltop I see a schoolhouse. I see students entering this house and I know I am expected to enter as well. For some reason, I decide not to go anymore. I sit on the green grass during the morning to see what will happen. As I sit there, I can feel joy and freedom. At the end of the morning, I see that the teacher is my analyst, who is now saying goodbye to the students. In the afternoon, I again make up my mind not to attend school. I now decide I will dare something new and go on a bicycle ride. On my way, I keep my eye on the school, but then I have to concentrate so much on pedaling uphill that I lose sight of it. For a moment I feel insecure and helpless, but then I decide to continue and I become really curious about what will come next. Now I feel really free and happy. At the same time, I know that the schoolhouse will always be there and I can always return if I need to.

The dream reflects an early behavior pattern of childhood. As we have seen in the previous chapter, the child, when separating from the mother, adopts a separation-reunion pattern so that it can be sure that the mother continues to exist even if she is no longer visible. The balancing of autonomy and dependency indicates a precursory stage to coping with later homesickness. The beautiful dream narrative provided the client with an archetypal story that helped her survive separation from home in analysis, and contains a motif generated from a behavior pattern practiced already in the early years of her life.

Why a schoolhouse? Perhaps this image expresses the dreamer's unconscious perception of analysis as being influenced and shaped by a particular school and never simply a repetition of an earlier family home. The actual analytic relationship might at times regress to a dyad, but for the analyst it is always triangular. Analysts cannot afford to retreat into isolation, but should maintain a collegial connection, which allows their work to be reflected, criticized, and supported among peers. An analyst may provide a home in analysis, but that home is embedded in the context of a professional community.

CHAPTER 7

Homes of Fate, Homes of Destiny: Individuation and the Transcendent Function

The sphere rolls; never can it be certainly known where a story has its original home, whether in heaven or on earth.[1]

—Thomas Mann

In chapter 5, I gave a partial outline of the complexity of early child development and the enormous significance of bonding with primal caretakers. I reviewed some of the devastating effects of abandonment, which may have a lifelong influence. I described a child's struggle to create defensive structures in order to prevent further damage. In chapter 6, I gave examples from my own work, emphasizing the importance of providing a containing space that allows long-forgotten, hidden potentials of the soul to surface and blossom in a person's life. This process may be supported in many ways: in work with fantasy, dream, transference, and the kind of relationship established in psychotherapy. Interpretation of psychological material is crucial, but only has lasting effects if both analyst and client can reach the deeper levels of kinship affinity. I illustrated these complex processes from clients' narratives that were intrinsically connected with the need for home. This chapter will focus on the impersonal, collective aspects of home symbolism as an emergent, archetypal reality, but nevertheless enmeshed in personal biography.

HOME: A PROCESS OF INDIVIDUATION

Many of the ideas, quotations, or anecdotes in this book describe the changing circumstances of home. Most of us have had not only one home, but several. Each home has its own story, and each story reveals an identity, formed and fashioned by the circumstances of that dwelling place. You may try to link the various homes and the different identities you have created by articulating narratives about them—tales of deterioration, tales of repetition, tales of individuation—as you attempt to grasp what holds your life together. Such tales are not always linear. They are usually serpentine and unfold as a labyrinth of narratives. You may not know if you are moving forward or backward. Some doubt, some persevere, others endure hardships, and there will be those who need support. Sometimes an unexpected encounter from within or without can provide the clue for the next stage of the journey.

It would be impossible to give an adequate assessment of all the ideas connected with the stages of human development. I have selected a few to serve as an introduction to this chapter. In Dostoyevsky's *The Brothers Karamazov*, the two brothers, Ivan and Alyosha, discuss midlife. In the first half of life, Ivan has drunk the cup of life and all becomes lawful: "to love life more than its meaning."[2] In the second half of life, through a profound awareness of human guilt towards all creation, Alyosha tells Ivan to turn to the resurrection of life, "to raise up your dead [who] may never perhaps have died." Another illustrious writer of the nineteenth century, Oscar Wilde, elegantly remarks on life's changing conditions. In the first half of life, "[t]he soul is born old, but grows young. That is the comedy of life." In the second half of life, "[t]he body is born young and grows old. That is life's tragedy."[3] James Joyce captures, with some remorse, the ambiguities of life's stages in a statement attributed to him: "The unlived dreams of one's youth become the unwanted realities of mid-life." The theologian Jürgen Moltmann sees life's pattern in four basic stages: trust in childhood, longing in youth, responsibility in maturity, wisdom in old age.[4] Confucius witnessed his life evolving in six stages:

> At 15, I set my heart on learning; at 30 I was firmly estab-
> lished; at 40, I had more doubts; at 50, I knew the will of

heaven; at 60, I was ready to listen to it; at 70, I could follow
my heart's desire without transgressing what was right.[5]

If we adopt Jung's individuation process as a model for ongoing life,
care is needed that it does not become an ideology or, worse still, a
power-program, dividing the sheep from the goats—those who can indi-
viduate from those who cannot. Life itself, in all its fullness, is individuation. Life is far too complex to follow an itinerary that expects everyone to
fulfill the biological needs in the first half of life and the spiritual in the
second half. If the necessary conditions are given, an individual life
evolves of its own accord. When we consider individuation from the perspective of a child, who gains a sense of self and of being at home in the
world at the end of the first three years of life, we can expect his or her life
narrative to unfold in authentic ways. Individuation evolves organically,
and is not dependent on the possession of a house, partner, family, or job.
The purpose of our childhood home is to provide the individual with a
foundation for surviving the loss of any particular home, which is to be
expected in the course of a lifetime. Plasticity has become a key biological
and psychological term expressing an inherent resilience of plant, animal,
and human nature for surviving loss and adapting to a new environment.
The aim of analysis is to facilitate those inner resources so that the move
from the old to the new home can evolve in an organic way.

Children encounter such changes more than once with the breakup
of a home and the consequent adjustment to new surroundings, new
schools, or new friends. The process usually continues into late puberty
and young adulthood, as a person attempts to move out of the parental
home and establish his or her own home. The young man or woman can
no longer identify with the world of their parents. Their impulse is to live
their own life. They start looking for a new home in a partner or profession, house or family, creed or party. The ancient rituals of initiations into
manhood or womanhood, sadly lacking in our time, helped the young
person to enact the transition from the old to the new—from the state of
being the child of parents to becoming an adult member of society.

In midlife, the glamour of outer success begins to fade. One may no
longer have the same energy to repair or improve the house, buy more furniture for cluttered rooms, struggle for the next promotion, or continue a
partnership that has lost its life-promoting energies. For some, the reality
of the soul may then become a focus of attention. Its whispers may be dis-
cerned from an inner voice or encountered in another person who bears a

different message than the one of previous relationships. The energies released from such encounters can either renew the faded life of the old home or signal the foundation of a new home, partnership, or profession—perhaps initiating a path of liberation from the urge to hoard and possess. At this stage, you may begin to let go—to relinquish power over people and possessions and, if necessary, an identity that no longer finds purpose or meaning in the old landscapes.

In the film *Face to Face*, Jung remarks that in old age the psyche behaves as if life continues, despite the ever-approaching certainty of physical death. During the final stage, you realize that you have to relinquish everything. All that you have carefully built up, all the attachments that you have made, all the homes you have experienced will be lost forever. Now arises the question of the continuity of life. Ultimately we do not seem to belong here. Where are we going? Do we have another home that is not of this world? Even if we doubt it, our dreams hint at the existence of that other home. I will never forget the words of an old woman, shortly before her death. She talked about all the people, the animals, and the places that she had loved during her long life. All of them had passed away. She had to mourn their loss and outwardly let them go. She said:

> I am going home. But before I die, I wanted to recall to my mind all those loved ones of my life, wrap them carefully in a basket and take them with me, for they are part of me forever.

The above examples portray the individuation process through the metaphor of home. There are of course many other symbolic images that describe this process. Individuation, from a Jungian point of view, arises from a relationship with one's unconscious. Following the example of Jung, many have experienced the unconscious not only as a repository of unresolved conflicts that manifest in disturbing images, feelings, or thoughts, but as a source of creativity. Deep within, the unconscious mind acts as a regulating principle that seems to know more about us than we are consciously aware of. Our mind is active day and night. Through dream, fantasy, intuition, or affect, it continually processes experiences, sifting them out and providing perspectives that give us hints on how to live a life that brings healing, hope, and wholeness.

The Swiss essayist François Bondy described modern man as broken man. Individuation often begins through an awareness of being lost, broken, divided, or abandoned. When we take the fragmented pieces of life seriously and start the work of repair, individuation has already begun.

One may encounter pitfalls and commit numerous errors; the search may be never-ending, continuing for a lifetime. As one travels this road, one encounters fellow seekers, individuals who know they don't have all the answers but understand the necessity of enduring the unpredictable. Sometimes Jungian analysts have to believe in the impossible—or, more correctly stated, in that which cannot yet be imagined. Jungian analysis is essentially work with the unconscious. Openness and flexibility in facing the unknown are required. Honoring psychic reality in oneself and others is a fundamental tenet, which is equivalent to honoring whatever a person considers to be true. It is a lonely work, but the analyst cannot fall into isolation. Clinical skills, professional experience, and collegial exchange have become increasingly important as knowledge of this dangerous profession advances.

From Homes of Fate to Homes of Destiny

Sooner or later, most people will cherish the fantasy of having two homes, the real one and the ideal one. As they grow older, many will feel an increasing tension between the two homes, between what is and what could be. The more one was forced to adapt to the caregivers of the first home, the more likely one will feel imprisoned, fatefully linked with a particular place or person whom one might even hate.

Fate is one of the most ancient beliefs of humankind. Fate is about an ordering principle of the universe and the patterns of life transcending conscious intention. Most humans have encountered the imprisoning powers of fate, knowing well that they contradict the notion of being a free agent. Fate can intervene in human life in many ways, at any time, anywhere—in individuals, communities, and entire cultures. It can appear as demonic or divine. Through the passion for love or war, the patterns of fate can possess individuals and nations. The great artists and narrators of culture have attempted to present fate within a human context, linking men and women with the hidden messages of the gods. Many struggle to discern fate's hidden message in order to grasp its pattern and avoid being its victim. Fate appears in individual destinies. Its destructive potential can be recognized in the pathologies carried within, yet these pathologies harbor a creative potential, once the gods or demons have been appreciated. In fate one may sense a calling, a vocation, that is not identical with and sometimes is opposed to conscious intention. Fate can become a call of destiny, often encountered in the biographies of famous people.

Many are the explanations of the powers of fate, which rule over the lives of individuals, households, and nations. Jung resorted to the theory of archetypes. As an impersonal, inherited disposition of the soul, the archetype imparts structure, value, and meaning to human life. Jung's theory of archetypes was first understood implicitly in 1909 as the power of fate, embodied in a father whose influence over his daughter appeared as "some demonic power at work controlling mortal destiny."[6] Only in 1912 were archetypes formulated as primordial images, and finally introduced as "archetypes" in 1919.[7] Without these structural dispositions, human life would be unthinkable and unimaginable. Despite the numinous power of archetypal reality, Jung continually warned against identification with an archetype, which would only lead to an inflation and severe impairment of individual autonomy. In a later work, he suggested that destiny could be interpreted in terms of archetypal influence.

> As we have already explained, the phenomena of the unconscious can be regarded as more or less spontaneous manifestations of autonomous archetypes…it is amply supported by the fact that the archetype has a numinous character: it exerts a fascination, it enters into active opposition to the conscious mind, and may be said in the long run to mould the destinies of individuals by unconsciously influencing their thinking, feeling, and behaviour, even if this influence is not recognized until long afterwards.[8]

Jung discovered the archetype at a specific moment; it evolved to become an explanatory model, linking multiple events and experiences into a pattern of meaning. The archetype, however, is not to be understood as an abstract concept that replaces the image; on the contrary, the universality of the archetype is colored, qualified, and enriched through the particular image. Jung avoided what Cassirer termed the mythic impulse towards "concentration" and "intensive compression" of the mythic image,[9] without negating "the active and creative energy of the fates" as described by F. M. Cornford.[10] Analytical psychology is known for being open to receiving direct inspirations from the soul; at the same time, it does not dispense with the all-inclusive context of rational discourse.

The purpose of this chapter is to describe the intimate spaces of home as realms where transpersonal, collective attachments emerge, embodied in our primary caretakers, our teachers, and our dreams, shaping our lives and attitudes to the world around us. Such attachments sustain home as a terrain of fate. It may be a home of love or a home of hate. Inevitably we are condemned to repeat them, if we cannot make conscious those early attachments that have determined the fabric of our being. Good enough interpretations challenge the powers of fate, prevent victimization, and create a context allowing a freer embrace of destiny.

There is often confusion in the meanings of the words "fate," "fatalism," and "destiny." James Hillman, writing about fate from a psychological point of view, has emphasized that the plurality of the Fates do not occupy the human psyche entirely, but only parts of it.[11] They are not to be confused with a belief system of fatalism, in which all of life has been predetermined, leaving no space for choice or freedom. On the other hand, the word "destiny" implies intention. The main difference between fate and destiny is that fate is connected with something that will happen to you and cannot be changed, while destiny is associated with intention, direction, and goal.[12] In the distinctions between fatalism, fate, and destiny, there seems to be an ascending order of control, choice, and consciousness, even if the gods or demons maintain the upper hand in the end. For Christopher Bollas, capricious fate was linked with cultures that were agrarian, in which there was great dependency on the seasons for survival.[13] With the rise of the middle classes, the positive significance of destiny increased, encouraging individual initiative and action in a world that is less thwarted by fate's capriciousness. Applying the role of fate and destiny to psychoanalysis, Bollas believes the fated person suffers from complexes that severely impair his capacity for work, pleasure, or relationships.[14] The role of the analyst is to unravel the latent meanings of fate, and help to free that person from the curse of ignorance. The true self of those who feel themselves to be victims of fate "has not been met and facilitated into lived experience."[15] Similar to Jung's notion of individuation, Bollas understands destiny as addressing the evolution of the true self, a force imminent in each person's "unique idiom of being." Likewise in contemporary psychotherapy, tapping a patient's internal resources has become a key factor in undoing the knots of pathology.

The following statements from various people illustrate victimization by the powers of fate, yet in those cries of anguish we hear also a protest.

"Everything has gone wrong again."

"My astrologist says that this month Saturn will devour my moon."

"I asked the I Ching about this man, and I got 'Withholding'"

"I am back to square one. My mother got me again and I binged."

"No matter what I do, analysis does not seem to have any effect on
my problem. Fate will never relieve me from my depressions."

Although these people feel themselves to be victimized, they seem to
know that something has gone wrong and that they have suffered injustice. For a long time they have struggled with fate, even if they felt they
were losers. They may have compared themselves with others: "Why can't
I have a life like them?" Their protest reaches back to their parents, to destiny, or to God. They sense that they were caught in a web of circumstances beyond their control. They raise questions about the origins of
good and evil, the meaning or meaninglessness of life. They protest about
the injustice suffered in homes they did not create. We may hear a story
about violence, abuse, or broken boundaries. A consciousness of self
could not be maintained and was constantly undermined by intrusive
impositions, often a confused amalgam of parents, culture, or God. Their
will is broken, and their sense of continuity and identity is continually
ruptured. One part of the self is pitted against the other, and that struggle,
too, is acknowledged to be part of one's fate. Their developmental process
having been severely impaired, they find themselves unable to remember
what went wrong, unable to distinguish the various parts of the puzzle,
and unable to recognize what belongs to parents, to culture, or to God.

At some time, a process of sorting out the transgressions begins, often
with the start of therapy. The work usually commences with the parents.
Sometimes we trace the complaints of clients—depressions, repetition
compulsions, or psychosomatic disorders—back to the primal relationship. Repressed emotions around cruel feeding schedules, strict toilet
training, trauma, abandonment issues, or non-empathetic parents are
bound to explode in therapy, particularly in transference, leaving both
analyst and client stunned. Many years of therapy, which include a heavy
dose of countertransference, are essential to a narrative context in which
the split-off feelings are relived in meaningful ways. Because these primary affects are unconscious, they often determine a person's life in fatalistic ways. Such affects are autonomous, repetitive, inhuman, and
impervious to reason or reality. Those who consider themselves victims of
fate utter statements like:

"I can't do anything, gods and demons control my life."

"I am so obsessed with myself that I will never have any friends."

"When I come to analysis, I can't help hating you, but when I am at home it is the opposite. That is total humiliation."

The more primitive the affects are, the less one can reason with them. Sometimes analysts simply have to accept the projections and be strong enough to carry them. The analyst must be careful not to identify with them; they often possess an all-convincing divine or demonic power. In working through repetitions of the non-empathetic parent's behavior, opportunities arise for analyst and client to break the inexorable power of a fated bondage, create a new narrative context that distinguishes the human from the super- or sub-human, and thus together contain the powers of fate. Once these are contained, transformational experiences are likely to happen, surprising both analyst and client. Handling the fates in this way may lead to a new understanding of the relationship between fate's patterns and personal destiny.

"They are responsible for everything that has gone wrong in my life." Such a statement places fate within a personal framework. In the sorting-out process, blame is first placed on the parents. On further analysis, one discovers that the parents, too, suffered under a similar fate, and you find yourself looking at one link in an endless chain. The person who carries the suffering of their family may be the very person whose destiny is to break the power of a fate that has dominated family life over generations. When healing takes place, many positive events happen to other family members—events that have no outer, causal connection.

In tracing the origins of fate, you are likely to discover its impersonal power embedded in identification with a parent figure. It is not only the parents, but also the power of fate that has such overwhelming influence. Inevitably, one discovers a collective issue at the core of the personal relationship. This may manifest as a complex, which in turn may take on characteristics of a cultural complex, transmitted through a collective memory, activated from a "hunger to belong."[16] It is autonomous, highly charged with emotion, and resists change. Such patterns have a massive influence on our attitude to home, and can be traced to ideologies that control people through fear; cultures that degrade women; societies that judge people by their skin color, religious affiliation, intelligence, or some other extraneous factor that has little to do with the well-being of the person as a whole. Sometimes we may trace the powers of fate to some collective catastrophe that has long been forgotten or repressed, such as famine, earthquakes, war, or the Holocaust. The following vignettes describe narratives of clients who were first caught in the imprisoning powers of fate, but could transform those prison houses into temples of freedom.

THE BANISHED GODDESS

Milena, a woman from Eastern Europe, suffered from anxiety attacks and lack of concentration (Attention Deficit Disorder-ADD). One day she brought to analysis the following dream, which she felt was connected with her complaint.

> I saw a small female doll standing by the radiator of my parent's house, just under the control faucet. She wore a shawl in the typical Russian fashion. Water leaked from the faucet, dripping onto her head. I feel anxious for her. I ask father to stop the water. Maybe he did something, maybe he did nothing. Suddenly the doll became a little child. Her head grew larger and larger. I felt anxious and started to cry. I awoke crying in despair.

The dream refers back to the time when Milena's nation was controlled by the Soviet Union. The radiator was in her parent's house. Sometimes it was so hot that it hurt if she touched it. The family had to continually take care of it. The dreamer remembers how the heating system for the entire town would break down two or three times a year.

Milena's mother maintained an important teaching position in Moscow. She would bring this kind of doll to her daughter whenever she returned from the city. Milena was happy to receive such a present. She now sees the gift as a compensation for being sent away to substitute parents or left alone when her mother departed. She was overcome with deep sadness when remembering the long absence of her mother. Milena described her father as being distant.

Following the associations, I first thought that the dream was about Milena's relationship with the mother. The radiator could symbolize the relationship that could give warmth but leaked, implying that her mother's affection was not consistent. Milena often felt like a helpless doll; she was entirely dependent on her parents, yet abandoned by them. This interpretation seemed to work, but we both felt it did not mirror the intensity of affect contained in the dream. Why did the dreamer's head grow larger and larger?

Not being able to make further progress, I decided to meditate and let my mind wander (Freud's nondirected attention). I found myself remembering the time I spent in Moscow, giving lectures and staying overnight with a university professor. It was autumn and I still remember the bitterly cold weather. The city's heating system was not turned on. My host was very angry at the city's central authority, which decided precisely when the heating system for the whole town would be switched on. It then dawned upon me that was the usual heating conditions for most people in Eastern Europe, including Milena's town.

Awakening from this reverie, I said to the Milena: "The heating system symbolizes the central control of the old Soviet government system." My conjecture brought immediate response. Milena remembered the terrible quarrels between her parents about the communist party during her childhood. Her mother was a communist; her father was not. Each time the city's centrally controlled heating system broke down, fights about communism would erupt. The feuds terrified little Milena. She could not understand what they were about. She felt helpless, flipped out, lost her powers of concentration, and felt her head becoming bigger and bigger.

Much of the dreamer's insecurity and difficulties in concentration could now be traced back to the parental conflicts. The parents' arguments for or against the communist system assumed an emotional intensity that terrified young Milena, preventing her from coping with the situation. In such moments, a cultural complex took possession of the parents: the mother rigidly defending communism, the father hating it. Both lost all sense of moderation and failed to take care of their frightened daughter. A political ideology that at one time controlled all of Eastern Europe literally leaked into Milena's home and, like the powers of fate, controlled in divisive ways the emotional life of her family. This was especially tragic, considering that the hearth is the realm of Hestia, the goddess who never partook in warfare. The communist control system banished Hestia and the values she represented from the family home.

The dream helped Milena become aware of the source of her anxiety and lack of concentration. The communist ideology harmed the conjugal life of her parents and her own emotional stability and confidence. Political arguments inflated the head and muted the heart. As Milena gradually weeded out the influence of that ideology, she could gain more confidence in her own feelings, especially when facing situations of potential conflict.

A HOME OF FEAR

The following narrative is about Adele, a young woman who became a victim of the imprisoning powers of fate, expressed in a cultural complex that controlled the family home over generations.[17] The family religion was a severe brand of Protestant pietism. They owned a large farm, which demanded all the energy and attention of her parents. Adele was the second-eldest daughter in a family of twelve siblings. She had to sacrifice many of her needs to care for her younger siblings. She qualified as a nurse and later moved to Zürich to study medicine. Since she had moved to the city, Adele suffered from depression, unsatisfactory relationships, and feelings of inferiority. She described herself as a "girl from the country," homeless and unable to fit in to the sophisticated atmosphere of Zürich. When depressed, she felt her grey urban surroundings to be an evil place, possessed by the devil, a place without spirituality or love. Adele felt victimized by this evil influence. Her dark feelings became acute shortly before taking an important exam. She was convinced that fate was against her, and failure imminent. One night, after a full day's work, she had the following dream:

> I come into the examination hall. The professor sits on a large chair. Those who are allowed to do the exam are sent to the right, and those who are not permitted to do so are sent to the left, to the gas chambers. I am sent to the left and I awake in terror.

When Adele brought her dream to me, she was extremely frightened and absolutely convinced that she would fail the exam. I recognized a disparity between the Christian motifs of the Last Judgment, located in a Nazi setting, and the actual exam situation, understood as a modern initiation into a professional identity. In several dramatic sessions, work focused on separating her actual fear of exams from the deeper anxiety of eternal damnation. It became a question of separating adulthood from childhood. I confirmed that her preparation for the exam was sufficiently thorough and her chances of success were excellent. The dream was pointing to another fear—a fear of an all-powerful, inhuman God, who had already pronounced judgment over her and the world.

For several sessions, we focused on the two forms of anxiety. Finally, in one session, Adele unexpectedly remembered the family governess in charge of the children's education. Every night, the governess gave the children a lecture on good behavior and warned them not to be bad or else the devil would come in the night and take them away—never to return home again. Each night of Adele's childhood was a night of terror. No matter what she did during the day, the all-powerful demon of the night would find fault with her. Her destiny was sealed; she had no way of defending herself. She had become a victim of a cruel fate permeating the family life over generations.

Amplifying the dream was crucial to our work. We discovered the root of the fatal bonding with the governess who had assumed the power of a God, imprisoning the dreamer's soul in a religion of guilt and fear. With the help of amplification, Adele could separate the inhuman from the human. This involved several discussions on sorting out "Christ's Last Judgment," "the Nazis," "the governess," and "the professor." In this process, she could internalize "the judge" and gain more confidence in her own capacity of self-evaluation. Eventually, she decided to disengage herself from the religion of her family, which had obscured the boundaries between God, the devil, and the governess. She began to believe in herself and her capacity to become a confident and less frightened member in a social framework of her own choosing. Adele succeeded in the exam and later in her profession.

The above narratives illustrate a blurring of boundaries between a parent figure and a cultural tradition, experienced in images of the banished goddess and the Last Judgment, which shaped the childhood home and maintained a fatal influence over a lifetime. Healing began through focus on powers of fate embodied by the early caretaker. The process of demythologizing the parent was crucial to the healing process. Children belong to their parents' world, which may be felt as a prison or a source of warmth and protection. They often do not have the capacity to create their own world except in a wish, dream, or fantasy. As witnessed above, the childhood home is not only made up of parents and siblings, but is an arena of trans-generational social, political, or religious ideologies that mold the emotional life of a family in fatalistic ways. Parents may not be conscious of this kind of influence, and pass it on to their children unaware of its detrimental influence. I have recognized fate's influence in fathers returning from war, mothers who were sexually abused in childhood, or men and women who were discriminated against because of their skin color. Unable to understand traumatic experiences, parents may unintentionally act out the brutalities that they once suffered on their children. The influence of fate may not always be dramatic; it may be witnessed in homes where parents sacrifice their individuality on the altar of ideals sanctioned by society, such as success, wealth, or fame. In such cases, their capacity to relate with their children in deep and authentic ways may be impaired. The spiral of fate becomes perpetuated. The power of fate, entangled in the relationship with the parents, has to be made conscious if change is to occur.

Homes of Destiny

One can scarcely underestimate those golden moments when parents convey to their children love, respect, and dignity of which an individual person is worthy. One has the impression that such parents have gained a sense of personhood, which prevents the family from being victims of a collective ideology. They are unlikely to pass on imprisoning cultural norms that cripple a child's budding individuality. Children from such homes feel seen and understood. Their sense of self is strengthened. Here, "self" is not to be understood as a permanent state of being—it is more like an awareness of a dynamic equilibrium or a regulating principle linking the fragments of our existence into a new whole, as we respond to the ever-changing circumstances of life. The sense of self is constantly shifting, colored and formed by the multitude of encounters in our waking and sleeping life. No word can adequately define what selfhood means. It is like an immanent potentiality that is more a surprise than a certainty. Home with good enough parents is later remembered as fountain of inner resources, a leaven for the various identities we have built up or cast aside. These influences, personal or impersonal, remain throughout a lifetime and are available as a source of imagination, reflection, and prolific emotional exchange. Individuals with this background feel connected with themselves and their history, and can work with the influences of the past in original and creative ways.

Ruggero's Olive Field

Some narratives about home are full of surprises. They can lift depression and bring healing to the momentary afflictions of a suffering soul. Ruggero, a client of mine, once told me about visits to his ancestral home in Southern Italy:

> We lived in town. When I was a child, we would often go back to the countryside and visit the ancestral home. My relatives were still living in the house. My grandmother was very powerful and strong. She never liked me climbing trees. She was afraid that the olive trees might be injured. I begged my father to buy a tree for me so that I could climb it. He bought a small plot of land with several olive trees. Now I could climb trees, our trees. I will never forget what my father did for me. We still own that plot of land. It is a little gold mine. Each year it provides several hundred liters of olive oil, more than enough for the whole family. Father was worried I might sell it one

day. I would never do that. I could sell everything else, but not the field. My olive field… It is like a church. It never changes, just like the surrounding landscape and the old people who live on the land. No matter what I do, they never change. They are reliable. When I go back to the village, meet my relatives, and see my olive field, I am at home.

Ruggero's narrative appears to advocate a return home as the most effective remedy for homesickness. He has, however, lived in several different countries and not suffered the profound sense of homelessness that causes confusion, disorientation, and loss of containment. He visits his beloved olive field only once in a while, and is under no compulsion to do so. Ruggero described his relationship with his parents as problematic. Outwardly, they were overprotective; inwardly, he felt misunderstood and neglected. Nevertheless, he remembered moments of vital exchange in which his whole being was reflected in their eyes. The purchase of the olive field was one such moment. It was highly significant that Ruggero's father supported him in defiance of his domineering grandmother, an act that strengthened Ruggero's identity as a man, so important in a culture in which females could be all-powerful in the family milieu. As he told his tale, it dawned upon him that his identity belonged to the far wider context of land, family, and culture. It created connection to his ancestors and promised a prosperous future. His soul gained a sense of continuity and belonging, experienced as an inner resourcefulness to face the challenges of the future. Home was not the olive field, but that field represented an outer and inner reality that survived change and brought to Ruggero a sense of being in the world that was reliable.

The olive field narrative illustrates a foundational experience of soul kinship with self and the world—with family, culture, and the surrounding countryside. Home became an inner reality that Ruggero could carry with him wherever he went. He could access the quality of those earlier attachments and affiliations to his original homeland so as to meet life's contingencies in appropriate and creative ways. The memory of the olive field was not stored as a fixed image, but as a rich source of meaning that could be activated when in need. Like the fertile fields of his homeland, it remained an undefined potential that brought to memory again and again the promises of springtime, particularly at moments when the darkness of winter seemed overwhelming. It became a source of hope and renewal that infused his being with a secure narrative perspective on who he was and who he could be.

THE THREE HOMES OF SAN

All too often, we think of our childhood home in terms of the intimacy we share with others. We have seen that no matter how intimate personal relationships can be, inevitably they are infused with collective, cultural patterns, transforming caregivers into demons or gods. If parents fail to integrate these cultural complexes appropriately, they are likely to influence their children in overwhelming ways, leaving little space for the freedom and autonomy necessary for their maturation process. This was not the case with Ruggero's olive tree. The olive tree became a church, a symbol of the bounty of nature, and an extended identity linking untold generations. Ruggero's father saw the olive tree as a source of his son's well-being and not as a possession of parents or grandparents. Mirroring nature's abundance, this generous man conveyed an invaluable heritage to his son.

Religion often tends to dominate family life, occasionally imposing lots of unhealthy restrictions on those who remain susceptible to its influence. Parents may assume the right not only to convert, but also to control their offspring in religious matters. Such environments foster the scourge of fundamentalism or radical skepticism, and prevent free access to those materials necessary for building one's own temple in honor of the sacred. Sometimes we are privileged to witness the religious significance of home through a dream, vision, or poetic utterance. Such revelations rarely represent the actual home we remember—they transform those very dwellings into temples of beauty and light. This is likely to happen if we have grown up in a culture where the sacred has remained a living reality, supported by parents, relatives, or friends, and transmitted to children in ways that respect them as individuals.

San, a former client, is Japanese. He was raised in the Buddhist religion. He was grateful to his parents for the deep and authentic sense of the sacred they had bequeathed to him without trying to control him. On that foundation, he could build his own temple and translate the ineffable dimensions of existence within the context of a professional vocation. Towards the end of his training to become an analyst, he told me the following dream:

> I was playing with several children. In the dream, I too was a young
> boy. We were playing in a big hall of a Buddhist temple, which
> looked like the one I used to visit with father when I was a child. We

were playing a game of tag. During the game, I came to the altar on which a big statue of the Amitabha Buddha was sitting. The altar was covered in a thick black cloth. I lifted up the cloth's bottom hem and saw that the altar was the secret entrance to another hall just below us. I gathered all the children and asked them if they were willing to go down with me. About half of them replied yes. So we went down through the entrance to the second temple underground. The inside of this second temple was very strange. It was lit with thousands and thousands of candles. The walls and ceiling were made of plated gold. As I looked closer, I saw that the walls were covered with reliefs of landscapes, describing the Buddhist paradise known in several of the Sutras. Everything in this room was made of gold; even the air seemed to be golden. We continued to walk along beside the tall walls, viewing the scenes on them. Suddenly, I was caught by a certain idea that there should be a further entrance to a much deeper world. Having separated myself from the group, I looked for clues to discover it. Finally, I found a small entrance in the wall. I opened it. Behind this secret door ran a narrow, dark path. From this dark corridor came a breeze, which felt so pleasant, filled with the fragrance of flowers. The breeze was cool and refreshing, quite a contrast to the golden room, which felt stifling. It was a dry wind. I asked my friends if they would follow me. They all declined. So I decided to go down the dark corridor alone. I was very sure that I would reach something absolutely authentic. The path formed a spiral that continued downwards counterclockwise. At last I reached a hall in the shape of a vast octagon. As the dream ended, I vaguely remember seeing a big lotus-shaped pedestal for the Buddha in the middle of the room.

It would be impossible to give a full account of the meaning of this visionary dream. It came at a time when San felt he had come to a new understanding of psychotherapy and the role of the psychotherapist. He was wondering how this relatively new profession could be related to the Buddhist tradition in which he grew up. In search of answers, he started to read the Buddhist Sutras. San's associations with the first temple brought back memories of childhood. It reminded him of the temple that he frequently visited with his father, who was a Buddhist priest. The temple was near the sea, where his father taught him how to swim. He recalled those moments as the most cherished experiences he shared with his father. He also remembered playing in the temple, even though it was forbidden to do so. He felt he could play there because he belonged to it. San understood this first temple to symbolize a spontaneous, emotional relationship with the Buddha. The temple was his first spiritual home.

The second temple reminded San of the Golden Pavilion in Kyoto, an edifice that is a popular tourist attraction. San noticed that the golden rooms of the dream were somewhat profane, and that the gold relief scenes, which were outwardly impressive, appealed to people who were well intentioned, hardworking, but perhaps naïve in their religious attitudes. The hall was for people who made themselves entirely dependent on the Buddha, and believed that paradise would be the reward for their faith and good deeds on earth.

The third temple reminded him of the eight-walled dream pavilion of prince Shotoko, near the ancient capital of Nara. Shotoko was the first great prince of Japan to introduce a sophisticated and highly developed form of Buddhism from China into his country. There were times when he would withdraw from public life to the octagon pavilion in order to relate to the Buddha on a personal level through dream and meditation. Throughout the dream, San said he was aware of the mysterious presence of the Amitabha Buddha. This was the Buddha of his father's religion, the Buddha who serves all who call his name. He is the most generous of the Buddhas and is present for all those in need of his help. In the discussion following the dream, San concluded that the Buddha is present on many levels of human existence. On the first level, his father's temple, Buddha is there to meet the child's need for play, beauty, and affection. He prepares them for life, encourages them to play with the forces of nature, and provides for them a sense of home and belonging. On the second level, he is present to compensate and bring relief to the hard lot of the multitude who seek reward for carrying the heavy burdens placed upon them during their life on earth. On the third level, he reveals himself as an unknown, transcendental presence. Each person has to find this Buddha in him- or herself alone. Encounters of this kind lie outside conventional rule and conduct. In the dream, there is just an empty lotus seat; Buddha radiates an invisible presence.

From this extraordinary dream, San found the clue to connect the beliefs of the past with the profession of his future. He had experienced three levels to his life—three homes, three identities—and wondered how they all fit together. The more deeply he understood the dream, the more it became for him a testimony to the divine love and unlimited generosity of the Amitabha Buddha, who showed San a way to hold his life together.

In his future work as a therapist, he would appreciate the reality of the child, the adult, and the mystic in all those whom he would meet. He was about to encounter the diverse needs of humanity on the levels of playful affection, tender compassion, and deep spirituality. The dream and the following discussion impressed upon him the necessity of being nonjudgmental, tolerant, and patient with the different kinds of people he would meet while working as a therapist. The professional home he was about to create would be made to house the generosity, compassion, and mysterious existence of a divine presence, so eminently present in the dream.

JUNG: MULTIPLE HOMES, MULTIPLE IDENTITIES

Jung spent his entire life translating diverse symbols that revealed many aspects of his own individuation process. Certain mythic motifs and dreams, such as the solar hero, the Gnostic Anthropos, the killing of Siegfried, and finally the multiple images of the *Mysterium Coniunctionis* became associated with the soul's capacity to provide new symbols, which brought healing and renewal to his divided life. The following is an attempt to outline aspects of Jung's individuation process from the imagery of the various dwelling places he inhabited.

The seeds of dividedness were already present in his first home, in the contrasting worlds of his parents. Jung describes his mother as having a "hearty animal warmth" and a depth that was "uncanny" and "frightening."[18] She was the daughter of an unconventional protestant pastor, who learned Hebrew believing it was the language of heaven, and a mother who regularly conversed with ghosts.[19] Jung's mother grew up in a household in which visionary experiences were an ordinary part of everyday life, and she was happiest "when telling some of the parish women about the ghosts and spirits who roamed the parsonage halls at night."[20] She had a powerful presence, possessed a sense of the occult and the uncanny, and certainly was a major influence on her son's lifelong interest in parapsychology, spiritualism, and medium-like women.[21]

Jung's relationship with his father was different. Paul Jung was a quiet, self-effacing, and scholarly man who lacked self-confidence and strength of character. He was the son of a famous medical doctor who failed to provide sufficient finances to further his son's academic career. Paul Jung became a pastor of the Swiss Reformed church. He served his church in the prescribed way, embodying a spirituality that was academic, lifeless, and without inner conviction. Paul Jung cared for his son "with the same kindness and concern he gave his parishioners."[22] Nevertheless, it was a relationship that remained reliable and "affectionately close." Paul took an interest in his son's education, and there was a period when the son adored his father.[23] This might have lasted up to his adolescence, when the precocious son recognized his father's religious doubts, power-lessness, and unwillingness to engage in open discussion. Nevertheless, despite Paul Jung's weakness, the foundations of a healthy father-son rela-tionship were laid. Jung's later dialogues with personality No. 1, his medi-cal degree, interest in science, and his allegiance to and final confrontation with Freud all point to a strong, mature, and conflict-sustaining libidinal attachment to the patriarchal world of culture, institutes, and profession.

Jung's experiences of a divided life became internalized in the secret homes of his childhood, and literally enacted in his conversations with what he called Personality No. 1 and Personality No. 2. The former rep-resented the reality principle, including associated qualities generated from the healthier aspects of a father-son relationship. The latter appeared as a dark, underworldly figure, uncanny and ambiguous, yet inspir-ing—and, like the mythical Mercurius, became known as the Lord of Dreams. This figure could be associated with his mother's ghosts, repre-senting otherworldly connections from which his father kept a safe dis-tance. The division was evident in his marriage with Emma, whom he obviously loved, but as she became more occupied with maternal respon-sibilities, the unattached portion of Jung's anima caused him to be attracted to medium-like women—first his cousin, Helly Preiswerk, and later Sabina Spielrein and Toni Wolff. Both Spielrein and Wolff were a source of inspiration, and were a powerful influence in framing the foun-dations of analytical psychology—Toni Wolff's influence and conflict-provoking presence in the family home lasting almost all of Jung's life. A divided world furthermore manifested in the two houses Jung built. At his beautiful home in Küsnacht, Jung devoted his energy to his family, friends, and work. In the other home, Bollingen, he was often alone or with close friends only. In the seclusion of Bollingen he could communi-cate with nature and the souls of the dead.

The division in Jung's psyche was evident in 1913, after he relin-quished prestigious positions in the outer world—the relationship with Freud, presidency of the International Psychoanalytic Association, and Lectureship at the University of Zürich. He was suddenly alone and iso-lated. This was the beginning of a period of deep self-questioning, outlined in *Memories, Dreams, Reflections*, which involved a surrender to inner dwelling places populated by strange figures who seemed in no way identical to those of the outer world. Jung was well aware that he might have lost his mind if he had not established two other identities to support him. Work in the consulting room and private family life continually made him aware that he was an ordinary human being who really existed and not just "a piece of paper blown by the winds of the spirit."

As the process continued (1913-1916), Jung confronted the unconscious directly by letting images arise from it. Inner personalities emerged, such as "Philemon" and "Salome"—figures which he later termed "self" and "anima"—which made him aware of the forces of wisdom and life contained in the unconscious. They taught him about the reality, objectivity, and structure of the psyche. If Jung had just stayed with the mythic images, his experiences would have remained mysterious, isolated, and private. He would only have developed a belief system of "Philemites" or "Salomites," adherents convinced of a cult because of the overwhelming visionary power of the master. Jung was not interested in creating a cult. He avoided the temptation of building a numinous edifice that might only have encouraged a fanatical or frustrated retinue.

No sooner had the process reached a climax than Jung began bridging the newly discovered inner identity with the outer world. In this phase, we witness a process of interweaving mythic vision and theoretical interpretation. The original images were not simply translated into abstract ideas. That would have killed their living quality. At first he created a symbolic space that allowed him to paint and play with the images and, like a child, he fashioned some of them into miniature stone buildings on the lakeside of Zürich. The remains of the little village are still to be seen today. The new experiences took on their own life. As ideograms they retained some of their original mythical attributes, common to expressive symbolism, such as play, mystery, paradox, and the power of the symbol to bring meaning and change to one's life. Despite his belief in the primacy of the image, he opted for distance from his own material and went in search of a universal significance of the visionary experiences. He refused his anima's invitation to become an artist, although he later admitted that an artistic approach to the psyche was just as plausible as a scientific one.

It took the rest of his life to find parallels, classify, compare, and finally formulate generalized symbolic forms in order to communicate the discoveries to his colleagues and to the world. This was the dawn of analytical psychology, which has become a professional home not only for Jung, but also for thousands of others. Through dream, vision, synchronistic phenomena, and through his extensive writings on alchemy, in particular on the figure of Mercurius, Jung formulated a psychology focused on bridging a divided life. Jungian psychology became a psychology of process, a psychology that focuses on an interaction between the various parts of the psychic puzzle. The notions of "self," "anima," "archetype," "transcendent function," and other concepts of analytical psychology evolved from this work. One could say that Jung created analytical psychology as a building under construction, which after the break with Freud became his professional home that housed not only his particular experiences of the soul, but also opened its doors to other disciplines. We can be grateful not only for the visions but also for Jung's theoretical work, which translated those visions into a contemporary context, creating a new culture in the world of soul healing.

Jung's search for home was not completed with the outline of the foundations of analytical psychology. Shortly afterwards, he was occupied with a series of dreams about unknown annexes attached to his house, one of which contained a wonderful library with folio volumes from the sixteenth and seventeenth centuries. He suspected that the series announced the presence of a new home. In a dream of 1926,[24] he found himself imprisoned in a seventeenth-century palace. He remembered the palace was built at the time when alchemy had reached its zenith of fame. Despite resistance and the certainty of knowing that most people regarded this discipline as sheer nonsense, he felt impelled to understand the meaning of its imagery. Alchemy was to become part of his personality. He accepted a destiny that required that he study it for many years.

> I had stumbled upon the historical counterpart of my psychology of the unconscious. The possibility of a comparison with alchemy…gave substance to my psychology. When I pored over these old texts everything fell into place: the fantasy-images, the empirical material I had gathered in my practice, and the conclusions I had drawn from it. I now began to understand what these psychic contents meant when seen in historical perspective.[25]

It was now clear that analytical psychology was not a discipline merely for solving personal problems. It evolved to become a psychology that grounds humans in a much larger historical context. Once connected to the archetypal imagery of the unconscious, modern man and woman gain a sense of belonging to an ancestral heritage transcending everyday concerns, even one's accustomed cultural perspective. The boundaries of home were now extended beyond their usual significance to embrace kinship with a forgotten tradition, alchemy, which had long been relegated to the dustbins of cultural history.

As Jung formulated the historical dimensions of the human psyche, he started with the construction of another home. Unsatisfied with putting his experiences in words and on paper, he began to build Bollingen, a house that would manifest his psychological process in stone.[26] He first built a round tower, resembling a primitive hut providing shelter for family life. Home became a primitive hearth, a place of maternal warmth, similar to the Roman conception of home as a sanctuary of Hestia. After further extensions, the idea arose to build a second tower where he could be alone in a space of spiritual concentration. Later came the need for containment, a place "open to the sky and to nature"; a courtyard and loggia were added. As Jung grew older, Bollingen metamorphosed into a sanctuary of seclusion away from the burdens of everyday life, an opportunity to return to the older, simpler ways of humanity. It was a locus where he could communicate with nature and the spirits of the dead. In Küsnacht, Jung remained the cautious psychologist, but in writing about Bollingen he describes experiences of an entirely different order of being.

Only after the death of his wife in 1955, Jung decided to add an upper story to the middle tract of the building. Concerning this psychological piece of architecture, he comments:

> I could no longer hide myself behind the "maternal" and the "spiritual" towers. So, in that same year, I added an upper story to this section, which represents myself, or my ego-personality. Earlier, I would not have been able to do this; I would have regarded it as presumptuous self-emphasis. Now it signified an extension of consciousness achieved in old age.[27]

Jung's experience of home expressed facets of a many-sided identity. Home became an inner and outer space to celebrate the mysteries of life and spirit. Expressed through symbol, home was not just an idea or image; as a symbolic experience, it incarnated the contrasting worlds of spirit and matter, head and hand, word and stone. Although at times ambivalent, claiming that alchemy was only a projection of the inner on the outer, Jung believed that the final goal of human endeavor was to embrace a pre-Newtonian unitary world, the *unus mundus* of alchemy, a psychoid realm that unifies the physical and spiritual.

Jung rediscovered the lost heritage of a unitary world on a trip to Africa. According to Roger Brooke, Jung knew about this world in his youth, forgot about it, but later re-discovered it in his dreams and in primeval Africa.[28] On the train journey from Mombasa to Nairobi, Jung, contemplating a lone dark figure with a spear standing on a rock at dawn, discovered what archetypal home could truly mean. It was not just a house, a person, or a particular place, but in Africa it became a unifying, symbolic reality, waiting for him over thousands of years. On Mount Elgon, he witnessed the dawn lighting up the world in all its magnificence, redeeming it from the silence of the night. Alone, except for the baboons, he faced the rising sun. In a state of awe, he was reminded "of the great baboons of the temple of Abu Simbel in Egypt, which perform the gesture of adoration."[29] The world became a temple and "the earth consecrated ground."[30] Archetypal home could no longer be interiorized within a European head. The mind regained its lost attachment to the living universe. Jung was initiated into a kinship with all that surrounded him, a moment of revelation echoed in the closing lines of his autobiography:

> The more uncertain I have felt about myself, the more there has grown up in me a feeling of kinship with all things. In fact it seems to me as if that alienation which so long separated me from the world has become transferred into my own inner world, and has revealed to me an unexpected unfamiliarity with myself.[31]

As Jung's life was approaching its final stages, he caught a glimpse of yet another home, definitely not of this world. In 1944, he suffered from a heart attack and, in a state of coma and close to death, witnessed in vision another house to which he would return one day. In the vision, he found himself high up in space, looking down on the subcontinent of India and the blue silvery shine of planet earth. He then came to a rock temple, in front of which was seated a black Hindu in a white gown. As Jung approached the steps leading up to the temple gate, he felt his earthly existence was being stripped away, but something remained. This was his core identity, a kind of "bundle" of who he was and what he had accomplished. He knew with certainty that if he entered the temple, he would meet all those people to whom he ultimately belonged.

> There I would at last understand…what historical nexus I or my life fitted into. I would know what had been before me, why I had come into being, and where my life was flowing. My life as I lived it had often seemed to me like a story that has no beginning and no end. I had the feeling that I was a historical fragment, an excerpt for which the preceding and succeeding text was missing.[32]

Jung's time to depart had not yet come. A voice called out to return to earth. With great reluctance, he realized he had to come back to the "box system" once again. Nevertheless, through the vision, Jung had the privilege of witnessing a dimension of home beyond normal human understanding. His long, rich, and intensive life permitted him to gain a rare insight into the multiple significance of home and, I might add, the multiple facets of human existence on earth and in the hereafter.

THE TRANSCENDENT FUNCTION

We have seen that Jung's long life provides an example of a man who dwelt in many houses, outer and inner, tangible and mythical, visible and invisible. His professional calling and inner necessity demanded that he not only live in these houses, but also offer to the world a method of construction so that others would have the opportunity to do likewise. Jung called this method the transcendent function. Most people in the West have had the opportunity to rent, buy, or build at least one dwelling place. The course of a person's life undergoes many changes—one day you may ask if you have felt sufficiently sheltered to meet those changes. What do you do when some other reality gnaws at your guts, making you feel restless, uprooted, and alienated from your surroundings, despite having an outer roof over your head or being surrounded by loved ones?

The transcendent function does not give us a home to live in; it is not the kind of method that provides neat answers for regaining home and a sense of belonging. Jung's description of it is abstract and relatively content-free; few examples serve to illustrate the process. The transcendent function resembles a scaffolding, giving us a hint of the contours of a new building and the necessary building materials to start the work.

Jung first wrote about the transcendent function in 1916, but this was only first published in 1957, and later extensively revised in a German edition of 1958.[33] The transcendent function is a description, in generalized form, of his personal confrontation with the unconscious. Having broken with previous professional attachments in the outer world, he began to formulate a psychology distinct from Freudian psychoanalysis. The transcendent function may be considered as a guideline to "come to terms in practice with the unconscious."[34] The goal is union between the unconscious and consciousness so that a new attitude is achieved. The use of the word "transcendent" is to describe a transition from one attitude to another, and "function" in Jungian psychology implies a process of making conscious certain contents of the unconscious.

Like a good builder, Jung poses two questions to get the process going: What materials are required to produce the transcendent function, and what is to be done with them? In answer to the first question, preference is given to fantasy, "thus laying the foundation of the transcendent function."[35] Here the unconscious is given the lead. It may express itself through image, voice, or body movement. The emotional disposition is crucial; the process often begins in a state of depression, discontent, or lack of meaning. True to his basic understanding of individuation, Jung is convinced that in the disturbance of affect lies the energy to heal and make whole. The answer to the second question is basically a matter of evaluating and interpreting the material gained so far. This may be achieved by creative expression or intellectual formulation. In his decisive confrontation with the unconscious (1913-1916), Jung did both, now witnessed with the recent publication of the *Red Book* (2009). An inner dialogue, a shuttling back and forth between the ego and the unconscious, takes place. By maintaining the tension of opposites, a uniting symbol emerges in dream, fantasy, or active imagination, eventually becoming integrated as part of a new attitude, a new way of life.

The transcendent function represents the cornerstone of Jungian psychology. Its origins are already evident in the figure of Ivenes in Jung's doctoral thesis,[36] and its dynamics evolved from Jung's personal confrontation with the unconscious, which lead to a formulation of the basic principles of analytical psychology. It is not to be applied in a mechanical way. It is a process inspired by the creative core of one's personhood, linking together what previously was deemed irreconcilable. When working with this method, the client and analyst may discover that the goal of analysis is not simply to achieve adaptation to the outer world, but to create circumstances that allow for the presence of soul in the world.

The transcendent function may be compared to a scaffolding, guideline, or map. However, these are not used simply to build prefabricated houses and or inform one what to do or where to go. The process indicates a practical means of coming to terms with the unconscious. Each person, group, or community—with or without the help of an analyst, guide, or leader—attempts to give expression, find meaning, and create new life in an encounter with that other reality we call the unconscious. It furthers the translation of fate into destiny. A theoretical description of the transcendent function is necessary to create a common ground of mutual understanding. To apply this principle of analytical psychology in a purely theoretical way, however, is like dwelling on scaffolding without building a house, or looking at a map without going on a journey. Nevertheless, scaffoldings or maps are useful to construct a building or start a journey.

A CLUMP IN THE CHEST

The transcendent function can happen in quite unexpected ways, even as a clump in the chest. It is not unusual that people complain of pressure or weight in that area of the body. Sometimes I ask clients to focus on that area, which they often describe as a congealed mass of tissue. At first they complain and see no purpose to such an exercise, and even get angry that I would suggest such a thing. If they maintain focus, images come to the surface: a lump of lead or a red ball of fire. Soon they may realize that the clump is alive and starts to communicate with them, as witnessed in the following examples.

Sandra started analysis feeling inadequate, inhibited, ashamed, and without any sense of having a life of her own. After several sessions, she had nothing more to say. I asked her to close her eyes and focus on one part of her body. She immediately was aware of pressure in the chest. An image followed of a congealed mass, heavy and closed. Keeping her attention on it, the mass turned into a being that was monstrous, tight, and dense. She felt fear, shame, and disgust, and wanted to stop the process. I encouraged her to stay with the image and, if possible, care for this helpless, unformed entity. She started crying. At that moment, a memory of early childhood came to consciousness. The monstrous creature was herself, who had shut down because she could not stand rigid feeding schedules and the fathomless emptiness emerging from dependency on a nonresponsive, depressed mother. With time, the monstrous being became a child in need of care, and again Sandra recognized the child to be that part of her that had existed before she shut down. With continuous analysis, we could build on that foundation to the point where Sandra became aware that she was no longer a person who felt inadequate, ashamed, and frightened. With a secured base, she gradually gained more confidence in her professional and private life.

Hans had served his firm for many years. One day, on overhearing a conversation among his superiors, he suspected they were planning his dismissal. He was reassured that this would not be the case, but depression set in and he could not get rid of it. After he had complained about a weight in his chest, I asked him to concentrate on that area. An image of a red ball appeared. There followed conversations between him and the ball. Images of the past surfaced. Finally a memory of one particular event entered consciousness. As a young man, he fell in love with the daughter of a wealthy family. He did not have sufficient means to provide for her and was dismissed by her family. He suppressed the incident and eventually forgot about it. In the following discussion, it became clear that from that time on his belief in love and his confidence in himself and his work had greatly suffered. The discovery of the connection between his depression, his lost love, and lost honor brought relief, and he could let go of a vigilant attitude that always expected the worse.

The transcendent function may manifest in any part of the body, in strange affects, dreams, or surprising symbolic imagery. Memories of the past are encapsulated in the body. When the strangers within are welcomed and raised to consciousness, they link up with other segments of the personality to become facets of one's identity, chapters in one's life narrative. As identity is a process in continual formation, symbolic imagery may use the past as a springboard for future intentions. We have seen how an unacknowledged identity was imprisoned in the protests and anxieties of Milena and Adele, who had been victimized in homes of fate shaped by Soviet state policy and the terrors of Hell. In each case, the conscious ego needed to be grounded before confronting the overwhelming powers of the past. Ruggero's olive field or San's three temples are examples of how the transcendent function appears in memory and dream, prefiguring a destiny that molds identity, forges a new attitude to life, and provides a sense of home in oneself and the world.

Of course, the transcendent function is not a home—but it serves as a practical instrument for each person to build his or her own home. Jung's biography provides an outline of the kinds of homes one can build. They are intrinsically related to the diverse identities that are created in the course of a lifetime. Homes appear and disappear, and yet indicate a foundation that survives life's transitions. We gain awareness of it in the instinctive need to belong, continually experienced as the source of the various identities we have created. Jung's various homes—his childhood home, a professional home, an inner home, a home embedded in an historical nexus, home as kinship with our living planet, and home in the hereafter—represent threads of a mysterious pattern, which he describes as follows:

> I know only that I was born and exist, and it seems to me that I have been carried along. I exist on the foundation of something I do not know. In spite of all uncertainties, I feel a solidity underlying all existence and a continuity in my mode of being.[37]

Martin Heidegger once wrote that modern man's homelessness could not be understood purely in terms of the lack of housing, the destruction of war, or an increase of population. Heidegger concluded that, understood philosophically,

> The real dwelling plight lies in this, that mortals ever search anew for the nature of dwelling, that they must ever learn to dwell. What if man's homelessness consisted in this, that man still does not even think of the real plight of dwelling as the plight? Yet as soon as man gives thought to his homelessness, it is a misery no longer…it is the sole summons that calls mortals into their dwelling.[38]

You might experience anxiety and insecurity in moments of transition, when there is a separation from the old and a search for the new begins. Perhaps these are moments when you sense the true significance of what home can be and what it means to be human. The meaning of home enters consciousness in those in-between states of mind where you experience the paradox of being or not being at home in the world. Individuation is never complete. As a process that furthers consciousness, it thrives on the tension between concordance and discordance. In the drama between fate and destiny, between what is and what can be, the story of your life gains color, form, and definition. The house you are building is woven from the fabric of your soul, truly your own—of this world, yet not of this world.

PART IV

HOME: AN ODYSSEY THROUGH MANY LANDS

CHAPTER 8

Lost Homes, Lost Nations

> The man who sat on the ground in his tipi meditating on life and its meaning, accepting the kinship of all creatures and acknowledging unity with the universe of things, was infusing into his being the true essence of civilization. And when native man left off this form of government, his humanization was retarded in growth.
>
> —Statement of Chief Luther Standing Bear[1]

Lost Homes

James Joyce chose to live in exile. His life narrative was chartered by an unconventional odyssey lasting a lifetime. By the time he was twenty-two, his family had moved thirteen times. Joyce continued this pattern of moving from place to place, sometimes due to eviction, war, or lack of funds. The unconventional was his inspiration. His restless spirit could not find a home in one dwelling place, but sought satisfaction in artistic creation—the most famous being *Ulysses*, an odyssey of the human mind coming to terms with ever-changing circumstances of life. He never seemed to have suffered from the homesickness connected with the loss of an outer home. Nevertheless, the final chapter of *Ulysses* describes the recovery of a lost love and a lost home. Very few have the capacity to transform home into a passion for artistic creation.

As home is intrinsically connected to a sense of self, its loss may have devastating effects on people's lives. Homesickness prevents us from forgetting what has been lost. Its unrelenting pain demands that we transform lost worlds into new landscapes, as witnessed in the following statement of a client, Hanna.

> My parents never told me that we were going to leave our home in the Middle East. We went on a boat and I arrived in the cold North. The Middle East was my home, the home of my childhood. I miss the smell of the eucalyptus, the rocks, the mountains, and the gardens. When I was six years old, all that beauty was ripped away from me, and since then I could hardly put my feet on the ground. This began to change when I became aware of what I had missed in my earlier life.

As Hanna talked, her face was covered in tears and her mind flooded with images of her original homeland. She had often moved houses in her lifetime, but each time she came to a new place, pain spread in her feet. They did not want to touch the ground. The pain became a testimony to the loss she had suffered in childhood. Her parents had tried to cover it up; but Hanna's body would not be deceived. The memory of that loss was stored in bodily cells. Her body preserved her identity and history, and refused to believe in the deception of others.

A SICKNESS UNTO DEATH?

Saint Bernard of Clairvaux once wrote: "You will find more in the forests than in books. The trees and the rocks will teach you things that no sage can tell you." Jung believed that not only do we learn from nature, but nature, our original mother, can nourish us in other ways than providing food—a belief cherished by many Shamanist traditions. In 1465, Nicholas von Flue, the Swiss patron saint, left his family home and lived in a hermitage for the last twenty years of his life. Subjecting himself to a total fast for twenty years, he devoted his entire life to God, prayer, and counseling those who sought his advice. The hermitage can be visited today, located at the bottom of a beautiful Alpine valley surrounded by snow-capped mountains. In this place of peace one hears the call of the birds, the murmurings of a stream, and the occasional sound of a church bell, interrupting a serenity extending beyond the visible world. Here the Middle Ages have survived, untouched by modern civilization. In an article on Saint Nicholas, Jung conjectured that he drew sustenance from the powers of his natural environment.[2] This statement would be hard to prove. Its validity, however, can be confirmed by historical evidence of the great suffering caused by homesickness, which eventually could lead to death, once people were deprived of the sustaining resources of their natural surroundings.

When I started to write about homesickness, an incident had occurred that unexpectedly brought to mind the power of land as a nourishing environment. A seventy-eight-year-old man, known to me, had become demented. No one could look after him any longer in his own house, located in an Alpine village. He was moved to an old people's home. When I visited him a few days later, he had aged ten years. He had become utterly disoriented. His spirit seemed to know that life was not worth living in the new conditions. Without any clear medical reason, he died within a few weeks. The incident brought to mind an even more poignant memory of an old woman who lived in a small house at the foot of the Alps. She was forced to leave her house because it did not measure up to the fire safety standards of Switzerland. The woman—who lived as people did in the Middle Ages, and whose identity was intimately bound to her house, her land, and her flock of sheep—was put into a psychiatric hospital by the health authorities. The nurses bathed and dressed her for the first time in her life. Her heart was broken. She looked miserable, uprooted, homeless, and frightened of the alien environment in which she found herself—an environment with which she could in no way identify. The shock of the forced eviction did irreparable damage. When I visited her a few weeks later, all she could say was "Take me home." I could see she had begun to withdraw from life, and within two months she had died.

One is reminded of European descriptions of homesickness from the eighteenth and nineteenth centuries. There are many documents that read as tales of a broken heart, particularly among Swiss men, many of whom were forced to leave their Alpine homelands. They had no choice but to depart from the small mountain farms that could no longer support ever-growing families and become mercenaries in foreign armies. An abbreviated description taken from an encyclopedia published in the nineteenth century describes the effects of homesickness as follows:

> It is a form of grief at separation from the native soil and may
> become in men of great sensibility a real disease. It shows itself
> by a deep melancholy, difficult respiration, sighs, deadly pale-

ness, immoderate heartbeats, and loss of appetite. Sleep flies
away, or consists of dreams, which are filled with scenes left
behind. Sudden death sometimes puts an end to this situation. A return home is the most effectual remedy.[3]

Already in 1688 Johannes Hofer writes in his *Dissertatio Medico der
Nostalgia* about homesickness as the special illness of the Swiss. In those
times, poverty or famine tore the young men away from their beloved
homeland, only to serve as mercenaries in the legions of the greater powers that surrounded their country. Hofer observed that they pined for
"motherly care and the freedom of the fatherland." They fell victims to
homesickness, then considered a disease with fatal consequences. Hofer
mentions Swiss folk music, in particular the *Kuhreihen*, which released a
powerful longing for home, causing them to desert from the army. In
view of this danger, the death penalty was given to soldiers caught whistling or singing the tune. Hofer outlines several psychosomatic symptoms
that accompany homesickness: melancholy, nervousness, lethargy, loss of
appetite, and fever.[4]

Johann Scheuchzer, writing in 1705, supported Hofer's thesis on
homesickness, and believed that it was a special illness of the Swiss. In a
popular weekly journal, he asked:

> Why does it happen that the Swiss, who are such a free,
> strong, and courageous people, are overtaken by an illness that
> one would rather expect to find among the French, Italian, or
> other peoples whose bodies are tender and therefore more sus-
> ceptible to homesickness?[5]

Scheuchzer was convinced that he had to resolve this matter so as to
save the reputation of the Swiss nation. He believed that homesickness
among the Swiss is a medical condition and comes from inhaling the
denser air of the lowlands, which they, being used to the rarefied and subtle air of the Alps, are unable to adjust to. In the lowlands, the heavier,
compact air exerts pressure on their blood circulation and thus slows
down the whole system. They suffer from heart palpitations, insomnia,
sadness, and a longing to return to the lighter air of the mountains. A further proof of the wonders of the Swiss air "is in the seldom occurrence of
the Pest, and other dangerous illnesses, as well as the health of old men
and the fertility of women."[6] He claimed that all those who breathe the
murky air of the lowlands are usually not exposed to the dangers of home-

sickness when traveling in Switzerland. "The Dutch, French, Germans, or Italians bring with them dense air compressed in the arteries, which in the subtle Alpine air expands and releases the juices of life, leading to a lightness and freshness."[7] Scheuchzer recommended cures for those Swiss who live in the lowlands and suffer from this illness. They are to be encouraged to return home or, if that is not possible, to climb a high mountain or tower. He concluded if mountains or towers fail to cure homesickness, the doctor could prescribe saltpeter, a substance containing compressed air, which is supposed to increase the air pressure in the arteries and thus counteract the pressure from the dense outside air. If that is not available, a small dose of gunpowder! There seems to be no evidence that gunpowder was a successful cure.

In the nineteenth century, a psychological explanation of homesickness replaced the medical model, even though Scheuchzer's dense air theory continued to be in vogue until the end of the eighteenth century.[8] Johann Ebel, a medical doctor from Silesia who settled in Switzerland, was convinced that the inhabitants of the Alps were the happiest and freest people of Europe. He believed that homesickness is more likely to occur in the simpler, nonintellectual person, whose feelings are the main source of satisfaction. The soul of such a person finds more gratification in feelings of the heart than in intellectual development. The unsophisticated but happy inhabitants of the Alps are particularly prone to the illness when deprived of the world they love—their family, their goats, their cows, and the beautiful, towering mountains that surround them. It is no wonder, claimed Ebel, that they fall prey to homesickness when they are confined to a barracks and forced to serve as soldiers under the strict discipline of an authoritarian commander. Surrounded only by men, who show no affection or tenderness, they feel alone, confused, and lost in a world unknown to them. They withdraw, become apathetic and bored. Their heart lives only on images of the past, and a longing for home overcomes them. Ebel cites one instance in which displaced Swiss workers succeeded in keeping homesickness at bay:

> Some years ago men from Entlibuch were brought to Paris to work in a large Swiss Sennerie for the manufacturing of dairy products. They were content as long as they were working with cows and milk products, but as soon as the dairying ceased, they were troubled with homesickness.[9]

The Swiss *Kuhreihen*, a folk melody used to call home cattle, dating back to the sixteenth century, is well known in the history of folk music. Chronicles inform us that this music had the power to make the strongest men cry, lay down their arms, desert from the army, even die. Hofer reported that the mercenaries were strictly forbidden to whistle or play the *Kuhreihen* on the flute, in case it awakened the "Delirium Melancholicum." Ebel claimed that this music derived its power to evoke extreme nostalgia less from its melody than from its capacity to awaken memories of herding cows and goats, which was part of Swiss life from childhood.

> This music enters the soul of the men of the Alps like a streak of lightning, creating images of the mountains, valleys, herds of cattle, family and friends.[10]

Ebel was convinced that the *Kuhreihen* was so powerful that it could even affect Swiss cows.

> When the cows are parted from the country of their birth and hear this song, all the images of the past suddenly become alive in their brain. They become excited with a longing for home, toss up their tails, start to stampede, break fences and go completely mad. That is why near the town of St Gall it was forbidden to sing or whistle the Kuhreihen in the presence of Appenzeller cows that have been separated from their homeland.[11]

During the nineteenth century, the popularity of this music knew no bounds. There were several regional versions of the *Kuhreihen* (also known as the *Ranz des Vaches*). Already in 1791 the Siebenthal version was reproduced in the first act of Rossini's *Guillaume Tell*. In 1821, Joseph Bovet arranged the Gruyère version for men's chorus; it soon achieved great popularity in Switzerland. Other variations appeared in the shepherd's piping of Beethoven's *Pastoral Symphony* (1807), in Berlioz's *Scène aux Champs*, Schumann's *Manfred* (1848), Liszt's *Album d'un Voyageur* (1835), and Wagner's *Tristan and Isolde*.[12]

Not only the Swiss, but people throughout history have resorted to folk songs reminding them of their native land, bringing relief to the pain of homesickness. During the nineteenth century, innumerable songs expressed a longing for preindustrial, Arcadian landscapes—compositions that were often beautiful, vibrant, and sentimental. We can still hear today the music of the exiled Irish in pubs in America and Australia, singing for a lost lover or a lost homeland. Pathetic or joyful, the old tunes full of sadness inevitably strike the uprooted heart. In Germany, some of these songs began to sow dangerous seeds for a future glorification of the fatherland. Today we might witness the influence of new sounds and rhythms, sung and danced by immigrants from Eastern Europe and other countries of the world.

The Swiss, of course, were not the only ones suffering from homesickness. Ebel mentions the case of Laplanders who, with their reindeer, were sent by the King of Sweden to the King of Spain. When the reindeer lived, the Lapps remained healthy and content, but as soon as the animals died, they were struck by homesickness and would have perished if they had not been sent back to their native homeland. *Zeewee* is a Dutch term used today to describe a seaman's longing for the sea when he is living ashore.[13] Homesickness was a widespread theme in the literature of the nineteenth century. Among the heroes and heroines of Dickens, Charlotte Brontë, and Thomas Hardy, one encounters figures filled with sadness and melancholy when forced to leave their rural homelands in order to gain a livelihood in the great mansions and cities of those times. The people of Victorian England were plagued with homesickness. They knew in their hearts that the implacable advance of industrialization would break up traditional community life and destroy the age-old kinship between self and homeland.

HOMESICKNESS: THE GREAT THEME OF LITERATURE AND FILM

Literature and poetry abound with examples of the human struggle to come to terms with the enigmas of attachment and loss. This was a major theme in two of Dostoyevsky's most famous novels. The great Russian writer measures the spiritual height and chthonic depth of home and homelessness. *Crime and Punishment* portrays Raskolnikov as a hero who commits a murder, motivated by a "modern belief" in the superior value of the individual over collective morality. He has finally to bow down and kiss the holy soil of Russia. He must acquiesce to a profound sense of guilt for the crime he committed. In the end, he comprehends that he is only one particle of a much greater whole. Sonja, the woman who loves this broken, exiled man, knows that his crime can be redeemed and God will give him new life. In *The Brothers Karamazov*, the final testimony of the elder, Zosima, reminds humanity of a mysterious connection to a higher, celestial world. Humans must cultivate the seeds of that other world, which grow to become the very roots of their thoughts and emotions; otherwise, they become indifferent to all that surrounds them. The elder Zosima exhorts man and woman to remember those ancient roots:

> Know the limit, know the seasons….And remaining in solitariness, pray. Love to bow down to the earth and kiss her. Kiss the earth and untiringly, insatiably, love all creatures, love all things, seek this ecstasy and this frenzy. Moisten the earth with the tears of your joy and love those tears of yours.[14]

Leopold Bloom and Hans Castrop, creations of James Joyce's *Ulysses* and Thomas Mann's *Magic Mountain,* represent emblematic figures who find little satisfaction in isolated heroic achievements. Toward the end of the novels, they seem to lose their profile as individuals. One returns to his home and wife, a goddess-like woman who celebrates the glories of nature, and the other participates in a wider historical framework— Bloom in the fertile landscape of the wife/goddess, Molly; Castrop, together with his comrades, on the battlefields of World War I. These few examples illustrate how the sounds and symmetries of belonging affect humans in an immense variety of ways.

During the last few decades of the twentieth century, the glorification of heroes, who have served a civilization bent on achieving mastery over nature, has reached a zenith. The "killers of redskins," the "tamers of savages," or the "slayers of wild beasts" impress contemporary humanity no more. On the contrary, a great struggle has commenced with those forces that continue to destroy humanity's natural habitat. Sincere efforts are being made to save what remains of the last areas of wilderness and the heritage of the older cultures that still revere the sacredness of nature. Many now seem to realize that, once deprived of a deep connection with nature, the human soul is in danger of losing a fundamental source of nourishment that has kept it alive and well throughout the ages.

Many heroes of modern literature and film embody the search for home. The immense popularity of heroes' quest for a lost homeland, as described in Alex Haley's *Roots* or Stephen Spielberg's *E.T.*, indicates a continuing archetypal need of our time. Haley describes a search for roots through the pursuit of an oral history linking continents, customs, and family over seven generations. Haley's story about origins creates a narrative of defiance and reconciliation, bridging worlds beyond an individual's lifetime. He paints his ancestors' attachment to their village and land of origin as if it was yesterday. "This is our village. No other well has such sweet water. No other trees' shade is as pleasant. No other kitchens smell of the cooking of our women."[15] In a no less heartrending fashion, Haley depicts the cruel exile from the shores of Africa, as his people, treated like animals herded and chained together, were sold into slavery: "My brothers and I watched many fall onto their bellies, clawing and eating the sand, as if to get one last hold and bite of their own home."[16] In the film *E.T.*, a Christ-like hero descends from heaven; teaches children about love; is persecuted, dies, and is resurrected; to finally ascend to a home among the stars. The long finger of the strange little spaceman, pointing upward to his lost home, awakens thoughts of a final dwelling place beyond the horizon of human understanding, a home not of this world.

Published in 2003, Jhumpa Lahiri's award-winning novel *The Namesake* describes the fate of an immigrant Indian family in the USA, over two generations. In moving ways, the author tells about Ashima and Ashoke, first-generation parents, who have spent most of their life in America. Having achieved an outwardly successful life, they remain estranged from their environment, an estrangement compensated for by upholding the traditions of their Bengali homeland with a "makeshift family" comprising other immigrants from India. Sadness looms over the couple as they realize their son and daughter are incapable of surviving in India; they outwardly adapt to their American surroundings and become estranged from their parents' customs. The book's focus is on the fate of the second generation. Gogol, the son whose life straddles two cultures, develops two identities—one validated by personal pleasure and freedom; the other, in spite of rebellion, by a deep bond of loyalty to his family of origin. Exposed to a "string of accidents, unforeseen, unintended," Gogol struggles to find a third space in order to "reinvent" his identity. Jhumpa Lahiri portrays the inner terrain not only of Gogol, but also of today's many immigrants who are caught in an identical struggle.

> And yet these events formed Gogol, shaped him, determined who he is. They were the things for which it was impossible to prepare but which one spent a lifetime looking back, trying to accept, interpret, comprehend. Things that should never have happened, that seemed out of place and wrong, these were what prevailed, what endured in the end.[17]

This extraordinary book describes the transitional life of members of an immigrant family in our times. In realistic and sensitive ways, the author brings to life the ambivalence, uncertainties, and conflicts among members of second-generation immigrant families. They are at home in neither one nor the other culture. Unlike the first generation, they do not suffer from homesickness, and "a return home" is certainly not an alternative. In the Lahiri story, the straddling of Indian and American cultures becomes a search for identity. Belonging to neither cultural heritage, many have no alternative but to create a third space in which to filter the old and the new. Jhumpa Lahiri reminds us that in our time identity can no longer be a fixed certainty, is no longer fueled by an untainted cultural memory, or molded by a landscape, tradition, or culture formed over generations.

Ken Loach has beautifully captured this theme in the film *Just a Kiss* (2004). Portrayed is the story of a love relationship between Cassim, a Pakistani Muslim who has to assent to an arranged marriage following family tradition, and Roisin, an independent young Irish woman employed at a Catholic school. Cassim will destroy the honor of his family and Roisin will be dismissed from the school should they continue their relationship. The drama of the film focuses on Cassim's battle with himself, as the strife between conflicting cultures tears him apart. In Lahiri's book and Loach's film, identity appears to emerge as an unexpected creation, a tapestry woven by chance events as they fit or do not fit into a trans-generational heritage imposed upon each person since birth. For most people today, there is no longer a simple remedy to relieve homelessness. The homeless figures on today's stage of cultural transitions often are not aware of being homesick. There is nowhere to go, except inside—but that, too, can lead to further isolation. Allowing space for the ambivalent is perhaps the only way modern migrants can create an identity to bridge worlds without betraying their innermost being.

In the past, homesickness was kindled by the memories of a lost universe: songs of an Alpine landscape, kissing the holy soil of Russia, eating the sands of Africa. From these tales, we learn that homesickness is not only about the loss of a house, but of a whole world. These memories, conscious or unconscious, still haunt us today. As they fade, the tenuous connection to a deeper self that holds diverse worlds together begins to recede from consciousness. If connection to that deeper world is not possible, the juices of life run dry and there is insufficient energy to translate old heritages in terms of the new. If a return home is impossible, one is in danger of loss of identity. The despair, boredom, and emptiness among the uprooted can be partially alleviated by re-creating the original home in ghettoes or in tightly knit rituals that structure homo-ethnic communities. The first-generation immigrants' attempts to maintain a rigid connection with the original homeland hardly offers a feasible alternative, particularly when the second generation has already integrated much of the customs and culture of its host country.

Very often, immigrants drift between worlds and have no option but to invent an identity that has been described as *contrapunctual*, to use an expression of Edward Said. In weaving the tapestry of their lives, the second generation will use threads of the old and the new; however, the threads alone will not create the pattern. Although much of their identity will require inventiveness, its creation cannot be arbitrary. It may be compared to a work of translation or a rendering transparent of one text in terms of another. Family history, culture, and ultimately the biological disposition of human nature will influence the outcome. No doubt the quest for identity can be assisted by resort to the unconscious, the storehouse of ancestral memory that acts not only as the containing structure of our personal and collective history but also can provide innovative and timely responses to the dilemma of straddling different worlds. The images, symbols, and affects that emerge from the depth do not necessarily have a fixed meaning, but serve as a source of inspiration to link the multiple facets of an emerging identity. They can help translate old attachment in terms of ever-shifting environments. "Home" is an old word, but a good word to describe this process. It implies that, whatever threads are added to the pattern, you may feel they are rooted in an inclusive depth, embracing generations. The new and the old become part of who you are and want to be.

Perhaps Not unto Death

Homesickness can be devastating. If the loss of the original home is not redeemed, it can determine behavior for a lifetime. Memories of a lost home can be a curse or a blessing, depending on how one has experienced that deprivation. If it is abrupt and forced, the pain of loss can be so great that memories of the original homeland become suppressed, only to surface in a variety of psychosomatic and psychological symptoms.

Contemporary studies, on which I can only make brief comments, have yielded more precise descriptions of homesickness than those of previous centuries. Enrique Yepes describes not only its negative characteristics, but also its prospective significance. According to Yepes, homesickness can create a variety of experiences, ranging from "suicidal depression" to an expansive feeling "of going forward in the direction of an ultimate purpose, or of a vital core, as when a study is finally homing in on the mystery that it wanted to unveil."[18] Miranda Van Tilburg elucidates with great clarity some of the differentiating characteristics of homesickness, distinguishing it from related phenomena such as nostalgia, depression, and separation anxiety. Nostalgia is "bittersweet," and expresses "a yearning or longing for a bygone day." The overwhelming sadness of homesickness, however, is uniquely related to being away from home. Whereas many homesick symptoms overlap with depression, especially reactive depression, "the ruminative and obsessive thoughts about home and the desire to return home" are particular to homesickness. In the *DSM IV*, separation anxiety is listed as a youth disorder, along with school phobia and homesickness. Fear and avoidance are prominent in all three categories: in separation anxiety they are activated in connection with an attachment figure, in school phobia with school, and in homesickness with home.[19]

Furthermore, Van Tilburg views the "experience of homesickness" under four interrelated aspects: "the antecedent situation, the person, the response and reactions, and social regulation control." Her research on adults and children in the antecedent situation confirms that separation from the old environment rather than the process of adapting to the new "elicits homesickness." A person who tends to be "rigid," or has a previous history of insecure attachments, is more likely to be prone to homesickness than others. Reactions similar to the older descriptions of homesickness include depression, apathy, loss of appetite and sleep, and psychosomatic symptoms. Social regulations can be harmful, especially "when homesick children are encouraged to suppress their feelings."[20]

The early separation from the mother as outlined by Mahler, the pain of the homesick child, the plight of immigrants, or the ending of home in analysis affirm that loss of home should not be abrupt or forced. Concerned with the recovery of the homesick child, Christopher Thurber stresses the need to balance autonomy and dependency. Forcing separation from home can strengthen "aversion to future separations"; acquiescing to an early return home can augment "overdependence"; recognizing the benefits of separation can lead to an "enhanced sense of competence."[21] The autonomy/dependency dilemmas of a homesick child bear remarkable resemblance to dilemmas of the adult immigrant as he or she transits from one home to another. Salman Akhtar has outlined several psychosocial variables that accompany the immigrants' loss of home. In evaluating future prospects of integration, it is important to know if the transition has been "temporary or permanent," if it was chosen "freely or forced," if there was a possibility of "revisiting the previous home," and to ascertain the "reasons for leaving" one's original home.[22] The dilemmas of the homesick child and the adult immigrant reveal the need of a context that assures them of the possibility of adopting a separation-reunion behavior pattern, as described by Mahler, which was once exercised in early childhood and is designed to ensure the survival of identity despite outer loss.

Homesickness is not simply about loss of a particular person, place, or object in the outer world. Nor can it be reduced to a classification of symptoms, although such research is important so that homesickness is not confused with other disorders. From a Jungian point of view, it is also a symbolic event, intrinsically connected with loss of one's affinity with caregivers, family, community, nation, culture, and cosmos. As Jungian psychology tends to be less concentrated on the symptom and more on the whole person when it comes to treatment, the individual and his or her relationship with the unconscious becomes the central focus of atten-tion. Home and homesickness, understood symbolically, take on a wide variety of meanings. From a symbolic point of view any object, event, or person can represent home, once they are invested with kinship libido or feelings resembling the earlier attachments of childhood.

In working with adults, the Jungian-oriented analyst may also dis-cover an "inner homesick child." This clinical child may strike one as being rigid and vulnerable—similar to the descriptions of homesick chil-dren mentioned above. All too often, the inner child of the adult reveals a history of insecure attachments concealed by a powerful defense system. If a good enough relationship is established between the analyst and the inner child, the client will eventually reveal its preciously guarded secrets. One may discover that the client as a child invented home in hidden places—in the garden, the house, the stable, the woods, or the local chapel. Home may have been embodied in a beloved grandparent, neigh-bor, or family friend. Early symbolic constructions of home not only indi-cate what was missing in the original family, but also represent symbols of the Self, understood as a predisposition to hold conflicting worlds

together. In those shrines of safety, children could find relief from the torments of their unloved heart and express feelings not permitted in the
parental household. The "homesick child" in the adult needs a new space
in which to make conscious those unhoused parts of the self that were
never seen or heard in the original home. Early attachments of childhood
are relived in relation to the analyst. In relating to the "homesick child" of
the adult, the analyst must listen for the sounds and symmetries of
belonging. When the analytic space becomes home, allowance must be
made for a slow weaning process. There can be no abrupt end. All who
have lost their home—children, adults, clients—need to be reassured that
they can always return to a place they once called home, even if that cannot be realized in one lifetime.

LOST NATIONS

Over the past one hundred and fifty years, the plight of the homeless
has manifested on a gigantic scale. Every continent has woeful tales to tell.
Living in central Europe, I have had the opportunity to witness many stories of the dispossessed. Several of my friends and clients were victims of
mass deportations carried out under Hitler's or Stalin's orders. I have
worked with victims of the Holocaust and have listened to horrific tales
about the loss of an entire family, village, nation, and culture. Life in Hitler's death camps incarnates an antithesis to home, a place where "there is
no such thing as father, brother, friend. Each of us lives and dies alone."[23]
Elie Wiesel's testimony, among many others, helps us never to forget the
damage perpetrated on humans when they are systematically deprived of
every form of attachment, of every centimeter of that space we call
"home," without which it is hardly possible to remain human. It is impossible to measure the extent of a crime done to a young man that termi-
nated in the death of his family, his innocence, and his God.

Many Germans suffered the loss of home after Hitler was defeated.
Twelve million people, the largest deportation in World War II, were
forced to move from their Eastern European homes. They had lived in
Prussia, Pomerania, Silesia, and Czechoslovakia, and were part of the history of those lands for a thousand years. Those who settled in
Communist-controlled Eastern Germany were strictly prohibited from
using the term "dispossessed" or calling themselves "refugees." The only
term permitted was *Umsiedler*, implying one who is simply changing his
address. Soviet policy at that time did everything to prevent those unfor-

tunate people from making any claim to their lost heritage. They were forced to accept a life of deception. And they are not the only ones who were dispossessed of their physical homeland and suffered destruction of their history, culture, and identity. The haunting music of the Armenians, massacred in the name of nationalistic ideology, or the lyrical songs of the exiled Greeks, deported from Asia Minor, express the soul's lament for lost homelands that had lasted several thousand years. These tragedies, usually executed by ruthless politicians in the name of some fundamentalist brand of nationalism, are scarcely reversible. Nevertheless, the historical reality of such events cannot be denied. In such matters, the human soul will not tolerate deception. Crimes of this nature must be subject to disclosure, so that loss can be mourned and later generations can come to terms with having been deprived of a home and culture, which cannot be justified.

HOME: A POLITICAL REALITY

Nationalistic ideologies have reigned in Europe since the latter half of the eighteenth century. They were refined and developed during the nineteenth century. Previously, peoples' communal loyalty was to a city-state, feudal lord, dynasty, or a universal secular or religious principle such as the Roman Empire or Medieval Christendom. The theories about the origins of nationalism are manifold. H. G. Wells believed that nationalism developed as a reaction to the congress of Vienna in 1815, which attempted to carve up Europe into states without natural ethnic boundaries.[24] Loyalty to the state was, through education and law, imposed from above. Eric Hobsbawm[25] believes that the origins of nationalism came from below, and argues that national ideologies developed out of those earliest experiences of having a place of birth, a homeland, *la Patrie*, or *das Volk*. Community kinship evolved out of a common cultural heritage, which was experienced in attachment to one's own family, local clan, village, or landscape. As nations evolved, the diversity of cultural life was threatened. Certain cultural attributes dominated and others were destroyed. The more grandiose the ideals of nationalism, the more minority races, local customs, or dialects were stamped out or relegated to subordinate positions. "Nation" became a political ideology creating new bonds of commonality, which soon replaced earlier ones to homeland, local culture, and local community. Nation making was more successful when the new unity integrated enough local material from below—from the diverse cultural traditions.

Towards the end of the eighteenth century, homesickness was no longer considered a medical illness, as discussed at the beginning of this chapter. During the nineteenth century, Romantics described it as a sweet but bitter longing for an irretrievable world. Lost homes, idealized and sentimentalized, became a lost paradise, celebrated in literature and music. As the unity between self and a local homeland was fading into oblivion, nationalism gained in strength. The idealized state took over those uprooted archetypal energies that had belonged to the original homeland. As a result of this change, the state gained enormous power over the world of human feelings. Home became a political reality.

Nations tended to split apart when local cultures were not tolerated or were entirely suppressed in the name of some unifying ideology. The more abstract national ideology became, the less it was capable of survival. With the passing of time, the inflated ideologies lost their gripping power of attraction and often turned out to be the antithesis of culture and life, creations of men incapable of any authentic attachment whatsoever. One revealing example was the "blood and earth" ideology of Adolf Hitler. Erich Fromm understood Hitler's endless war games, control of youth gangs, inflated dreams of becoming an artist, and falsification of reality as a confirmation and consistent toughening of early narcissism.[26] Hitler's inability to form any real attachments eventually found full substitution in the idealized party and nation. His personality had identified so strongly with the nation that an objective appreciation of the roots and history of that nation and the life of its individual members was no longer an option. When Hitler's nation crumbled under the strain of war, he revealed a pathological mistrust and hatred toward the same German people who had served his morbid fantasies. As defeat in Stalingrad drew near, Hitler promoted general Paulus to the rank of field marshal, thinking that was the suitable reward for his martyrdom. After he learned that Paulus had surrendered, Hitler remarked:

> They have surrendered there…they should have closed ranks and shot themselves with their last bullet….What is life? Life is the nation. The individual must die anyway. Beyond the life of the individual is the nation….So many people have to die, and then a man like that besmirches the heroism of so many others at the last minute. He could have freed himself from all

> sorrow and ascended into eternity and national immortality,
> but he prefers to go to Moscow.[27]

Hitler's statement seemed to foretell his own end—his suicide, his last commands to destroy what remained of Germany, and his final blaming of the German people who had betrayed him. This was a man who replaced concrete human life, human history, human suffering, and human hope by a pseudo-religious abstraction, the creation of a man who had lost all sense of kinship with the world and with his fellow humans. A "Hitler" may be lurking in us all. All sensitivity vanishes whenever we repress the heart's vulnerability and become so hardened that we believe ourselves to be invincible.

Home, understood as a political reality, has changed radically in the past fifty years in Western Europe. Old national boundaries fell and a new cohesive multinational identity is being born. In the West, the unifying national ideologies of the nineteenth and early twentieth centuries have lost much of their significance. The appeal to origins and descent—common ethnic roots, tradition, language, religion—has been seriously undermined by the outrages of Nazi Germany and reduced in significance through the political unification of Europe and the massive advance in economic growth, communication, and mobility in the latter quarter of the twentieth century. Citizens of Eastern European countries faced a different situation. Following the collapse of the Soviet empire, the people of the former communist bloc rediscovered a lost identity with the restoration of national boundaries. In post-communist Eastern Europe, the international ideology of communism failed to provide authentic bonds of commonality. In the final decade of the twentieth century, the peoples of the ex-Soviet Union retraced their history to find a common cultural heritage. This journey provided many occasions for celebration, but it also reaped a grim harvest of mass destruction, ethnic cleansing, and a new wave of refugees with the breaking up of Yugoslavia.

Today, the forces of democracy and capitalism have been acclaimed in both East and West. They too are not without shadow, depriving many peoples of their home in the name of progress and economic development. Some states and civil societies of Eastern Europe have not always been successful in harnessing the new ideologies of democracy and capitalism through a secure and reliable definition of citizenship, thus endangering the civic rights of minorities and marginalized groups.[28] Cultural regression can reinforce the identity of a nation, but unfortunately in ways that may exclude those who do not possess the same creed, language, or ethnic heritage. Citizens of those nations who have suffered under the megalomania of Stalinism will find it difficult to invest libido in a state advocating social inclusion. It is possible that a cultural complex, reacting to the forced adaptation of the mass collectivism of Soviet ideologies, will be activated in individuals and groups. Under the spell of the complex, they will find it easier to identify with a local, more familiar sense of nationhood, advocating social exclusion. In such conditions, primitive tribal forces can erupt. Home risks becoming an ideology, transforming former neighbors into enemies.

In both Eastern and Western Europe, new forms of nationalism have recently emerged. Fear of loss of former privileges has unleashed xeno-phobic forms of nationalism that have a divisive effect on society and manifest in violent reactions to an alien other, often perceived in the unwanted immigrant. One might ask, what has happened to the nation-state? Why have so many lost belief in its integrating function and are no longer able to identify with it as a whole? Obviously, one needs to trust and be convinced that loyalty and service to the nation serve a greater cause, even if one is not always in agreement with state policies. The nation-state has always transcended the individual interests of its group members. Loss of nationhood is not simply an outer political event, but also a loss of a sense of service to a greater whole. National policies will not always gratify our needs and, considering the complexity of today's socie-ties, will not be intelligible for a large section of the population.

Adolf Guggenbühl attempted to understand the connection between psyche and nation—less from a factual point of view, but more in terms of an idea, fantasy, or value. A nation represents all aspects of human life: old and young, rich and poor, saints and criminals.[29] The individual psy-che can only grasp the complexity of humanity (*Menschenbild*) in ways that include the indispensability of boundaries and restraint, hence the idea of nationhood as a more comprehensible and concrete variation of the Anthropos, an image implying "humanity as a whole." Nations are symbols of a greater self, which "incarnates" in communities, societies, or nations. Seen from this point of view, nationhood represents an enclosed reality. Yet nationhood as an incarnation of the Anthropos ultimately rep-resents universal human values and thus leaves an opening to other nations in matters concerning humanity as a whole.

Considering the above, let us raise the question of whether the soul's inability or unwillingness to identify with nationhood implies a loss of connection with the Anthropos, producing indifference to issues beyond benefits for specific individuals or groups. In engagements with a particular community, society, or nation, it is important to recognize that you are serving a greater whole, one that requires dedication, loyalty, trust, and endurance. In this way you serve your own soul, which seeks home not only in a family, society, or nation, but in the experience of a greater self that transcends individual or group interests, embracing a mysterious reality that is all-inclusive, even if only grasped in rare moments of inspiration. Jung's notion of the Self as the source of identity approximates to images of God, which have been a source of all-inclusive meaning and integration even if often acted upon in ways that exclude others.

We learn from history that nationhood has always posed a threat to justice and individual freedom. The danger comes not only from the outside, but also from within. Nationhood as a symbol can achieve godlike dimensions and may possess the ego, obliterating its powers of discrimination. A healthy relationship between the individual and the nation depends on the recognition of its symbolic dimensions. Symbols are not the possession of the ego. They provide nourishment for the soul, having been formed over generations as collective representations of value and meaning. Almost every race or nation believe, at some time, that they are the chosen ones—nevertheless, the archetypal significance of native soil cannot be exhausted in loyalty to a particular homeland, nation, prophet, or Führer. A critical attitude to cultic worship requires awareness of its symbolic dimensions. Symbols are intentional and point beyond themselves. Objects may embody symbols, but can never exhaust their full meaning. Loss of the object does not mean loss of the ability to be at home somewhere, with somebody. As humans, we need to attach ourselves to people, groups, and places so that we may feel at home in the world. We need to know and love them in such a way that we can let go of them when called upon to do so—ultimately, in the face of death, the stranger who can visit us anytime, anywhere.

Louis XIV once said, "I am France," and Hitler, "Life is the nation." Here is a denial of boundaries and of the ability to remain truly human. An ideology of this kind persuaded the German psychoanalyst Alexander Mitscherlich to define home as "the martyrdom of identity." Identification with an archetype—in this case, nation as home—leads to the control and manipulation of others and distorts enterprises serving a greater whole. Its victims live a life of terror—once an object or fixed dogma replaces the interior images and associations of the soul, the ability to reflect and evaluate experience is endangered and may be imprisoned by some object or ideal that limits human freedom, creativity, and openness to a world of multiple values. Home's potential for further significance, for a plurality of meanings, becomes severely restricted. Intellectual and imaginative life is crippled. Our ability to assimilate the world, form new attachments, and continue translating the interior language of the soul in terms of new cultural landscapes risks impairment.

Visiting Russia and America

In a visit to Moscow in 1996, I was shown some of the remaining monuments of a fallen empire. Stalin's triumphal architecture, celebrating a collective utopia, is visible everywhere in the city—in monumental blocks of flats, in grandiose skyscrapers, and in the interior of the Underground stations. The vast halls of one station are decorated with colonnades of larger-than-life bronze statues—soldiers and laborers of both sexes poised for action, all with the same anonymous heroic expression. Human endeavor is sculptured as a struggle for survival and conquest. Soviet men and women had to embody the virtues of sacrifice and endurance. I could hardly find a sign of this grim ideology in the fun-loving, busy, affluent, depressed, or broken faces of contemporary Muscovites, who seemed unconnected and indifferent to the memorials of their past.

Another remarkable monument to Soviet ideology can be witnessed in the grounds of the magnificent Monastery to the Virgin (Novodewitschij Monastyr). Its graveyard has been reserved as a last resting place of Russia's most famous people. Here one finds the unpretentious graves of Pushkin, Chekhov, Prokofiev, and Shostakovich. The largest part of the cemetery is set apart for elite members of the communist party. The graves are of black marble; from the headstones loom bronze heads and sometimes the full bodies of deceased marshals, generals, and party leaders. They are well sculptured, and I could clearly recognize Khrushchev, Molotov, Gromyko, and Furtseva. Hundreds of dark heads or standing bodies look down upon the visitors, as they once stood on the Lenin mausoleum watching the military parades of the October Revolution pass by. There is an eerie atmosphere to this place. It is strange and uncanny to walk among the mighty of a fallen empire. Those who were once familiar and foreboding have now become petrified in stone or bronze effigies. My

Russian companions could not withhold their pride and deep affection for the great musicians and writers of their nation, but were embarrassed and visibly disturbed as we walked among the tombs of their most recent history.

American history contains many narratives about the loss and gain of home and nationhood. North America has been a great melting pot for many nations. The space, freedom, and generosity of that land have provided millions of homes for the uprooted. The United States has been a land of hope for many. Its population is not mono-ethnic, and therefore it is much easier for an immigrant to become an "American" in the United States, than to become German, Swiss, or French.[30]

Social scientists are increasingly aware of the limits, particularly with regard to Europe, of the American model of assimilation in which all immigrants are to be assimilated into one society. Previous assimilation in the United States was less complicated due to the extent of available land. Elena Liotta, writing on "The Soul of the Earth," suggests that the "aggregating power" of territory in the United States tended to unite different minorities, forming a cohesive group "identified by a common land, and common lifestyle." This policy, however, was mostly reserved for European whites. With the diminishing availability of land, conflicts are bound to increase. Liotta implies that not only the soul of the land but a change of attitude is crucial, if minorities are to live in peace with one another:

> The problem today in a society that considers itself multicultural lies not in the growing coexistence of different ethnic groups…but in the distortion of collective relationships, carried out by groups, corporatism, various kinds of terrorism…animated by the dynamics of power.[31]

Despite the success in creating a multicultural society in North America, successful integration will depend on the attitude of the host country towards the newcomer. Those who feel rejected will create new ghettos, and social exclusion will continue to pose problems for future generations.

Every nation has its shadows. American history, infused with the settlers' ideology of land possession, brought destruction to the Native American nations. One shadow that still lingers over America can be described by the words of Chief Plenty-Coups, in his farewell address of 1909 at the Little Bighorn council in Montana. The words of this Native

American chief stand as a testimony to an unbroken yet endangered identity between land, culture, and people.

> The ground on which we stand is sacred ground. It is the dust and blood of our ancestors. On these plains the Great White Father at Washington sent his soldiers armed with long knives and rifles to slay the Indian….A few more passing suns will see us here no more, and our dust and bones will mingle with these same prairies. I see as in a vision the dying spark of our council fires, the ashes cold and white….I hear no longer the songs of the women as they prepare the meal….The white man's medicine is stronger than ours; his iron horse rushes over the buffalo trail. He talks to us through his "whispering spirit" [the telephone]. We are like birds with a broken wing.[32]

Despite war, poverty, and segregation, the First Nations of North America have survived and continue to smoke the peace pipe. The ideal of nationhood among these peoples still carries echoes of their once-lived nomadic existence, and is more inclusive than a traditional Eurocentric one. The "Lakota Nation" includes not only the people of the Lakota tribe, their laws, or their lands. Whenever there is a smoking of the peace pipe, kinship with the entire universe is established:

> The pipe consists of four parts: the stone bowl, which stands for (is) the earth; the stem, which is everything that grows upon the earth; the animal carvings on the stem, which are the four-legged creatures; and the eagle feathers and pipe smoke, which together are everything that flies and lives above.[33]

When the Lakota people smoke the peace pipe, they draw smoke into the lungs, which is then sent as prayer to the heavens, making a connection between the Great Spirit above and the Earth Mother below. Nationhood for the Lakota people is founded on a deep spirituality, embracing a wholeness that respects the sacredness of all life. Less burdened by the conflicts of European civilization, they listen to the sounds and symmetries of their natural habitat and their voices still sing the song of the universe, a home common to all humanity.

When I visited the Pueblo village of Taos in New Mexico, several years ago, I had in mind Jung's visit to the village in 1925 and his encounter with Mountain Lake, an elder of the Pueblo tribe. This man impressed upon Jung the distinction between thoughts of the head and thoughts of the heart. Jung learned some of the tribal secrets, which expressed a deep kinship between the people and the powers of nature. In one revealing exchange, Jung was told that the sun was their father, and if they discontinued practicing their religion, the sun, their father, would rise no longer. In my visit to Taos, instead of meeting a "wise old man," I unexpectedly met a young Native American who had lived on the reservation for most of his life. He had been to university, and was full of praise for President Nixon, who granted his people rights to possess their ancient lands again. The young Native American was convinced that his people would survive. This encounter changed my attitude towards the First Nations of America—I felt a fresh wind blowing through these lands, among these people. Threatened indigenous cultures hardly need to be continually reminded about their losses, which only supports an attitude of imprisoning defeatism and melancholy about a lost home. Instead of retaining romantic images of the past, it may be more helpful to encourage an attitude of hope that these people will regain their rightful place among the peoples of the world. We have much to learn from them. Each time I have visited the United States, I have experienced premonitions that overwhelm me with a mysterious power, connected with the ancestors of the Native American. I sometimes wonder if the deep kinship with the land, upheld by all indigenous cultures, speaks to us in our dreams. One night, just before I began a lecture tour of Australia, a little aboriginal man appeared to me in a dream, saying: "Don't forget us."

The kind of homesickness expressed in the words of an old chief faced with the impending loss of nation and identity stands in stark contrast with the homesickness of contemporary humanity. John Updike describes ordinary life in America with a realism that makes it extraordinary. He takes to task the American dream of having your own home. Rabbit, the hero of his famous fourfold novel, achieves the dream, but soon feels trapped by the pressures of domestic life:

> It just felt like the whole business was fetching and hauling, all the time trying to hold this mess together she was making all the time....it seemed like I was glued with a lot of busted toys and empty glasses and the television going and meals late or never and no way of getting out.[34]

Rabbit tries to escape—first by driving south, then through affairs. Updike's brilliant description of homes that go wrong reminds one about many tales of unacknowledged violence and abuse done to children in what may seem an ordinary household. In many of today's urban homes, both parents are in full-time jobs. Often regular meals are replaced by "grazing," a process of devouring frozen, precooked meals, made edible by microwave, whenever one is hungry. Conversation is rarely personal, and relaxation is provided by all kinds of electronic gadgets. The hearth and the table are gone—two powerful elements that held homes together. This kind of mediocre, boring, and superficial family life breeds escapism. Sunday worship—which Updike describes as "people in their best clothes….it seems a visual proof of the unseen world"[35]—rarely provides relief. The soul withdraws from a reality that no longer provides sustenance. There is a rabbit within all of us who will take every opportunity to create an alternative existence—which, if not grounded, is likely to have divisive effects on later social life.

Social integration cannot be the only answer to fantasies of an alternative existence. Many years ago, a man who had lived most of his life in the United States came to see me with the complaint that he could never cry. He had spent most of his life achieving outer success, but knew something was missing. His domestic life had been one of broken promises. The only time when he came close to tears was in reading poetry. Robert Frost's "Death of a Hired Man"[36] was the one poem that made him cry. It tells a very different tale about what homesickness can be. The poem is about Silas, a wanderer and a man of the land who could build the best load of hay that any man could. One day he returned to Mary and Warren, a couple who ran a farm and had hired Silas many times. Warren did not want him back because Silas was old and unreliable. She coaxed her husband to employ him and go talk to him about ditching the meadow. Warren returned as clouds approached the moon. He had only one word to say: Dead. Frost describes the hospitality of a home that is unreservedly reliable, even in dire circumstances: "Home is the place where, when you have to go there / They have to take you in."[37]

I have known many people who have grown up in a home that was no home. Like the hero of Updike's novels, they suffered from the pressures of domestic life and attempted to escape them by working, traveling, or sex. Frost's poem, however, pays homage to the wanderer in all humanity. It implies that, despite all diversions and distractions of an unsettled life, the sounds and symmetries of belonging call us to some place we call home. The hymns to the universe, as witnessed among the First Nations of America, provide a foundation for all those who find no home in family, profession, or nation. They express an archetypal theme: all living beings belong to the earth and to the heavens; all are encouraged to sing the song of the universe, especially when the waters of the earth mirror the stars of the night, promising a return to the home of the ancestors.

The integration of the black population and minority nations in the United States remains an unfinished tale. Even though the black population of that country received citizenship a hundred and fifty years ago, segregation continued for many decades. The black population still remains underprivileged compared to the rest of the nation. A new chapter has opened with the election of the first black president, Barack Obama. The hope of many is now linked with an incredible man who has African, Cherokee, English, and Scotch blood in his veins—whose identity has been formed by the cultures of Hawaii, Indonesia, Kenya, and North America, and who has seen members of his family becoming victims of violence and sexism. He has "dug beneath the surface of things"[38] to witness poverty, racism, and the undisguised misuse of power at his doorstep. He learned from his grandfather about a form of worship that "drew on the scriptures of all the great religions,"[39] and from his stepfather about "a brand of Islam that could make room for the remnants of more ancient animist and Hindu faiths."[40] In times of crisis, a man has appeared who has had the courage and strength to forge a character consisting of diverse identities that many consider to be incompatible, and who has kept alive the memory of those loved ones who have passed away before him. Whatever Barack Obama achieves, his message stands for a brighter future, one that welcomes racial and cultural diversity as a means of ennobling the human spirit.[41]

A TURKISH GARDEN: RESTORING ISLAM'S SACRED HERITAGE

Sometimes loss of a childhood home awakens bitter memories. They may be registered on a personal level, but on further probing reveal the loss of a valuable cultural heritage passed down through generations. A few years ago, I worked with a group of twenty-five people in the precincts of the ancient Greek amphitheater of Pergamon, Turkey. The work consisted of theme-centered psychodrama, which took place in open tents with a view of the surrounding landscape. The protagonist, Alara, was a thirty-year-old woman who wanted to work on "loss of home." Something was missing in her life. She felt detached from her family, culture, and nation.

Alara began the psychodrama by contemplating the beautiful sun-burnt landscape in a deep silence, only interrupted by the songs of the birds. After some time, she felt the presence of the garden of her child-hood home. So she asked various participants to embody the entire garden: the birds singing, a well in the middle of the garden, the small fence surrounding it (embodied by three people), a vine clinging to a wall, and a big tree in its corner. Alara warmed up those who volunteered for the assigned roles, as follows:

> The bird must sing; the well must whisper, "I am cool and refreshing in the summer and full of water in the winter"; the fences say, "We love the roses and vines that grow upon us"; the vine says, "Come and eat my grapes, enjoy my sweetness"; the big tree invites children to climb on its branches.

First Alara listened to the many voices of her beloved garden from the outside. Then she entered the garden and spoke with loving words to the birds, the well, the fence, the vine, and the tree. When the exchange came to an end, tears filled her eyes. She told the group that the garden no longer exists. It was destroyed, broken up by construction work; only the well remains. We made a pause, allowing time for the protagonist to recover. Everybody present felt this woman's pain, and that something was missing. Was the garden irretrievably lost? Was her fate simply to mourn the loss of the garden? We tried again, and it was as if everybody in their assigned roles intuitively understood what needed to happen. Alara entered her garden once again. Each person, embodying the various parts of the garden, had something new to say.

> The bird tells her that if she is quiet, she will always hear its beautiful songs; the well whispers, "The water of the well will always be available for you to create new life and new gardens"; the fences say, "The fence is part of your soul, protecting your beautiful roses"; the vine declares, "I am in you, you experience me whenever you feel nourished and nourish others"; and the tree adds: "I come to life in you, whenever you play as a child."

Alara felt relief, and realized for the first time that she had not lost her garden. It is her home forever, an "eternal memory of a child's heart," as proclaimed in the final chapter of Dostoyevsky's *The Brothers Karamazov*. The garden became the voice of her soul, providing assurance it would never leave her. A cruel fate deprived her of the garden of her childhood; her destiny was to discover that the purpose of her life was to remember, cherish, and cultivate that same garden. The garden, created in psycho-drama, became an inspiration to regain a lost heritage. It represented a soul landscape, a cultural memory, and a vision of wholeness. It embodied the garden of paradise, so prominent in her Islamic culture, preserving and protecting a spiritual tradition that hopefully one day will be strong enough to counteract the unbridled energies of contemporary affluence.

NEW HORIZONS

Homesickness has many faces. All too often, it has been associated with children who miss their home and family and whose young lives have to face the dilemma of dependency versus autonomy. When it appears in adults, society has often sanctioned it as being childish, overde-pendent, and nostalgic—interpretations from a patriarchal system that has little appreciation of values of the heart. We have seen how it was con-sidered an illness that could be fatal, due to separation from family, com-munity, or natural landscape, elements of a mosaic that molded identity over generations. Homesickness signified the loss of a whole world, a unity of self and surroundings that nourished one's being and preserved the will to live. As pastoral cultures slowly disappeared with the advance of industry and urbanization, the archetypal disposition to identify with one's surroundings underwent a change—attention shifted from nature to nation. Home became idealized in the principles of the nation-state. The archetypal energies previously invested in the cultural, mythic, or religious significance of family, house, gardens, village, animals, moun-tains, rivers, and lakes were trapped in another framework, which in the first half of the twentieth century flourished in nations ruled by generals and dictators. The energies were in some instances focused on one man who embodied the ideal of the nation, much to the chagrin of minorities and other nations who were suppressed by force. The death camps were monstrous examples of creating dehumanized spaces in which every sense of home was systematically destroyed. In those jails of horror, any senti-ments expressing homesickness, loss of loved ones, and values of the heart quickly reduced one's chances of survival.

Every human being has a right to be at home in the world. The instinctive and cultural affinity for home finds expression in attachment and connectedness, observed in all living beings, and in the specifically human need to create a world of shared meaning. Possibly the founda-tions of feeling at home in the world are to be found in those experiences of deep connectedness between a child and its primal caretakers, and later in one's family, social, cultural, and natural environment. In earlier societies, this unity embraced the history and traditions of a community, as witnessed in the creation of sacred space. Nature and culture were not separate realms. In the history of Western thought, an intellectual detachment from natural environment already began with the philosophers of the Renaissance. With the rise of nationalism in the nineteenth century, the older unity between self and the familiarity of a local, natural, and cultural landscape received another setback, and was gradually replaced by a unity between self and nation on a mass scale. After 1945, there followed the modern age of detachment and alienation, an age that also permits new possibilities of being at home in the world.

Contemporary humanity is no longer required to remain bound by tradition to one particular home or nation. Modern man and woman are free to move out and find other homes, even though their childhood home might always remain the most significant. Today, one has the opportunity of finding a home not in only one place, but anywhere, with any person or community where a world of shared meaningful experiences can be discovered—where the interior language of the soul can celebrate a diversity of worlds. An inner ear must learn to listen for home, not only in the familiar, but also in unfamiliar narratives initiating new horizons of consciousness. To facilitate this process, let us hope that the world we are creating will become more humane, generous, and respectful, so that as many people as possible can find a way of being at home in it. Salman Rushdie warns us not to get caught in a ghetto mentality and not to confine ourselves within narrowly defined cultural frontiers, but to remember that there is a world beyond the community to which we belong: "For God's sake, open the universe a little more!"[42]

HOMESICKNESS: ITS SECRET INTENT

Home expresses the paradox of dependency and autonomy, containment and freedom to explore new horizons, trust in the familiar and readiness to defend or extend boundaries. Despite the increasing atomization of society, many still define themselves within the context of a local environment with all its personal, social, and cultural affiliations. If you feel homesick, particularly in moments of transition, you may see it as a sign that you are still curious about what is missing in your life. You still long to be related, to love and be loved; yet you will want to maintain a level of competence, autonomy, and control. Homesickness prepares you to build new friends, new families, new villages, and a new relationship to humanity as a whole. Homesickness emerges from the transcendent source of your own being. It manifests as the soul's natural disposition to connect in respectful, profound, and loving ways with landscape, city, family, community, and Planet Earth. If one's story of homesickness is heard, it can be the seeds of a new, shared understanding with others who have suffered a similar fate—creating a world of common meaning, a world of respect and affection that includes individual freedom as well as the desire to explore the full potential of one's animate and inanimate surroundings.

Home and homesickness are ancient words. Everyone has some sense of what it means to be at home or not at home in the world. Home and homesickness may be used to describe objective realities, but also an inner, subjective disposition. The meaning of home cannot be exhausted by modern words such as "assimilation," "integration," or "acculturation." If you have felt the joy of being at home somewhere with someone, or suffered the pangs of homesickness, you never forget those experiences because your whole self is involved. You may have been grasped by an ineffable joy or sorrow that defies any reductive interpretation. Home or homesickness refer not only to the gain or loss of a particular person, status, or object. They are an inner archetypal disposition expressing a connectedness or disconnectedness between you and the world, your home or its loss. Home and homesickness are symbols of the Self, transcending the various identities you have created, experienced in moments when the deepest levels of your being are reflected or rejected in the world that surrounds you.

Should you identify a friend, a family, a community, or a landscape as your home, then you shall surely care for them, protect them, nourish them, and support their full potential. Likewise, as you see yourself reflected in them, your very being begins to blossom. The meaning of home and homesickness as a symbol is inexhaustible. When you are faced with death and the possibility of survival beyond death, once again homesickness may reveal new secrets. Perhaps that will remain the final challenge of this enigma we call "home." If you find yourself dwelling not only on life, but also on death, you might begin to understand the paradox of the truly human, as once did Rilke:

Earth, is not just this that you want: to arise
invisibly in us? Is not your dream
To be one day invisible? Earth! Invisible!
What is your urgent command, if not transformation?
…Beyond all names I am yours, and have been for ages.
You were always right, and your holiest inspiration
Is Death, that friendly Death.[43]

CHAPTER 9

Ireland: Contemplating a Nation from a Place of Exile

Identity is seldom straightforward and given, more often a
matter of negotiation and exchange.
—Declan Kiberd, *Inventing Ireland*[1]

A Tenuous Project

National identity embodies an aspect of home that, for many, represents a reality they never had to doubt. For me, it was never self-evident. I was born into a cultural heritage that could be described as both a blessing and a burden. If I was to survive, I had no option but to translate that heritage in terms of new narratives that became the life I was to lead. Cultural norms of behavior are mediated to us at an age when we are highly susceptible to outside influence. We take over innumerable behavior patterns—from parents, teachers, priests, language, or religion—which become an intrinsic part of a shared identity. We define ourselves in terms of a collective memory of which we are hardly conscious. We are only one small link in a long chain that we have not created. In recent history, humans have become increasingly exposed to a multiplicity of new cultural landscapes, very different from the ones they have acquired from their parents. Already in adolescence, youths rebel against the familiar and attempt to define themselves with new cultural or counterculture acquisitions. This can be a process continuing over a lifetime. Some assume this is simply a question of choosing an alternative life style, but such an attitude can lead to dissociation between the older and the new identities. The art of translating a traditional inheritance in terms of a contemporary context is more complicated than simple choice. It is not easy to give up cherished beliefs, relationships, status, or lifestyles, even if they encumber the unfolding of personality. Transition points can be dangerous, especially where there is an urge to suppress the old or deny the new.

There was a moment in my history when I could no longer bear the narrow confines of my familiar home surroundings. When I heard the stories of ancient Ireland and traveled to its West Coast, narrative and landscape conveyed to me a very different reality than the one I had known. Something in me responded, and I felt nourished by a sustenance that had little in common with the daily life of an Anglo-Irish family. The new language was not about the racecourse, golf links, or cocktail parties; the imagery of Romantic Ireland portrayed passionate men and women in continual exchange with the invisible world of spirits. There was more than the banality of my everyday life. Gods and goddesses, heroes and heroines, fairies, monsters, ghosts, and mysterious landscapes were more successful in activating deeper levels of the psyche than well-worn creeds, intellectual learning, or polite conversations. Before I could appreciate the new sounds and symmetries of belonging, schoolboy pranks soon prevented any idealization of being purely Irish—at the age of twelve, I was sent for a year to a "rough" school run by the Presentation Brothers, in order to learn the Irish language. The usual games in the school break were fights between the English and Irish. As one of the less popular boys, I was given no choice but to be made a member of the "British army," who would inevitably be bashed up by the boys representing the "I.R.A."

Years later, I studied aspects of Irish heritage in order to discover what an Irish identity could possibly mean. I am grateful to the many writers and poets who have reworked that heritage in terms of a contemporary context. Gradually, I understood the significance of the old myths as a source of inspiration, molding new perspectives. If there is such a thing as a racial or national identity, it can only be understood in terms of a process that translates historical material in ways that transcend the actual history of a nation. I have attempted to do this, mostly within the context of psychology. Psychological reflection has enabled me to interpret the underlying messages of ancient myth in the flesh and blood of today.

Jung's poetical thought about there being no psychology without a myth confirmed this approach:

> [T]he man who thinks he can live without a myth, or outside it, is an exception. He is one uprooted, having no true link either with the past or with the ancestral life, which continues within him, or yet with contemporary human society....The psyche is not of today; its ancestry goes back many millions of years.[2]

When I first heard some of the stories of ancient Ireland, my young mind responded with passion and interest. They seemed to capture a world not just made up of endless historical events, but one that appealed to the hopes and fantasies of a soul imprisoned in a world of convention and tradition. Here was described another home, utterly different from the one I had known in childhood.

One day, on a visit to the General Post Office in Dublin, I received some confirmation of that other home. Inside the main hall is a bronze statue of a dying warrior tied to a post with a raven perched upon his shoulder. I soon discovered that this statue embodied a powerful myth that had determined the course of Irish history. The statue represents the death of Cuculainn, enshrined in an effigy to Irish nationalism, dedicated to the martyrs of the 1916 Rebellion. For the first time, I was able to make a connection between ancient stories of a long forgotten past and historical events in the real world. What was this connection? How did it come about? Could there be a link between myth and reality? Could my soul be searching for another station that had little in common with the home of my parents? A lifetime work of translating the pre-Christian legacy of my Irish heritage into the psychological reality of today began.

Despite my fascination with Cuculainn, I did not forget the bashings by the "I.R.A." boys at school, and viewed the nationalist interpretation of Irish mythological history with suspicion. Nationalist movements of Ireland have long sought to legitimatize their ideals and objectives by referring to the ancestral myths of Celtic heroism. Members of the I.R.A. have seen themselves as upholders of an Irish cause that can be traced back to archaic Celtic civilization. When the Troubles in Northern Ireland started in the 1970s, my attention was drawn to an incident that affirmed my suspicion of movements fuelled by mythic motifs. Although the stories of the ancient Irish heroes liberated me from an adherence to conventional expectations, the incident made me acutely aware of dark shadows spawned from a life motivated by mythic material.

WEAVING THE THREADS OF A NATION

In the early years of the Troubles in Northern Ireland, an Irish girl, belonging to the Catholic minority, became engaged to a British soldier. The women of her community cut off the unfortunate girl's hair, bathed her head in tar, covered her with feathers, and ostracized her from the community. Did these women know what they were doing? Probably they were unaware of an underlying mythology that led them to commit the crime. A national mythology, sustained by bonding memories, has structured the cultural and political history of Ireland over generations. The girl, laden with a burden no individual should bear, became a goddess, the land of Ireland, who had sold herself to England. Her innocent love affair with the British soldier represented in the eyes of her persecutors the hated union with England. With the distinction between the human and the archetypal obliterated, she suffered a drama extending beyond her personal identity. Both victim and perpetrators were imprisoned by a cult that identifies woman with land. The Irish girl had blemished the purity of Mother Ireland, a betrayal that had to be revenged. I intend to explore the historical and psychological significance of that event within the context of national identity.

Nationality is one of the many ways in which humans define themselves as members of a group. We take our national identity for granted, but when it comes to defining it, we tend to find ourselves at a loss. This is especially true when it comes to appreciating degrees of loyalty, patriotism, or solidarity with the marginalized. Obviously, many different elements constitute national identity, as Andrew Samuels has pointed out.[3] A collective identity is nourished and strengthened through shared taste, food, space, language, character, history, or culture. Nationhood is impoverished if reduced to a single dimension, such as one particular race, language, or religion. The less inclusive a nationhood, the more will excluded elements inhabit a shadow realm, causing splits and preventing social integration.

According to Eric Hobsbawm, nationhood is "a work in the making."[4] Destruction and creation, deconstruction and reconstruction, apply not only to the social framework but also to myths and rituals, which originally inspired and structured the fabric of a particular nation.

The history of Ireland offers an arena in which to study the transgenerational influence of a mythic notion of national identity. It is one of the few nations to possess a mythic belief system, embedded in a cultural memory that has upheld a particular brand of nationalism, shaping its history over centuries. The aim of this chapter is to outline the origins, influence, and diverse functions of that mythic system. I will describe its slow evolution, its power as a breeding ground of cultural complexes, its imagery as a source of poetic inspiration, and its inherent, liberating capacity to transform collective consciousness.

Let me begin by narrating a twelfth-century tale, of which there are many versions, that probably refers back to Celtic Ireland of the fourth century:[5]

> An old king is dying and sends out his five sons to find the water of life. The first son comes to a well guarded by an old hag. She will give him the water of life, if he will lie with her. He dismisses her and she refuses him the magic potion. The same happens with the next three sons. The fifth son, Niall, consents to lie with her, and the old hag becomes a beautiful young maiden. She calls herself Mise Flathius na h-Erinn (I am the Sovereignty of Ireland). She promises to give Niall the kingship of the land. Peace will prevail and the land will be fertile: the crops shall be manifold; the cows will give forth more milk; the rivers will be full of fish.

Scholars have considered the tale to be an offspring of the universal *hierosgamos* motif, and has been subject to innumerable interpretations—a joining of heaven and earth, a synchronizing the energies of life with the norms of society, or, more specifically, as evidence of a tension and reciprocity between an earlier goddess-oriented culture and later Celtic patriarchal culture. Despite the relatively late dating of the tale, and despite its usage as a political instrument to justify the legitimacy of the UiNeill dynasty, the narrative contains distinctive mythic elements. The union of king and goddess is narrated in terms of the great cycle of life, death, and rebirth. In ancient Ireland, the king is inaugurated in a state of sacred intoxication and, through union with the goddess of the land, achieves royal charisma.[6] When a king's reign is about to begin, he encounters a young maiden who offers him the waters of life. When it ends, he meets an old hag, and the rivers of the land run dry. "Sovereignty," as the old hag or young maiden, represents the earth goddess. As an old hag, she represents life's bareness and infertility; as a young maiden, its springtime and abundance.

It would be a mistake to think that the union of king and goddess can be interpreted as an example of only a seasonal vegetative cult. There are texts that indicate a deeper significance. In the *Book of Invasions*, and other texts,[7] we witness a mytho-geographical account of the formation of a people's conception of a shared collective identity. Each legendary invader brings a distinct cultural asset to the land. The earliest invaders are associated with magic and the mysteries of the underworld. The next newcomers, the people of Nemed, develop agriculture and are connected with the principle of abundance and the virtue of generosity. The Fir Bolg are next, a warrior caste whose supreme virtue is courage and bravery in battle. The Tuath deDanaan follow, bringing metal craft, art, and druidic wisdom. According to the myth, each invader settles in one part of the land. Thus the four provinces of Ireland come into existence: Connaught, Ulster, Leinster, and Munster. In one text, *The Settling of the Manor of Tara*, Ireland is divided into four quarters and a center—"knowledge in the west, battle in the north, prosperity in the east, music in the south, kingship in the centre"—the king representing, respectively, the four virtues of wisdom, bravery, generosity, and connection with the Underworld.[8] In another text, the sons of Mil, the last of the invaders, have to assent to the wishes of the three goddesses of the land in order to gain the kingship.[9] As each invader succeeds the other, the newcomers have to come to terms with preceding invaders in order to rule and guarantee the fertility of the land. The preceding invaders, once defeated, go underground and become the fairies, goblins, or spirits inhabiting caves, mounds, and offshore islands. They represent a feminine principle and confront the new masters of the land in the form of otherworldly female beings. The union of king and goddess implies far more than a fertility cult; the narratives indicate that the union symbolizes a connection to the ancestors and a psychic inheritance embedded in the land.

Concerning this theme, Proinsias MacCana once wrote:

> Just as the land lies barren and desolate in the absence of its destined ruler and is quickly restored to life by his coming, so the goddess who personifies the kingdom often appears ugly and unkempt and destitute until united with her rightful lord.[10]

In ancient Ireland, the rightful consort of the goddess has to incarnate the virtues of wisdom, bravery, generosity, and knowledge of the Underworld. The legends imply that the goddess of the land, often a tutelary figure of a clan, mediates the ideals of an ancestral heritage to the king or hero whose royal charisma then embodies them. The union of king and goddess represents a local, nonpolitical, spiritual point of reference and meaning, which, as MacCana implies, sheds significance on the Celtic notion of cultural identity and continuity.[11] It represents an early collective ideal of human virtue, rooted in local landscape and ancestral history. The Celtic ideal of perfection achieved neither the status of a national creed nor an abstract purity separated from the contingencies of life's changing circumstances, clearly distinguishing it from the canons of later patriarchal culture. The ideal was mediated to the rulers, usually the chiefs of petty tribal kingdoms, by powers beyond their control. Formed within a cyclic conception of life, they could embody it for a limited period only. Their right to rule did not depend on abstract principles, but on a deeper, local, underground ancestral reality, imaged as a connection with spirits and otherworldly female beings—a realm that resembles today's unconscious. Perhaps this is one reason why the Celts are fond of magic and myth, why the mysteries of the soul and of life are so fully present in their stories and legends, and why the landscape evokes tales of wonder and beauty of an ancient heritage lost in the mists of time. The Celtic values of the tribe, represented in kingship, were subject to a continual process of transition. Everything, including the virtues, must live, die, and be reborn so that the clan's cultural norms and beliefs retain their freshness and vitality. Meaning must renew body and soul. Expressed in contemporary language, the encounter with the old hag implies not only death and destruction—a loving embrace of the repressed, unwanted, or excluded parts of one's personal psyche and one's cultural heritage promises renewal.

Ireland as a nation has struggled with the dark and light aspects of a mythology that has personified the land as a *puella senilis*, a beautiful maiden or old hag. It is one of the few countries in Europe whose history has been determined by mythology in an unbroken way. After the destruction of the old Gaelic order at the beginning of the eighteenth century, the myths, stories, and rituals continued to survive among the indigenous people. Storytellers, bards, and poets kept the old ways alive, reminding the people of their ancient heritage, knowing well that a loss of story meant a loss of national identity. Many poems of the eighteenth century adopted the union of the goddess of the land with her consort as their chief motif. The *hierosgamos* was transformed into a political instrument, losing much of its deeper psychological significance, but nevertheless generating the struggle for independence.

In the *Speir Bhean* of Egan O'Rahilly,[12] the poet bewails the exile of the Stuart pretender. In the poem, he falls into a swoon, and in a dream sees the figure of a bright and stately woman revealing herself as the land of Erin. She expresses her sorrow for her true lover who is exiled beyond the seas. There follows a voyage to a druid place, where the poet finds a woman seated beside a clown. He longs to embrace her and free her from her shameful marriage to a tyrant. The political intent of the poem is obvious. The beautiful woman is the land of Ireland, which had been ravished by the Williamite conquest and finally bonded to the yoke of English supremacy. The old Gaelic order has been defeated; the Catholic Stuarts driven into exile. The poet's longing to embrace the mysterious woman expressed a political message: the Gaels alone are the consort of the goddess and the rightful lords of the land. The struggle for a national identity and freedom from England was about to begin.

At the turn of the twentieth century, the Sovereignty myth found full expression in the writings of W. B. Yeats. In 1902, the play *Cathleen ni Houlahan*[13] had its first performance. It was inspired by a dream of its author, in which Ireland appears as an old woman in a cottage where people are talking of a coming marriage. In the play, Delia Cahel is to marry Michael Gillane. The parents want to know if Delia will bring enough money into the house, if Michael has a nice pair of clean clothes, and if the priest has given his approval. An old woman appears, who neither wants food nor money, but Michael himself. If he follows her, he will be remembered forever. Michael hesitates, but when the sounds of battle are heard, he runs out of the house in search of the old woman. In the end, Michael's father asks his younger son if he saw an old woman leaving the house and the answer is: "No, but I saw a young woman and she had the walk of a queen." Yeats's play signaled to the Irish the coming of revolution. It was a message to his fellow countrymen to wake up and free themselves from the lethargies of civilization and the bourgeois ideals of clean clothes, money, and priestly approval. Yeats rejected the mediocrity of conventional society and welcomed a return of ancestral heritage, ancient heroism, and primitive mythological energy. He released a dormant pagan energy that set the spark to revolution. "A terrible beauty was born."

What for Yeats was a literary and cultural vision became for Patrick Pearse a political and military reality. Pearse, the founder of the I.R.A. movement, embodied the heroic ideal in his poem "Mise Erinn" (I am Ireland):[14]

> I am Ireland
> I am older than the old woman of Beara.
> Great my glory
> I that bore Cuculainn.
> Great my shame
> My own children that sold their mother.
> I am Ireland
> I am lonelier than the old woman of Beara.

The old woman of Beara was a legendary figure of ancient Ireland. It is said that when she was young she loved neither gold nor silver but the young men of the land. She lived through untold generations, drank mead with the warriors, and was married to no less than six kings of Ireland. Pearse was aware that this figure had the same attributes as the legendary goddess-queens of the land, and was none other than a manifestation of the old Celtic goddess. He also knew that Cuculainn, a kind of Irish Achilles, chose to die young rather than allow his heroism be blemished. The shameful children of the old woman of Beara were those Irishmen who refused the heroic and had betrayed the Irish cause for personal gain. They were not only the well-known historical figures, but also modern Irishmen who chose the comforts of bourgeois society over the struggle for freedom.

Pearse, like the romantic poets before him, rejected the dullness and security of industrial civilization. His soul was identified with "Mother Ireland," and he saw himself as the man who embodied the Cuculainn myth. It has been said that when he was ten years old and first read about this hero, he knelt down and vowed to devote the rest of his life to liberating Ireland. Believing this was his destiny, he participated in the archetypal axis of goddess and hero-consort. The hero's greatest glory was to live and die for Ireland. In the 1916 Rebellion, Pearse literally enacted the myth. The Rebellion was one of poets and idealists who consciously chose martyrdom so that the land would be liberated and national identity restored. Pearse, as consort of the goddess, became the new king and priest of Ireland. At that time, most people believed that the insurgents were crazy in challenging the world's most powerful empire. England's mistake was to execute the leaders of the rebellion, thereby fueling a cult of martyrdom. Confirming Winston Churchill's warning, "grass does not grow over the gallows," the death of Pearse and his followers lit the torch of Ireland's war of independence.

Civil war (1922) followed the creation of the Free State, in which the romantic ideal of Gaelic Ireland lost its mystical significance. Instead of choosing martyrdom to defend "Holy Ireland," the modern heroes began to butcher themselves with automatic machine guns. In the mystical nationalism of Yeats and Pearse, there evolved a purist ideal of mythological Ireland and her ancient heroes that excluded all evil. Ireland itself became a goddess, and her oracles were embodied in heroes ready to die for her. The words and actions of these men were unquestionable, and anything opposed to the cause was considered evil. Evil was first projected onto the common enemy, England, but once the Free State was established, and the inner dimensions of the amity/enmity split had not been resolved, evil became embodied in the opposing opinions of former comrades in arms.

The remnants of this split ideology continued to survive in the conflicts of Northern Ireland. The extremists of both sides have perpetuated opposing mythological conceptions of their land. Their conceptions are hardly Christian, but rather include vestiges of the ancient goddess-hero cult. In the purist visions of the Loyalist and Republican communities, evil is excluded and projected onto the enemy. Both visions are inhuman, intolerant, and fanatical. In the physical-force schools of both sides, there is a belief in violence to end all violence. Deaths, commemorations, and a firm holding to the past are part of these ideologies. The Loyalist extremists maintain a logic of triumph, and the Republican extremists a logic of sacrifice. The former hold festivities in commemoration of the battle of the Boyne and the siege of Derry; the latter revere the defeat of Wolf Tone, the martyrdom of Pearse, the hunger strikes, and the massacre of civilians on Bloody Sunday 1972. The Protestants rely on patriarchal structure and tradition; the Catholics on the older, enduring myth of "Mother Ireland," for whom her sons must die. The archetypal identification with either king or goddess in the Northern Ireland conflict reveals a split in the original *hierosgamos* motif. As long as individuals identify with one or the other pole, with the archetypal father or mother of a nationalized mythology, there is little hope that a unity between civic order and ancestral heritage can be achieved.

New Tapestries with Old Threads

One might ask what causes modern man and woman to become possessed by the archaic heritage of their culture? What leads to the breakdown of boundaries between the human and archetypal? What drives humans into those fatal attractions that force them to surrender their hard-won individuality and identify with collective, mass movements? What makes humans identify with a Hitler, a Stalin, a bin Laden? One obvious answer is that their capacity to reflect, evaluate, and make balanced judgments is severely impaired. They may become obsessed with an idea, lose an appreciation of cultural refinement, and fail to discriminate between good and evil. Imprisoned in a bonding memory, animated by lore, commemorations, and annual rituals celebrating victory or defeat, they instrumentalize cultural history to serve divisive purposes. A leader whose inner and outer worlds are split and whose narcissistic grandiosity resonates with unfulfilled ambitions of a collective body may enthrall many followers. Such splits permeate the social framework, fragmenting it into the haves and have-nots, the superior and inferior, victor and victim. As atrocities multiply, people will hopefully resort to countermeasures. In my country, the politicized *puella senilis* herself became subject to the cyclic process of life, death, and rebirth. In search of "the art that mends nature,"[15] the poets embraced and re-worked the myth's outdated, nationalistic moldings. Many Irish artists and intellectuals transformed it, which, if unchanged, would only continue to imprison people in ideologies that have long served their purpose.

Reflecting on a mythology that has incited humans to become callous and intolerant, two Irish authors exposed the delusions and limits of Irish nationalism. Their works dramatically describe the effect of a mythic power that no longer serves the real needs of the people. When a period of skepticism sets in, the old myths are discredited and the process of demythologizing becomes inevitable, perhaps to yield new meaning. *The Plough and the Stars*, by Sean O'Casey, expresses the artist's hatred of Cathleen Ni Houlahan and the heroes who serve her. Jack, the hero of the drama, departs after a month of marriage "when the wonder of woman wears off," and joins the I.R.A. He is disappointed in real love, real life, and a real woman, and chooses an ideal woman, "Mother Ireland," and thus participates in a death cult. The revolution fails; Jack is on the run and becomes a man of brutality. He mistreats his wife and accidentally kills his yet-unborn child. In this play, it is the men who fail, and the women take over. Jack's wife realizes that all men are afraid, and that they are out fighting, not because they are brave, but because they are cowards who wish to prove themselves brave in the eyes of the collective.[16] O'Casey has no compassion for the soldiers, but for the civilians who suffer from men's inhuman, heroic ideals.

James Joyce was even more radical in his criticism of the goddess-hero myth that has determined Irish history. In the "Circe" episode of *Ulysses*, Joyce's mother appears as a ghost. With warnings of the fires of hell, she tries to get her son to mend his ways and to return to the Catholic Church. Later, "Mother Ireland" appears in the figure of "Old Gummy Granny."[17] She is a descendant of the old Celtic goddess, but one that has lost contact with the renewing powers of the unconscious. She no longer represents a cyclic conception of life, death, and rebirth, but has become an emblem of political nationalism. For Joyce, these figures embody a death cult. Stephen (Joyce himself) refuses their overtures. Following the urges of his soul, he chooses to celebrate life.[18]

O'Casey and Joyce condemn all forms of fanatic nationalism and fundamentalism. The identification with a mythic figure, in this case Mother Ireland, prevents mature relationships and blurs the distinction between the ideal and the real. Hero worship tends to become rigid and fatalistic, thus hindering change in the lives of real people. In O'Casey's work, heroism results from the failure to relate to real women on an individual basis. Power and love become idealized, and the frightened men who serve those ideals are now forced to prove their manhood on a collective basis. The powers of fate, transmitted through the idealized mother, wind themselves around the fallen hero, who becomes incapable of ethical accountability. Joyce locates the source of collective heroism in the inability to displease the mother and defy her anxiety-provoking tactics. Like many people today, he favors a life of exile rather than serve a home, church, or state that rules over people's lives with fear and terror.[19]

Many contemporary writers continue to focus on this theme. The philosopher and novelist Richard Kearney, writing in the 1980s, outlines much of the collective psychology that has dominated postcolonial Ireland up to recent times. Sectarian violence has been carried out in the name of a religious affiliation of the opposing communities. But the

I.R.A. and U.D.A. "extremists don't care about the theological doctrines of the respective religious traditions."[20] The conflict is more about violence, tribal fidelity, and economic class interests. Religious labels—Catholic or Protestant—are "sublimated symbols," ideologies split off from the real lives of the people. In Southern Ireland, a purist ideal of Holy Ireland evolved after Independence and the Civil War. Everything Irish—Irish Catholicism, Irish language, and Irish morality—was good. Evil, previously projected onto England, became projected onto alien practices of foreigners. Non-Catholic intellectuals and those who indulge in "immoral practices," especially of a sexual nature, became the scapegoats, victimized by a split psychology. The Irish state enforced these codes in various law enactments: rigid censorship, divorce prohibition, the banning of contraceptives and abortion, and severe regulations of dance halls, without awareness that "Holy Mother Ireland" would eventually produce a terrible shadow. In 2009, the systematic abuse of thousands of children by priests, nuns, and members of various Catholic institutions was made public in the Ryan report.

For Kearney, it was clear that there must be a change in the religious identity of the Irish people. He appealed to Irish Catholicism to "detribalize its purist ideology,"[21] which only encourages a double-standard morality and reinforces religious sectarianism. The Catholic Church can no longer consider itself as the sole protector of "Holy Mother Ireland," enforcing its doctrines in state laws to the disadvantage of minorities. Kearney appeals to the Protestant churches to repudiate the purist ideal of Protestantism as inherently superior to Catholicism, and to "live instead the liberating heritage bequeathed by such Irish Protestants as Berkeley, Tone, Davis, Mitchel, Ferguson, Parnell, Hyde, Yeats, etc."[22] According to Kearney, this would include a fostering of the Protestant enlightenment as a guarantee of civil and religious liberties.

The work of artists, intellectuals, and politicians, the Peace Movement, and the sufferings of women and families on both sides have changed much in Ireland in the last few years. Their work has redeemed many from anxiety-provoking ideologies: Puritanism and sacrificial violence. A spirit of optimism prevails since the Good Friday Agreement, 1998. This agreement was reached in extraordinary ways. Senator George Mitchell prepared both parties by inviting them to sumptuous meals at the U.S. embassy in London, and Prime Minister Tony Blair kept the parties at the negotiating table until they might have been willing to sign anything to get a good night's sleep. Maybe the basic values of life, food, and sleep, so significant in the primal relationship with the mother, played a hidden role. Needs of the body, such as food and sleep, entice humans to relate on more intimate levels, initiate a shared identity, and further the appreciation of alternative values often denied by fundamentalist ideologies. There is an interesting parallel to ancient Celtic law, in which both plaintiff and defendant would deny themselves sleep and fast from sunset to sunrise in order to gain mutual sympathy for the other's cause, and promote agreement to arbitration. These ways of communication are rarely used in a society where rational discourse alone is valued. They express the hidden power of a mother tongue, our first language, the language of mother and child, of lovers or close friends. It is a language of the body, expressed in polyphonic intonations coupled with a myriad of facial expressions and bodily gestures. Food and sleep belong to its repertoire. It is a relational language through which we express intimate connectedness with another person, a gentle language where we find ourselves exposed and vulnerable. It is also a language of the heart, a language that can affirm that we are at home with self and other, and can extend the boundaries of a shared identity beyond tribal nationalism.

The poets of Ireland continue to work on the *hierosgamos* motif in terms of contemporary culture. Whereas the mythic pattern has been defrocked of its nationalistic attire in the poems of Eavan Boland and Paul Durcan, it has been reworked by Seamus Heaney and John Hewitt in the context of the Northern Ireland crisis. Eavan Boland's work expresses a radical indictment of the Ireland-as-woman tradition. The opening line of her poem "Mise Eire," no doubt a parody of Pearse's poem, begins with: "I won't go back." Boland will not assent to "the songs that bandage up the history / the words / that make a rhythm of the crime."[23] Her roots are "brutal," and do not stem from the nationalistic image of a woman liberated by soldiers. Instead, the poem draws attention to the shadow aspect of such imagery—the camp prostitute who offers her services in exchange for "rice-colored silk," and the emigrant woman on board the Mary Belle, holding "her half dead baby," expressing the sad reality of many Irish women, victims of war and famine. According to Boland, nationalistic myths simplify and distort reality, especially the reality of woman. The genderizing of national identity colonizes a woman's body, transforming her into an emblematic decoration—"she becomes the passive projection of a national idea."[24] Nationalistic images of woman can no longer serve a patriarchal society in promising men victory, nor should they be used as a means of getting men to die for their land. Such images are not natural but fabricated, mostly by men who swear allegiance to an ideology that supposedly represents an unquestionable truth.

In his poem "The Haulier's Wife Meets Jesus on the Road near Moone," Paul Durcan describes a woman who embodies the beauty and wildness of nature: "I am thirty-three years old / In the prime of my womanhood / The mountain stream of my sex / In spate and darkly foaming / The white hills of my breasts / Brimful and breathing / The tall trees of my eyes / Screening blue sky."[25] As the poem continues, the reader learns that the beautiful woman is neglected. Her husband, a "popular and wealthy" man, only makes love to her twice a year, "tanked up with seventeen pints of beer." The marriage cannot be dissolved because of clients, neighbors, and the children. The haulier's wife goes off alone on a weekend to Dublin, subconsciously hoping she will become somebody's *femme fatale*. Instead she meets Jesus, a man "entirely sensitive to a woman's world." He kisses her passionately, but refuses her invitation to spend the night with her, saying: "Our night will come."

Durcan uses the land-as-woman motif within the context of contemporary Irish affluence. Seen in terms of the *hierosgamos*, the land and its consort have become indifferent to one another. Natural woman, a striking anima image of the human soul in the prime of her beauty, is neglected, while her consort, entrenched in patriarchal traditions, pursues materialistic interests. Although a mythic motif is implicit, the poem describes the reality of problematic marriages within the context of the Celtic Tiger. The poem suggests that Ireland's new wealthy class lack spirituality, fail in relationships, and are therefore not the rightful consort for the land. The mythic ideal has now retreated into the hopes and fantasies of women. In those fantasies, a new attitude to life is described as one that is sensitive to a woman's world—one might add, sensitive to the soul, the heart, and human relationships. Durcan's poem reveals human qualities that have been sadly lacking in male-dominated notions of national identity—the male tyrant in days gone by, the new managerial class of an affluent society today.

The Bog Poems of Seamus Heaney revive the image of the land-as-woman, shaping it into an entirely original and new perspective on the Northern Ireland conflict. In "The Tolund Man," Heaney contemplates the fate of the Iron Age corpses that have been preserved for over two thousand years in the bogs of Northern Denmark. Heaney's poems are inspired by P. V. Glob's *The Bog People*. Glob was convinced that the rope nooses around the corpses' necks and the gruel in their stomachs, containing no summer or autumn fruits, hence suggesting they were killed in winter, provide evidence that the corpses were sacrificial victims offered to the goddess Nerthus in order to ensure fertility for the coming year. Heaney's Tolund Man, "bridegroom to the goddess," becomes a metaphor for those sacrificed for Mother Ireland. The bogs of Denmark and Ireland preserve the history of those countries. The land itself is experienced as a storehouse of collective memory, Ireland's collective unconscious, revealing "an archetypal pattern."[26] It expresses also a hope that something can evolve from all the senseless killings: "Consecrate the cauldron bog / Our holy ground and pray / Him to make germinate[.]"[27]

Heaney's poem has been described as a prayer, a kind of lament for all those victims of atrocities committed in the name of some political or religious ideology. Heaney refuses to act as a tribal bard, taking sides in the Northern Irish conflict. Yet he remains attached to the fate of his people. The last lines of "The Tolund Man"[28] express the agony of the poet, torn between two modes of consciousness, between reprobation of senseless bloodshed and deep attachment to his land and people.

> Out there in Jutland
> In the old man-killing parishes
> I will feel lost,
> Unhappy and at home.

Heaney's Bog Poems have been criticized for suggesting that sacrifice is needed for peace to be restored in Northern Ireland. In my view, this purely political interpretation of the poems in no way corresponds to the intentions of the poet. Heaney's "prayer-poems" attempt to include the dead, the ancestors, and the realm of spirit. Poetry gains access to the unseen world; politicians usually are not sufficiently gifted to appreciate this level of existence. It has been the domain of the prophet, priest, and poet. They are the ones who have voiced the universal conviction that an appeal to the dead can influence worldly matters in beneficial ways. Perhaps they are the only ones who know how to embrace the old hag, so that she can release the seeds of new life.

Heaney's humaneness, honesty, and sympathy for the persecuted shines forth in a poem dedicated to those female victims, sacrificed to the goddess. "Punishment," a poem for an Iron Age girl found in a Schleswig bog—blindfolded, with cropped hair, and weighed down with a stone—expresses the poet's hesitant but tender affection for "my poor scapegoat." Once again, Heaney links the fate of the Iron Age girl, probably punished as an adulteress, with that of the Northern Irish woman whose head was cropped, tarred, and feathered. Her innocent love for an Englishman had transformed her into an "adulteress" who had betrayed the Republican cause. In the eyes of the tribe, she became the goddess of the land, whose complicity with the enemy had to be revenged.

The Northern Irish poet John Hewitt has no use for the land-as-woman motif when it serves divisive forms of tribalism that segregate confessions and ancestry. In "Ireland," however, he does address "the Celtic wave" and hence a Celtic identity that is structured by the motif of the ebb and flow of "the waters of life." In the poem, Hewitt draws attention to the origins, ongoing history, and changing circumstances of the Celtic people. He describes the inevitable breaking up of parish boundaries, and the extending of the notion of national identity beyond the restrictions of a specific cultural or religious tradition, intimating the hope of a transnational and trans-confessional shared identity on the horizon of human consciousness:

> …We are not native here or anywhere.
> We were the Keltic wave that broke over Europe,
> and ran up this bleak beach among these stones:
> but when the tide ebbed, were left stranded here
> in crevices, and ledge-protected pools
> that have grown salter with the drying up
> of the great common flow that kept us sweet
> with fresh cold draughts from deep down in the ocean.
>
> So we are bitter, and are dying out
> in terrible harshness in this lonely place,
> and what we think is love for usual rock,
> or old affection for our customary ledge,
> is but forgotten longing for the sea
> that cries far out and calls us to partake
> in his great tidal movements round the earth.[29]

Another of Hewitt's poems, "Bloody Brae,"[30] is inspired by a legend about a Cromwellian soldier called John Hill (no relative, I believe), who was plagued with guilt after killing a native Catholic woman with his trooper's sword. She appears as a ghost and forgives him, while reminding him of the irretrievable consequences of his action. Seen from a horizontal plane, one motif of the drama carries a political message concerning reconciliation between Catholics and Protestants of Northern Ireland. The vertical axis of the poem reverts back to a much earlier function of the goddess-of-the-land stories. In the older myths, she mediated to the new invaders the ancestral heritage of Ireland in order to guarantee that the land be fertile and peace reign in the hearts of men. Today, one might ask: Can a change of attitude happen without a meeting of the horizontal and the vertical, the outer and the inner, political negotiation and poetic inspiration? Can peace and justice take root in the minds and hearts of the people of Ulster, without entertaining the ghosts of history and ancestral heritage?

The tarring and feathering of an innocent Irish girl, mentioned at the beginning of this chapter, is an historical event, the roots of which stretch back into Ireland's mythic history. It is linked with the Sovereignty myth, a variant of the Indo-European *hierosgamos* that has possessed an archetypal significance for numerous peoples of the world. In Ireland, it became synonym for a particular form of national identity, an identity formed in opposition to an occupying power. It served as a motivating force, creating group solidarity that inspired Ireland's struggle for independence, and eventually became for many a righteous and justifiable cause for action. At what stage did it outlive its function of liberating Ireland from foreign oppression? When do mythic systems lose their connection with reality and abrogate justice and ethical accountability? How does one explain such rigid mythological systems, fired by hatred, emerging from splits within and causing divisions without, and denigrating the human capacity to enter the arena of discourse in order to critically reflect and evaluate ideas, events, and situations in the spirit of Enlightenment? Psychologically, when do they overwhelm a person or a group, unleash an amity/enmity split, and assimilate the emotional characteristics of a cultural complex that tends "to be repetitive, autonomous, resist consciousness, and collect experience that confirms their historical point of view"?[31] Once the complex is activated, an idealization of a collective self and devaluation of a collective other follow—accompanied by projection, displacement, and scapegoating of the innocent. I suggest that the famous incident of tarring and feathering is an example of a cultural complex fueled by a bonding memory that prevents bridge-building to the denied other—within or without—producing a politics of discord and causing intolerance, strife, and suffering for all who are involved.

Ireland is a nation in the making. The horrors of the civil war and the troubles in Northern Ireland have inspired the poets of Ireland to review the motif of land-as-woman. The juices of creativity are still flowing in that land. Notions of national identity continue to be criticized, refined, extended, and deepened to embrace realms of the shadow, the marginal, and what has been excluded. The old myths have been revoked by some, or remodeled by others. For Boland, national identity can no longer be genderized. She has little use for the myths, which have been of no service to women but have furthered their abuse and the distortion of their historical reality. Durcan addresses the plight of women in a world of affluence. His poem suggests that the national identity of corporate Ireland still serves rigid patriarchal structures, is intent on economic prosperity, lacks spirituality, neglects feminine values, and fails in human relationships. Heaney's view of national identity is more complex—one that is rooted in kinship attachment, allows ambiguous uncertainties, includes the world of the unseen without abrogating the use of reason and ethical accountability. Identity in the poems of Hewitt implies a shared identity that recognizes its origins as being non-insular, one that celebrates open boundaries, includes a European identity, and appreciates a common human heritage. Looking back, he draws attention to a collective identity prior to the divisions of Catholic and Protestant; looking forward, he intimates an emerging identity that cannot be exclusively national but approximates to a patchwork identity including the trans-confessional and transnational realities of contemporary culture.

Having lived in Central Europe for most of my life, national identity, as seen from a place of exile, has undergone many transformations. Of course, attachment to my native Ireland remains strong, but the old myth of land-as-woman no longer defines my Irish identity in an exclusive way. That mythic narrative has haunted me, pursued me, and transformed me—finally convincing me that the sounds and symmetries of belonging reveal an inner disposition of the soul that we carry within, wherever we go. The *puella senilis* narrative may or may not determine the history of a particular nation, but as an inner disposition it can structure our lives, appearing in unexpected ways in dreams, fantasies, and affects. Stripped of a purely nationalistic interpretation, it becomes an image of the human soul, reminding us of psyche's transformative powers—forever dying, forever creating, urging us to submit to the ebb and flow of the waters of life.

An Unexpected Composition

I will end this chapter with a dream of a young man from Northern Ireland. The dream and following discussion testify to the creative powers of the psyche, which can provide new perspectives on identity, tribal loyalty, and the conflict in Northern Ireland.

The dreamer felt his life to be in the grip of two opposing powers: on the one hand, he suffered from depression, shyness, and feelings of inferiority; on the other hand, he was terrified of his own fits of violence. I was impressed by the way his dreams could reveal in condensed narrative the hidden mythic, religious, and social influence of "Mother Ireland." The following discussion illustrates not only his mother's influence in shaping the national and religious identity of her sons, but hints also at a new, life-affirming context that helped this man gain a mature attitude toward those nationalist mythologies that kept him in a state of fear and fatally bound him to the psychology of his mother.

> In newspaper articles there were scenes of Irish heroes and the rural countryside. Accompanying these scenes were poems from various Sinn Fein leaders. My mother was showing me republican newspapers with propaganda pictures of the I.R.A. in Northern Ireland. One article in the paper complained that one of the statues of Our Lady in the Catholic area of Belfast had been removed. We Catholics were outraged at this attack on our Catholicism, yet at the same time, I say to myself, "What harm will it do?" Going up the ruined streets, I see what looks like a new cross being built, but it is only the unfinished part of a nice new shop.

The dreamer offered the following comments. "*Mother shows me republican newspapers.*" He remembered how his mother dominated family life. She openly endorsed the I.R.A. movement and expected the family to do likewise. Her husband and children dared not cross her. She was prone to fits of fury against any person who opposed the minority cause. Once she got the whole family to laugh when a member of the Protestant community was killed. "*Our Lady is removed.*" The dreamer recalled the rigid and strict way his mother practiced her Catholic faith. He felt her worship of the Virgin Mary justified her purist idealism and determined the severity of her moral judgments. The dreamer further remembered how the siblings were divided—two brothers identified with the mother's aggression and became members of the political wing of the I.R.A., while the other brothers avoided aggression and adapted to the rules and expectations of the mother's Catholic faith. The dreamer himself belonged to this latter group and was the "good boy" of the family. He was sure that the removal of Our Lady meant a further separation from his mother. "*The unfinished new shop.*" This image brought happy associations. The dreamer remembered the bombed-out, drab buildings in the poverty-stricken Catholic areas of Belfast. The bleak scenes on the streets stood in direct contrast with the life and excitement shared by all in the local shops.

The dream and the associations revealed the dreamer's underlying identification with his mother. The mother's psyche seemed to have been controlled by two powerful influences: the church and the I.R.A. According to her son, she was either compliant and submissive to the rulings of the church or violent and aggressive in her support of the I.R.A. This split psychology was transferred to her sons, serving either the church or the I.R.A. The dreamer felt this division within himself. On the one hand, he was passive and self-effacing; on the other hand, when pushed too far, he would explode with violent temper tantrums. The violent behavior appeared in fantasies of a wild black stallion, activating associations to a famous totem animal of Cuculainn, the Black of Saingliu. Every time he tried to be too good, he would see the black stallion rearing, lunging, kicking, and ready to destroy everything around it. The dreamer, full of guilt and frightened of his aggression, was torn between two fates: Irish Catholicism and the pre-Christian mythologies of his cultural inheritance.

The removal of the Virgin confirmed a development the dreamer had experienced in the course of therapy: he had learned to gain distance from the all-powerful psychology of his mother. He saw that his life no longer needed to be ruled by either the pious, self-effacing demands of nineteenth-century Catholicism, or by the violent, heroic death cults of modern paganism. He understood that the mother embodied two powerful goddess-like figures: the goddess of the land and the Virgin Mary. What could a son do against such powerful figures? A process of demythologizing the mother commenced. His aggression was given support in the analytic interaction, and he learned to be assertive in appropriate, realistic ways. He began to find the right words and ways to express his anger, addressing the actual circumstances of a conflict. Instead of remaining trapped in a fate involving identification with the mother and the collective ideals she embodied, he became more active, creative, and could penetrate the issues of the moment. He began to succeed where his father had failed. It was this change that found expression in the Virgin being replaced by a cross and a nice new shop. This suggests that through suffering (the cross), a new participation in life (the shop) could blossom. As already stated, the shop brought happy associations. Instead of a death cult, witnessed in the bombed buildings, the shop became a temple of life, a place where one relates to others, exchanges goods, and participates in the richness and complexities of human society. Feeling less confined by the incestuous bonds of family politics, and in search of new meanings to home, he could begin to explore other directions in shared community life.

The dream exemplifies a creative capacity of the unconscious. Drawing on ancient mythic resources and embodying them in a contemporary context, the dream reveals an unexpected version of the *puella senilis*. With the rejuvenation of the old hag—as witnessed in the transformation of the mother's "Virgin Mary," symbolizing a tribal purity that incites liquidation of an adversary, into a "new shop," a place associated with refreshing and joyful memories of human exchange—the dreamer became conscious of the soul's capacity to bring renewal to a collective ideology that influenced much of the family life. The dream indicates that the unconscious does not only hold one in bondage to an archaic heritage, but can provide innovative and timely responses to the horrors of war and violence. It inspires new social perspectives, supporting a national identity in a process of individuation.

Between a Solid Rock and the Wild Seas of Imagination

Contemplating Ireland from a place of exile has helped me interiorize a country that has remained close to my heart. It was my cradle, and perhaps in the end will be my tomb. I am grateful for the hospitality of Switzerland. Although I have spent most of my life in that country, sometimes I feel I am only a guest. Its majestic mountains, dark forests, calm lakes, and quaint villages are of great beauty. Yet they cannot compare with the wild seas, windblown hawthorns, and racing clouds of my land of origin. I appreciate Switzerland as a solid rock; the winds and waters of Ireland evoke the music of my soul. I have learnt moderation and the gifts of reason in my host country; I speak with the gods, the fairies, and the dead in the land of my birth. If Ireland has been a mother, Switzerland has certainly been a father. I have tilled the soil of my motherland with the instruments I have learned from dwelling in a fatherland. I do not regret exile. It has helped me cherish and articulate the gifts I have received from two different countries, cultures, and people. My life and work have been an attempt to build a bridge between two homes I have known and loved so dearly.

PART V

HOME: RESPONSIBILITY IN UNSETTLED TIMES

CHAPTER 10

At Home in a Global Society?

> Most people are principally aware of one culture, one setting, one home; exiles are aware of at least two, and this plurality of vision gives rise to an awareness of simultaneous dimensions, an awareness that, to borrow a phrase from music, is *contrapuntal*. For an exile, habits of life, expression, or activity in the new environment inevitably occur against the memory of these things in another environment.[1]
>
> —Edward Said

Loss of Symbol as Loss of Home?

Echoing the opening lines of Tolstoy's *Anna Karenina*, Edward Said, in writing about the four million Palestinian Arabs scattered throughout the world, remarks that narratives about happy families are very similar, but the unhappy ones are always different. He quotes the poignant story of an elderly Palestinian refugee whose husband was shot and whom she buried in the village cemetery. Later, from her exile in Syria, she could not stop worrying whether she had buried him in the accustomed manner. Said bears witness to the fact that each story of his dispossessed people is like one out of three and a half million variations of the same theme.[2] Today's global movements have compelled many to rethink their sense of belonging to family, community, nation, and Planet

Earth. In 2008, it was estimated that there were approximately 190 million voluntary migrants worldwide.[3] Not included in that number were 42 million people uprooted by force, of which 26 million were internally displaced in their own country.[4] Despite the plight of millions, each tale about the loss of home is unique, bearing witness to each person's experience of devastation. Within millions of unhappy narratives, the significance of home remains an inimitable and intensely personal experience.

In this chapter, I will first outline some of the many faces of homelessness in our times. The suffering involved in the loss of home and nationhood has become a daily occurrence, producing major social and political issues. Except in cases of trauma, today's loss of home does not seem to have the devastating effects of the homesickness of the eighteenth and nineteenth centuries. The records of those times imply that the victims of homesickness were acutely aware of the cause of their suffering: deprivation of family, village, and surrounding landscapes. Homesickness at that time did not only mean loss of particular objects or possessions, but rather the loss of a deep bonding with an unchanging environment that had nourished and formed one's identity over generations. In the past, personhood was inseparable from one's surroundings. Family, village, and landscape embodied a *symbolic* space, the privation of which involved loss of identity and meaning. Does contemporary homelessness imply loss of the ability to appropriate the world symbolically? Can the absence of a symbolic understanding of one's home in the world diminish character and sense of self? As the chapter proceeds, I will describe some of the symbolic dimensions crucial to structuring citizenship and social integration where people of differing cultural and social identities are living in ever-increasing proximity. Once again we must learn to see ourselves in the world around us. In the past, nature was the great mirror of identity. Can today's urban landscapes ever perform a similar function?

A WORLD WITHOUT SYMBOL

Homelessness in our times has become more diffuse, having a confusing effect on its victims. Many do not know why they feel uprooted, unconnected, or incapable of deeper attachment to anybody or anything. This is partly due to the restless, distracted, bustling atmosphere of a world that has become increasingly urbanized, sequestered from the natural landscape that once shaped the life and character of men and women over hundreds of years. The sounds and symmetries of nature, emulated in myths and rituals of bygone civilizations, sustained awareness of the contingencies and depth of human existence. The edifices and activities of the contemporary urban environment rarely nourish the soul in the same way.

Today's homelessness appears with many faces. Overpopulation, intolerance, poverty, the concentration of wealth among the few, the speed of information, and the ease of transportation have unleashed world migrations of unparalleled dimensions. Tens of millions are uprooted and seeking new homes. They may be refugees who have been forced to leave their land due to political repression, economic insecurity, or natural disaster. Perhaps they are seasonal workers, adopted children, sex slaves, or even individuals who have been forced to move from one place to another because their job demands it. These people do not always travel alone, but in most cases with entire families.

The complex, impersonal urban culture of prosperous nations has cast a deep shadow on the lives of its inhabitants. More and more, people live in conditions of alienation from their surroundings. Our natural environment has been cemented over. Its riches are exploited for economic gain. We find ourselves more and more in bondage to artificial worlds of technology. The complexity of modern civilization requires high-level maintenance. Signs are replacing symbols; the factual has become the determinant of truth and meaning. Old and young have to fill their heads with innumerable facts and figures, leaving too little breathing space for deeper, more bonded connections to themselves and their surroundings. Values of a multinational corporate society are supplanting the older ways of civilization. Many are forced to live in the sprawling suburbs, which are detached from any historic center. The shopping malls, filled with the latest brands, trends, and labels, become the public space of patchwork metropolises, creating superficial forms of attachment and affiliations that are determined by wealth and purchasing power.

Richard Sennett's *The Corrosion of Character* expresses a radical critique of contemporary corporate society with its celebration of flexibility, change, freedom from geographic location, disjointed time, short-term commitments, and superficial teamwork. Such lifestyles corrode the more lasting values of "trust, loyalty, and mutual commitment."[5] Sennett continues:

> The conditions of time in the new capitalism have created a
> conflict between character and experience, the experience of

disjointed time threatening the ability of people to form their characters into sustained narratives....What's peculiar about uncertainty today is that it exists without any looming historical disaster; instead it is woven into the everyday practices of a vigorous capitalism. Instability is meant to be normal.[6]

In a world without symbolic attachment, people can easily find themselves adrift—without anchor, bearing, or center. For example, how can one be at home in one's profession if employment is under continual threat? Under such circumstances it is difficult to cultivate attachment, commitment, or care for one's work. Continually changing lifestyles without permanent values may satisfy the few, but a standardized, superficial mode of behavior will hardly provide inspiration for an evolving society that reflects diverse cultural traditions, or do justice to the human need for bonding that is gratifying, sustaining, and meaningful.

An experience of family, community, and nationhood remains indispensable to humans. There still is a powerful need in most people to maintain kinship with fellow humans through appreciation of a common landscape, dwelling place, physical appearance, language, religion, and other cultural values. Identity is fortified through continual confirmation of habits, tastes, values, or beliefs shared by a community in a shared meaningful world. If too many changes infiltrate familiar and local surroundings, many perceive their identity to be threatened, and sometimes resort to violence in order to defend it. Reflecting on such upheavals, Susanne Langer, writing in the 1940s, indicated the devastating consequences due to loss of a symbolic connection to environment:

> The mind, like all other organs, can draw its sustenance only from the surrounding world; our metaphysical symbols must spring from reality....If, now, the field of our unconscious symbolic orientation is suddenly plowed up by tremendous changes in the external world and in the social order, we lose our hold, our convictions, and therewith our effectual purposes. In modern civilization there are two great threats to mental security: the new mode of living, which has made the old nature-symbols alien to our minds, and the new mode of working, which makes personal activity meaningless, inacceptable to the hungry imagination....Most people have no home that is a symbol of their childhood, not even a definite memory of one place to serve that purpose. Many no longer know the language that was once their mother-tongue.[7]

Richard Sennett confirmed this point in a recent book, *The Craftsman*. He regrets the slow decline of handcraft, which "focuses on the intimate connection between the hand and the head."[8] In earlier times, humans took delight in their relationship with the materials they worked with, perfecting their craft and gaining mastery in their specialized field of accomplishment. They had time to create objects that reflected facets of their identity. Distinction in good work harvests satisfaction and boosts self-esteem. This positive effect is lost among those who are permanently pressured to increase production or who are repeatedly on standby for a job transfer. Both Langer and Sennett believe these changes occurred due to people's estrangement from their material local environment. Home and work are the two aspects of life that bring most gratification. They are intrinsically linked with intimacy and identity; their continuity and sustainability are essential for one's very being to be nourished and reflected in meaningful ways.

Accessing Home in a Global Age

There is hardly one satisfactory political solution for the millions of homeless in the near future. On the contrary, considering the increasing gaps between rich and poor in the industrial nations, as well as the considerable cultural diversity in the new waves of immigration from Third World countries, one can only expect a dramatic increase of problems. Instead of expecting a top-down solution, more effort has to be put into local community and individual exchange. As we approach the symbolic dimensions of social integration, it is crucial to understand that identity is not something encapsulated within a person, nor conditioned only by outer circumstances. The old inner/outer split is only too likely to favor alienation, by casting away unwanted parts of the self onto the stranger through the mechanisms of projection, displacement, or scapegoating—as witnessed in certain communities prone to fundamentalism. Identity remains a paradox. In my view, it does have an archetypal core, which Jung understood to be an inner disposition for wholeness that regulates one's mental and emotional life. Identity is, however, a social reality that is "invented" and "formed *between*, rather than *within* persons."[9] Relying on the work of Norbert Elias, who dismisses a Western approach to identity as being independent of the social nexus, Steph Lawler continues: "'Without you I'm nothing': without a nexus of others, none of us could be 'who we are.'"[10]

Extending the notion of identity to the realm of social discourse raises many questions. How do you establish a genuine cross-cultural dialogue? How can you help newcomers translate the manifold meanings of their interior language into the terms of their new local surroundings? How do you find commonality in diverse cultural heritages? In cross-cultural exchange, caution is advocated in attempting intercultural bridge building. Faced with highly charged emotional issues, you cannot respond with specialized and abstract theories; it is more a question of creating a safe context that permits soul searching, working beneath the surface, and listening for a deeper connectedness that supports rather than divides intercommunication. In search of that space between "I" and "the other"—a space that makes accessible an identity in a process of formation—one must be careful not to get entrapped in mythical, religious, or racial beliefs of superiority. This kind of attitude creates homes that are unduly exclusive and dissociated from society as a whole, and may lead to projection of all that is inferior onto an unsuspecting other. Exclusivity will continue to define cultural traditions. Exclusivity only becomes problematic when culture becomes rigid and one-sided, when communication and dialogue are not sustained, when the voice of the unconscious, witnessed in dreams, fantasies, artistic creation, or novel insights, no longer inhabits the space between the I and the other. Exclusivity does not necessarily imply fundamentalism. One should not forget that there is a fundamentalist attitude lurking in each one of us, structuring our sense of belonging to a particular community, society, or culture. Every person is entitled to maintain his or her fundamental beliefs, but "fundamentalism" is different—it is a social phenomenon that determines the space between different people, beliefs, and cultures. In fundamentalism, identification replaces identity. The space between different people, beliefs, or cultures that allows for discrimination and communication is taken over by a powerful ideology that is unable or unwilling to tolerate difference.

In the narratives of today's homeless, one discovers the deeper causes of why social integration fails. Home is not only about the loss of a place, but also the loss of Self. The Self, understood from a Jungian point of view, transcends ego-consciousness. It can be experienced as a creative principle and the source of symbols that regulate psychological life and endow it with meaning and depth. Individuals caught in transitional spaces may become victims of a psychological regression, which causes a splitting of the personality. A coherent identity may no longer be available. In their attempt to adapt to a new environment, homeless people may find themselves torn apart by a series of conflicting identities. They have lost connection with something that most of us take for granted—a psychological factor that allows one to hold different worlds together in a dynamic equilibrium. Faced with such challenges, Jungian psychotherapists try to find ways to activate the inner human potential to create symbols. Allowing space for new symbols to emerge, one might detect an archetypal structuring principle, the Self, which provides a foundation for bridging differences previously considered irreconcilable.

SELF AND EGO: BETWEEN THE ONE AND THE MANY

One needs to be Janus-faced in order to understand the plight of today's homeless—to be able to look both within and without. In order to link the divided worlds of the homeless, understanding the inner psychological state is just as necessary as taking measures to alleviate the difficulties of their outer, existential circumstances. One cannot take for granted that human identity consists of a conscious rational mind that always acts with impartial and unbiased judgments. Already in 1904, C. G. Jung developed the notion of multiple identities in his work on the association experiment. Complexes "behave like independent beings"[11] and possess an autonomy that enables them to act independently from ego-consciousness. Their content is emotionally charged, and reveals the historical records of one's attachment to significant others. In Jungian psychology, the ego is itself a complex and, as the center of consciousness, includes not only the discriminating functions of consciousness but also "the drive towards separateness, uniqueness, identity, and achievement."[12] It often finds itself in a state of conflict with other complexes. According to Jung, the Self, and not the ego, is the underlying unifying principle within the human psyche. The Self is not to be understood as a permanent state of being, but rather as a dynamic process that acts as a self-regulating principle between conflicting complexes, eventually providing new symbols of identity. If the ego cooperates with the new symbol and translates its meaning in terms of a person's actual life, a new attitude emerges. One achieves sufficient maturity to integrate complexes that were previously dissociated from one another. Jung termed this process the transcendent function, which I have discussed above.

As seen in previous chapters, the content of a complex consists not only of personal, but also collective determinants. Bonding myths and memories can fuel cultural complexes, revealing conflicting visions of reality that transcend personal biography. A cultural complex must be distinguished from culture proper. Although structured by cultural content, the complex inhabits the unconscious, erupts unexpectedly, is emotionally charged, acts autonomously, tends to be repetitive, and distracts, inhibits, or blocks the normal functioning of ego-consciousness. Tense situations—as when individuals and groups with differing cultural, social, or political backgrounds live in close proximity, or find themselves in a transitional space between cultures and societies—will not only accentuate differences, but also activate cultural complexes. Being highly charged with emotion, these are only partially conscious and resist change. Neutral injunctions or advice are hardly sufficient to counteract the power of a cultural complex. Communication easily breaks down, and one can no longer hold the interim space of becoming.

RECKONING WITH THE AMITY/ENMITY COMPLEX

Applying the above psychological perspective to certain aspects of today's multicultural societies, one must proceed with caution. The individual ego, unconscious complexes, and a sense of self are continually being structured in and through interactions with others, on personal or collective levels. Appropriate evaluation must account not only for the psychological frame of mind of the individual or group, but also for the social or political conditions that shape our daily lives. Obviously, there are vast differences in the social circumstances of the privileged few who can derive much satisfaction in transiting from one culture to another, when compared with economic or political immigrants. No doubt the privileged have problems of their own; nevertheless, they and their dependents receive ample help in making necessary adjustments—many international schools and social faculties are professionally geared to alleviate the pains of cultural change and cultural loss. Far worse is the plight of economic or political immigrants who have been forced to leave their original homeland. They begin their new life in a state of disorientation, often without any adequate aid in readjustment, and are usually unwelcome or stigmatized. Slums and ghettoes, racism, and sex tourism express some of the ugly living conditions of millions of men, women, and children who are forced to live in transitional spaces due to political persecution, the need for economic survival, or the destabilizing effects of exploitation of their land and culture by the richer nations of the industrial world. It has become increasingly difficult for immigrants from the Third World to achieve equal status with the citizens of their host country.

A Swedish author, Gellert Tamas, has described incidents of massive withdrawal among immigrant children in his book *De Apatiska* (The Apathetic). The book describes a phenomenon in immigrant families that occurs during transient periods when they await permission to stay or the decision that they be sent back to their country of origin. Apparently the children of these families just lie down in a state of apathy; they do not move or eat. This may be evidence of a severe form of anaclitic depression, but from a Jungian point of view it is as if the transcendent function is completely numbed. In such waiting periods, no real transition is possible, and the psyche's capacity to create integrative symbols of hope shuts down. Psychological and physiological nonmovement is a reaction to living in no-man's-land, and possibly expresses the child's way of keeping their parents active and concerned.[13]

The privileged few, often from a managerial class, receive much social support when transiting from one culture to another. They are less likely to suffer from psychological disruption than those who do not receive such support. Integration happens slowly, but more or less naturally, given the right circumstances. Scarcely harrowed by outer conditions, they can weave diverse threads into new patterns. When, however, the social framework is nonsupportive, uninviting, even alienating, there is a danger that the natural function of the Self to bridge divergent worlds is undermined. Deprived of that deeper sense of Self, the reflective capacity of the ego may also be impaired. For those unable to tolerate the social chasm, a splitting of the private and public spheres may ensue, obstructing entry into the public and social domain and creating collective identities that are restrictive or are defined in terms of reaction to the larger social body. In such instances, group bonding may be constituted by some unifying ideology opposing social integration.

France was long renowned for a tolerant policy of integration. Its republican principle of equality does not permit recognition of cultural difference in the public sphere. Multiculturalism is considered a private matter. This policy has unintentionally promoted a splitting within the social framework. The secular state has been unable to hold back the rising tide of ethnic and religious fundamentalism.[14] Recently, groups among third-generation immigrants, often underprivileged or unemployed, have resorted to forming communities with a strong Muslim ideology, reinforcing an identity in opposition to the secular state. Many social scientists of today are in the process of reevaluating the ideologies of a multicultural society of the 'seventies and 'eighties. Increasing segregation and ghetto mentality have become the harsh realities in many European cities, which in some cases have adopted severe repressive policies towards immigrants.

It is important to acknowledge the existence of these social conditions. They have a symbolic significance that may be relevant not only for immigrants, but also for many others trying to access home in a fragmented world of multiple identities, nations, and cultures. In one's interaction with the world, one discovers the same mechanism when encountering the stranger, within or without. Particularly when one feels threatened, defense mechanisms are activated, signaling a retreat from the world of dialogue and communication. In Jungian terms, the Self becomes overvalued at the expense of the ego, which leads to inflation and lack of differentiation. The need to feel "whole," "integrated," or to "fuse with others" prevents investing libido in the discriminating powers of the ego. A good enough functioning ego can reflect, and evaluate the uniqueness of each encounter and acknowledge difference. When the ego is connected with the deeper realms of the psyche, perhaps to discover values of a common collective heritage, a process of bridge building is conceivable.

With the splitting of self and other, emotionally charged complexes are inevitably activated. The reflective capacity of the ego is impaired and likely to succumb to unconscious defense mechanisms. Idealization of self and devaluation of the other, accompanied by projection, displacement, or scapegoating, indicate an inability to come to terms with all that one considers unacceptable, inferior, or disreputable. The activated complex prevents bridge building to the denied other, within or without. Colonialism, racism, fundamentalism, or religious and political sectarianism are well-known examples of the destructive power of the amity/enmity complex.[15] The longing for security, certainty, and a sense of belonging can stimulate all kinds of cultural complexes, which are then deemed to be part of one's identity. There is little evidence that a discursive process forms such creeds—their power is fueled by assumptions concerning the constitution of identity. Because identity is so fundamental, its loss may provoke chaotic and undifferentiated feelings, activating annihilation anxiety where survival can no longer be assumed.[16] Hence, intolerant political, social, or cultural assumptions structure a collective identity, formed in opposition to an alien other who threatens an already fragile existence.

Jürgen Habermas's speech on receiving the peace prize of the Deutscher Buchhandel, in October 2001, highlighted the enormous tension between the values of contemporary secular society and the fundamentalist religious tradition, following the events of September 11, 2001. In his view, contemporary fundamentalism, both East and West, arises from a lack of authentic roots, alienation from traditional values, and disenchantment with the rational values of the Enlightenment with its all-pervasive belief in progress. A radical secularism, excluding religious belief, will never have the power of conviction to counter "common sense," which treasures values beyond our understanding. What is the use of a secular ethic in countering the irreversible suffering and damage done on September 11? Must revenge be the only answer? With the loss of faith in life after death, a spiritual vacuum has emerged. In the older creeds, reparation and forgiveness were only imaginable within a belief system concerning life in a hereafter and a forgiving God.

Habermas appeals to the values of genuine common sense, which for most people uphold an equilibrium between science and religion. With the term "post-secular society," a critical reevaluation of secularization in the light of traditional ethical and religious beliefs is implied. Those who believe in a religious or mythic tradition and who enjoy and identify with the liberal values of contemporary society must "preclude the use of violence as an instrument of conversion" and uphold the values of the Enlightenment, which allow for critical reflection and evaluation of their beliefs within the dissonance of a pluralistic society. This would include acceptance of the "framework of knowledge and learning" and the constitution of the modern liberal state. The modified secular state must keep "sufficient distance" from the various belief systems in order to guarantee the freedom, security, and independence of those individuals who maintain them.[17]

The great challenge of the future will be to help people balance the mythic need for home and security with the reflective capacity to accept and appraise the reality of the other. Only when people learn this balancing act can a society be sustainably pluralistic and accept difference for the individual and group members. If humans in a post-secular society can sustain the tensions due to the ever-increasing proximity of different societies and cultures, without betraying their own inner sense of belonging to a particular heritage, one can expect a future that will yield new ideas, symbols, and attitudes regarding the interconnectedness of cosmos and polis. The outer approximation of diverse worlds must be complemented by understanding the inner dynamics of the human psyche, especially cultural complexes and bonding memories. They can be destructive or creative, furthering divisiveness or providing symbols of reconciliation. Symbols can inspire new attitudes to bridge separated worlds.

SHARING A COMMON DWELLING PLACE?

Processes of bridge building cannot be one-sided nor Eurocentric. Cultural pluralism invites each person to adjust in his or her own way to a world of different cultures, now located in ever-increasing proximity. The different traditions of eating, joking, dancing, dying, or thinking (thinking with the heart, the belly, the head) are among the greatest treasures of civilization. Perhaps, one day, we shall appreciate the strange contributions of peoples from distant traditions as opportunities for connecting with diverse cultural landscapes that practice what is missing in our own culture. We will be motivated to resist the pressure of a global movement where place is no longer a primary source of diversity and where traditions are homogenized, causing cultural confusion and anonymity. Leonardo Boff, returning from his spiritual exile, announced his conviction that the preservation of the Indio culture of South America may become of tremendous value for the well-being of all the peoples of the world. Their appreciation of God, the earth, and human society affirms a world that respects the sacredness of all life and is more ecology and community oriented than the cultures of Europe.[18]

The indigenous people of South America, as other peoples of the world, have the right to maintain their home and culture on Planet Earth—first of all geographically, then, if necessity requires, in an adjustment process that furthers a meaningful connection with other societies that respect and welcome their way of life. Long-term political and economic strategies are necessary to help people remain in their geographic location, strategies that go beyond the short-term economic interests of potential benefactors, strategies that are creations of the heart, strategies for posterity. Many humanitarian institutions have advocated investments in education, local agriculture, and local industry to benefit the integrity of a community.

What about those who emigrate in search of a new home? A lifelong work of translating their cultural heritage in terms of the new surroundings begins. It is a work that challenges guest and host to redefine their expectations of sharing a common dwelling place. This cannot be resolved by a program of "global goodness," to use an expression of Wolfgang Giegerich,[19] but must include solid "ground rules of engagement" to deal with the inevitable conflicts.[20] It is more a question of a balancing act between "the strange" and "the familiar." An empathetic approach that is attuned to the customs, history, and complexity of a cultural heritage can help make an emotionally toned complex conscious, which in turn facilitates a change of attitude. One U.S./Pakistani citizen—working in a non-governmental organization with the Taliban in the madrassas (Koran schools) of Pakistan and Afghanistan—once said that you cannot jump too soon to an appreciation of cultural differences. It is too much of a leap. The first step is to find similarity with the other, then develop tolerance and acceptance of the other, and only later the appreciation of difference. This is the cascade model. According to this man, "hate is not sustainable." Using the Koran to argue with the Taliban, he points out that it does not legitimize violence—only in life-threatening circumstances or serious infringements of justice may the use of force be contemplated.[21]

COSMOPOLITAN CITIZENSHIP:
SYMBOL OF A NEWLY EMERGING IDENTITY

Today's cities have now become home for most people in the world. As home is intimately connected with security and identity, home in a city or nation can no longer be separated from the notion of *citizenship*. With the waning of the older, cohesive forces of nationality, the civil, political, and social rights of citizenship have increasingly become an anchor of security for inhabitants of the multidimensional complexity of contemporary urban life. Many questions remain concerning the conditions of granting citizenship to the multicultural inhabitants of today's megacities. But how can those who are denied the basic rights of citizenship maintain any sense of home as a secure base in such places? Several of my expatriate friends living in Zürich feel dehumanized in having been denied the right to earn their living. How can citizenship be defined in order to respect diversity within urban populations? How can it take into consideration the cultural values of different nations and peoples without granting exclusivity to any one culture or nation? How can the lawmakers inspire the holders of citizenship to see beyond themselves and act in service of the greater whole? Citizenship is not simply a status, but a responsibility, even a way of life. Contemporary humanity will hardly be convinced of the significance of citizenship without internalizing its inner value and making conscious its symbolic meaning in daily life.

In earlier societies, belonging to a community usually meant being a "subject" of a particular dynasty or ruler. Citizenship originally implied being a freeman of a town or city. It later was identified with rights and privileges, as well as the recognition of formal equality in the public domain. In modern times, it became identified with nationality. Despite the brutal interruption by totalitarian regimes in the first half of the twentieth century, citizenship was granted a relatively secure status with the rise of the nation-state. In Western societies, democracy and capitalism, representing political and economic forces, became the nation's pillars of strength, both being partially restrained by the civic code of rights and duties of the particular society.[22]

According to Gerard Delanty and Richard Sennett, citizenship in a global age of fragmented communities can no longer ignore questions concerning cultural rights, the rights of the marginalized and underprivileged, the rights of women, and the rights of children. Citizenship must imply responsibility to one's fellow humans who are in less fortunate circumstances, and whose identity and means of livelihood are threatened by the unrestrained forces of global capitalism. As cities or nations no longer exist as isolated entities in a global age, citizenship must be extended to include responsibility for the preservation of animal and plant species and the natural resources of Planet Earth. Added to the list of rights are so-called "collective rights," extending beyond the confines of a particular city—as, for example, the rights of indigenous peoples, and rights concerning the protection of land, water, and language.[23] In daily newspapers we read about the tragic consequences when basic rights and responsibilities are denied or abused. Humans, animals, and the ecosphere have become the victims of a human hand that often lacks sensitivity and care for the diverse cultural and natural heritages of the world.

Delanty has argued that a conception of citizenship based on a one-sided, nineteenth-century civic code solely emphasizing rights and duties is inadequate. Recent discussion about the four main pillars of citizenship has highlighted the difference between rights and duties on the one hand,

and participation and identity on the other. The universal rights of the individual (liberal) or the state (conservative) regulate the relationship between the state and the individual in a formal way only.[24] Delanty reminds us that cosmopolitanism is not identical with globalization, corporate society, or the values of a secular state. Cosmopolitan citizenship must reflect the root meaning of the word "cosmopolitan," implying a sense of belonging to "cosmos" and "polis," to the universal and the local.[25] Civic cosmopolitanism must be "located in real lived communities" and "be rooted in civic communities, communities which are also discursively constituted."[26] The essence of community life is not mobility but communication, and must embrace commitment to social goals in order to counter the new forms of nationalism and fundamentalism, which are not unconnected with social discontent. In a discursive society, where many identities coexist, nationalism must become self-reflective.

Edward Said describes Huntington's clash of civilizations as an attempt to make "civilizations" and "identities" into what they are not: "shut-down, sealed-off entities that have been purged of the myriad currents and countercurrents that animate human history, and over centuries have made it possible for that history not only to contain wars of religion and imperial conquest but also to be one of exchange, cross-fertilization, and sharing."[27] Contemporary societies should make every effort to support communication that is critical, open-ended, and inclusive—perhaps to rediscover one day the gift of hospitality, the art of greeting the stranger, which has always been an intrinsic part of civilization. Recently, I was introduced to the Guestbook Project, directed by the philosopher and author Richard Kearney. This cross-cultural project explores the ambiguity of encounters with the stranger, a guest who is welcome or an enemy who is rejected. The project intends to further dialogue between self and the stranger, to provide opportunities for promising encounters between different nations, confessions, or cultures, and to elicit hospitality out of hostility, bearing in mind that both words have the same root.[28]

Reviving hospitality furthers the process of translating one home culture in terms of another. Delanty is convinced that cultural traditions, including nationhood, "can be seen both in terms of constructivism and essentialism, a reflected mode of thinking and a taken-for-granted mode of being. A culture of reflection and a culture of tradition are not exclusive but interwoven." As with Habermas's "post-secular society," Delanty contends that "post-national cosmopolitanism must not entail cultural negation or moral indifference but the ability to render cultural traditions transparent." From this point of view, "national identity contains a self-transcending dimension."[29] It is sensitive to local community, advocates pluralism of divergent political communities, and avoids the joint pitfalls of the disembodied universalism of liberalism and the communitarian romanticism of the private.[30] For Andrew Samuels, political and psychological thought today must include "the crucial interplay between the public and private dimensions of power."[31]

Cosmopolitan citizenship, as a symbol of a newly emerging identity, incarnates in the individual psyche, structuring affinities within a particular community, society, or nation. Representing human transnational values, it also creates an opening to citizens of other nations in matters concerning all of humanity, such as justice, equality, and the preservation of creation. Motivated by the inner symbolic meaning of citizenship, we learn to recognize that we are serving a greater whole, one that requires dedication, loyalty, trust, endurance, and responsibility. It is a way of serving the soul, which seeks home not only in a family, society, or nation, but in an identity that transcends individual or group consciousness, embracing a reality that is all-inclusive, even if only grasped in rare moments of inspiration. Jung's notion of the Self as the source of identity approximates to the images of God that have always been a source of all-inclusive meaning, cherished in a plurality of ways by the different peoples of the world. Unfortunately, throughout history, God-images have been appropriated in ways that activate an amity/enmity split. Once citizenship, however, takes on a broader cosmopolitan significance that would include cross-cultural fertilization, a whole range of privileges, responsibilities, and community participation opens new horizons of being at home in the world—preventing images of Divinity from becoming the exclusive property of one race, nation, or culture.

FACILITATING SOCIAL PARTICIPATION

Obviously, the emerging forms of communal participation require a psychology that reflects the new social realities of our times. Achieving meaningful relationships within a community cannot be based on rights and duties only, but ought to include differentiated notions of identity and participation, as witnessed in Delanty's concept of citizenship. This involves a process that invites each person to find new spaces between self and the other. It requires a considerable amount of self-knowledge and an ability to work through hidden anxieties that structure the well-known narcissistic defenses—denial, projection, or scapegoating. It also requires openness to "self-transcending dimensions." Such dimensions cannot be exclusively qualified as "national." They will also involve cultural traditions—religious or mythical, secular or sacred—that make up the fabric of national identity. They may actively structure the life of a society; they may be repressed; they may simply be archived in the unconscious. In this section I will continue to explore the self-transcending dimensions of the human psyche, which facilitate social integration without loss of self.

Rights and duties are part of any well-organized society with multiform functions. However, they are abstract and universal, and fail to account for the level of subjective participation in a society. Good governance demands some form of psychological assessment of an individual's subjective belief in and level of commitment to the community or nation. Depending on the size of the social framework, any assessment should distinguish the various levels of participation, whether through conscious consent, cultural heritage, a personal or cultural complex, or through archetypal myth or religious belief. This is "soul work," and obviously implies a balancing act between mind-sets: theoretical and mythic, knowledge and belief, reason and passion. It requires finding equilibrium between formal adherence to and genuine affective participation in a collective identity, as suggested by several authors quoted in this book. The play between the head and the heart is crucial to evoke social commitment and responsibility.

Whereas the notion of home was located in a local landscape, village, dynasty, or extended family in previous ages, in the nineteenth century home was increasingly identified with the nation-state. Today, with the diminished power of the state, the significance of home encompasses very different dimensions than the national collective values of a patriarchy-dominated society. Urban life has created many new organizations that sometimes are more important for today's citizens than belonging to a particular nation. One is now much more likely to encounter intense libidinal attachment to one's profession, or some kind of sub- or transnational organization that is concerned with matters of vital human interest. The significance of home, understood in the context of attachment to the newly emerging collective identities, has shifted from an exclusively national or political context to a professional, social, cultural, or environmental one.

Professional communities are often caught in conflicts having devastating consequences, leading to a loss of one's professional home. Many of my colleagues and I experienced this with the breakup of the C. G. Jung Institute of Zürich in 2004. It would be beyond the purpose of this book to analyze the dimensions of that long-drawn-out struggle. Part of the problem was the nondemocratic system of governance originally set up by Jung himself. One aspect of conflict, however, clearly comes to mind. One party emphasized formal rights and duties as the deciding factor of allegiance to the institute; the other valued communal bonding and a changing collective identity that demanded a higher degree of membership participation in governance of the institute, including the introduction of democratic structures. Many wondered what was left of Jungian psychology in all this—Where was there soul searching, a meeting of opposites, a new symbol? But even though we all were Jungians, no Jungian solution was possible. Communication between the parties eventually miscarried, resulting in a split—for many, the loss of the old professional home, but also the creation of a new one, now known as ISAPZurich.

Commenting on splits in Jungian societies, Aniela Jaffé once said, at a meeting of the Swiss Jungian society in the early 1970s, that Jungians are basically a loose body of individuals, having unconscious fantasies of their collective identity. At that time, the Jungian collective identity tended to be interpreted in terms of an intrapsychic reality—thus the danger of relegating communal relationships in the outer world to the shadow. Belonging to a collective organization was like adding on something to one's individuality that did not really form an intrinsic part of it. Since then, much has changed, due to the ease of communication and extensive publications on collective identities. Provided there is a good system of governance, participation in a group does not mean loss of individuality. On the contrary, with the recognition that identity is formed between persons, rather than within a person, participation in a collective identity can signal an enrichment of consciousness and an intrinsic extension of identity. Referring to communal participation, Andrew Samuels comments: "'We' will only be authentic to the extent the 'we' has been differentiated."[32]

Facilitating meaningful participation in collective identities requires not only good governance, but also a considerable amount of self-knowledge among the individual members, so that they maintain awareness of defense systems that when acted out will only harm the healthy functioning of a group or community. Individual work is often a prerequisite of meaningful participation in a collective identity. A purely rational approach—"the language of the father," a language of interpretation and explanation—can prevent the emergence of a new beginning in moments of transition. In those in-between spaces of social exchange, spontaneous and unexpected manifestations of the unconscious must be registered, reflected on, and eventually integrated into the newly emerging collective identity.

Working with individuals or smaller groups, the analyst or psychotherapist must not forget that his or her client is a fellow citizen. Avoiding the pitfalls of a superficial "we," the analyst must respect difference. Honoring the autonomy, rights, and beliefs of clients, the analyst will explore their mythic and religious affiliations—acknowledging their capacity to create deep bonding, unveiling their inhibiting influence, registering their potential for transformation, and eventually facilitating a constructive relationship between them and the new social realities of our time. This is not only a question of interpretation, but in the first place a facilitating of the reality of another person or another party. In balancing an essentialist and constructivist approach to the client's material, an internal world of meaning is established. Christopher Bollas terms these two processes the elaborative and deconstructive aspects of analysis. The former is a process of making present the client's internal world of meaning and his or her potential for change; the latter is a process of knowledge, interpretation, and the extension of meaning beyond subjectivity.[33]

I have offered examples describing the transformation of a mythic, religious, or ideological system in terms of new social participation, transcending social barriers, and embracing a larger social framework. Several contemporary poems about Ireland, inspiring new attitudes concerning the mythic motif of "land-as-woman," were discussed in the previous chapter. The Northern Irish man's dream of "the nice new shop" symbolized a new social perspective, transcending the tribal rivalries of Northern Ireland, and helped liberate the dreamer from the inhibiting ideological interpretation of the *puella sinilis*. In chapter 7 we encountered Milena, who, on becoming aware of the transgenerational influence of Soviet ideology, could eventually use her mind to make choices in order to undo the imprisoning influence of the Soviet heating system that had condemned her to a life of emotional insecurity. In the same chapter, we encountered

Adele, who was raised in a home of fear. She had to challenge the terrifying figure of "the Last Judgment," which had generated an unhealthy split between "good" and "evil." Only after internalizing "the judge" could she gain more confidence in her capacity of self-evaluation and her potential to become a more confident member within a social framework of her own choosing. Ruggero's olive field opened a new sense of kinship with self and the world—with family, culture, ancestral heritage, and landscape. Home became a rich, inner reality that Ruggero could take with him wherever he went, a conviction that he could mobilize in his capacity as a teacher in an international organization. The professional home that San was about to create would be made to house the generosity, compassion, and numinosity of the Buddha—a home to embrace the many different levels of society. In the above examples, symbolic material, political ideology, and traditional belief became transparent and transformed, providing libido necessary to substantiate an emerging identity that is not unconnected with contemporary notions of cosmopolitan citizenship. Each person, facing the challenges of social exclusion, discovered a new sense of freedom and became more confident in their capacity to evaluate and commit to a level of participation in a suitable social framework of their own choice.

Cosmos and Polis

In ending this chapter, I would like to return to the psychological relevance of the cosmopolitan citizen. Citizenship is not only to be understood as the possession of a privileged status. It is not just an ideal, but a process, a struggle, or one might even say, an event. Victor Turner describes ritual processes that bring new life and change within a social structure. Turner's concept of "communitas" is not about a fixed community. On the contrary, "communitas" is "a marginal and liminal reality." It is "an anti-structural moment" in social development, creating social bonds that are spontaneous, immediate, egalitarian, and nonrational. It is indissolubly linked with social structure, although it stands in opposition to it.[34] It brings possible and contrary forms into prominence and thus engenders reflexivity and change for the social and cultural system as a whole.[35] Likewise, today cosmopolitan citizenship happens in those moments when "context bound cultures encounter each other and undergo transformation as a result."[36] In other words, the newly emerging identity of contemporary humanity happens in a space between divergent realities, and is often achieved after having struggled with forces that resist change.

"Polis," representing the city, a community, or a society where human exchanges take place, opens itself up to "cosmos," representing the other, the stranger, the unknown, the entirety. Regarded from a symbolic point of view, this model of social development corresponds to some of Jung's basic tenets concerning the individuation process as a continual creative exchange between the ego and the Self. Polis represents much of ego activity—cities, communities, or societies are the realms where most of our daily interactions with the outside world occur and are usually contained within a manageable space. Cosmos approximates more to an experience of the Self. Encountering the universe of the unknown, either in an event or a person, is experienced as ruptures in daily life that appear threatening or inspiring, causing us to take flight or to stand firm and discover what the mystery is all about.

The meeting of cosmos and polis correlates with creative processes in every human psyche. They are the moments when the ego encounters the unconscious, within or without; when it can let go of rigid defenses, allow space for the unexpected that in turn can activate the unconscious to produce images and perspectives leading to the formation of a new attitude. Jung's transcendent function provides a psychological model of a "midpoint personality," a point of connection between me and the unknown other. Such moments are a far cry from a sentimental embrace of everyone. In this process, one cannot afford to neglect the discriminating powers of the individual ego that enable a person to appraise and evaluate the nature and purpose of such encounters. A discriminating ego, which is both grounded and sensitive to polis and cosmos, prevents idealization or dismissal of the stranger. The conscious ego frames such moments of encounter, either through artistic expression or through articulation of their meaning and value. We can never capture the entirety of the cosmos, be it a person or an event, but if we do not attempt to give it form we risk being overwhelmed by its immensity. Each person can only submit to this process in his or her own way, aware that opening oneself to the unknown can be perilous and bears responsibility. Nevertheless, creating instances of bridge building between the I and the stranger sustains cosmopolitan citizenship, experienced as an extension of consciousness that embraces what hitherto seemed irreconcilable.

Jungian psychology is not only an intrapsychic affair, a psychology for the elite or for the introverts. The transcendent function happens in us all, as we are out there encountering the real world, attempting to face it, understand it, and develop a new attitude that takes account of its complexity and its mysteries. Jung may well have had in mind the connection between polis and cosmos in the following quote:

> No, the collective unconscious is anything but an incapsulated personal system; it is sheer objectivity, as wide as the world and open to all the world. There I am the object of every subject, in complete reversal of my ordinary consciousness, where I am always the subject that has an object. There I am utterly one with the world, so much a part of it that I forget all too easily who I really am.[37]

Only after suffering and struggle do we gain awareness of that greater Self. This may mean going against convention, breaking taboos, or risking exclusion from one's community. Joanna Berry undertook that risk in coming to terms with the man who was responsible for the murder of her father. Sir Anthony Berry was a member of parliament who was killed by an IRA bomb at the conservative party conference in Brighton, England, in 1984. Having involuntarily been drawn into the Northern Irish conflict, Joanna Berry sought ways to work with that unaddressed collective trauma. Besides attending reconciliation groups, she made the decision to meet her father's killer, after he had been released from prison in 1999 as part of the Good Friday agreement. Concerning the decision, she had this to say:

> I knew that the saddest thing was that they were my brothers, not my enemies, that in truth there is no us and them, only you and me. I knew then that betrayal—the idea that we cannot be friends with the other side without being disloyal to our own—is a myth that keeps us from realizing that we are all brothers and sisters; in that moment I knew that the only real betrayal was the betrayal of my heart, which was telling me that we are all connected.[38]

A psychological understanding of cosmopolitan citizenship calls to mind certain aspects of the individuation process as understood by Jung. One has to start by facing the shadow within oneself. Julia Kristeva aptly expresses this when writing about new community bonds: "The foreigner is within us. And when we flee from or struggle against the foreigner, we are fighting our unconscious—that 'improper' facet of our impossible 'own and proper.'"[39] Work with the shadow, within and without, opens the door to awareness of a greater Self. Being a member of a community or a nation implies integration in a bounded realm and acceptance of its complexity. Citizenship opens up a vast range of experiences with otherness, which in turn stimulates open-mindedness to different communities and nations in matters concerning humanity as a whole, as Adolf Guggenbühl has implied. It may then dawn upon us that citizenship is not a possession, but an entry to other worlds—a moment of choice and responsibility to embrace shared values concerning ancestry, nationhood, and the universe.

CHAPTER 11

Traversing Cultural Boundaries

The difference between most people and myself is that for me
the "dividing walls" are transparent. That is my peculiarity.
Others find these walls so opaque that they see nothing behind them and therefore think nothing is there.[1]

—C. G. Jung

THERAPEUTIC CARE IN TRANSITIONAL PROCESSES

In a newspaper article, Christiane Schlötzer describes Mustafa Olpak's
incredible search for roots and origin. Olpak lives in Ayvalik, a small
town on the west coast of Turkey. He is Turkish, carries a Turkish
passport—and has suffered abuse because of his skin color. It took a long
time for him to discover why he was black. He remembered his grandfather, one winter, sitting for two whole days, just staring at the ocean without uttering a word. He wondered why his beloved grandfather could not
speak Turkish, only fluent Greek. He could not understand why he
would never take off his shirt in front of his grandchild, and why he would
whisper "Kenya, Kenya" whenever he would show his grandchild a map
of Africa. Mustafa Olpak finally discovered that his grandparents had
been slaves in the Ottoman Empire. Never having been taught in school
about the existence of slavery in the Turkish Empire, he gradually pieced
together his family lineage. His grandparents were imported to Crete in

the nineteenth century, sold as slaves to rich Muslim farmers, and finally brought to Turkey when the Turks relinquished sovereignty of Crete in 1923. Olpak found out that it was the shame of a slave's brand mark that prevented his grandfather from showing his naked torso. He could now decipher the meaning of those two days when his grandfather sat motionless before the sea, and why he whispered "Kenya, Kenya" in front of a map of Africa. Mustafa Olpak has had the courage to break a taboo, and has written a family biography with the Turkish title *Köle*, meaning "slave." The book begins with the words: "The first generation lived it, the second denied it, and the third researched it."[2]

There are many approaches to assessing the plight of today's immigrants. Suffice it here to sketch two directions that appear to evaluate questions of assimilation and acculturation from different viewpoints. One view is conservative, emphasizing the limits of integration due to wide cultural divergence; the other, pragmatic and optimistic. As a representative of the former view, the sociologist Hans-Joachim Hoffman-Nowotny, writing on the risks and opportunities in multicultural societies, warns about ideological positions that tend to overidealize the multicultural. In a process of assimilation the search for common links cannot exclude cultural divergence. Culture is not only about dress, food, or music. Human beings "need culture to create a symbolic construction of the world," which expresses itself through myths and ideologies that are normative and "regulate aspects of individual and social life."[3] One cannot expect immigrants to outwardly assimilate the social norms and practices of the host society, and maintain their cultural heritage solely within the domestic sphere. Culture cannot be "reduced to folklore." It is not just a personal or private affair, but extends into the public and social domain and includes a world of shared meaning, values, and norms that shape the life of a community. A splitting of private domestic and public social behavior will lead to further segregation, fundamentalism, and ghetto mentality. This becomes increasingly evident, the less compatible the cultural ideals and norms are between guest and host society.

A more optimistic view welcomes a newly emerging global culture. Although several empires have existed that included different nations and tolerated mass migration within their boundaries, never before has this phenomenon reached global proportions. Perhaps the children from immigrant families in today's global culture will tell us more about the significance of home than those of us who have always had the privilege of living in a secure social environment. Their lives may have a wider symbolic significance, relevant for the emerging social realities of our time. Immigrant children in today's global culture come from more than one cultural and language background. In Switzerland, they are known as "*Secundos*" or "global kids." A recent study shows that they tend to mix with other global kids. Even if they retain the local dialect and customs of the area in which they grew up, their identity can no longer be defined exclusively in terms of a particular village, family, or culture. They have an open and dynamic attitude to life. Their identity is to be understood as rather "a process of formation than a state of being."[4] Living between worlds inevitably causes doubt and vacillation, as young people try to survive the winds of change. In view of the material quoted throughout this book, the formation of cultural novelty involves a reinvention of identity, which in itself can be a lifelong pursuit.

Simona, a young woman of Italian descent with Swiss nationality, describes her ambivalent attitude to collective identity, which had already made its appearance in childhood.

> In 1994 I could become a Swiss citizen. I was nine years old. I said I don't want to have dual citizenship. I only want to be Swiss. Today I could slap myself in the face for saying such a thing. My parents maneuvered it; they wanted me to develop a feeling of belonging to Switzerland. They too became Swiss citizens.[5]

Much can be learned from psychotherapists' and social workers' engagement with immigrant populations. They continually witness the underlying innovative dynamics as the immigrant adjusts to new social and cultural conditions. In the process of achieving an authentic change of attitude toward self and society, professionals stress the slow process of integration, which takes place over several generations. Integration implies the ability to mourn what has been lost, to accept ambivalence, and to create an identity that might not fit the new or the old, but that is original, authentic, and sufficiently rooted to survive transitional processes. Change without a sense of self is unthinkable. Change implies a process of self-awareness and self-transformation that balances two fundamental tendencies of the human psyche: myth and reason, security and freedom, the symbolic attachment to home and the ability to translate that attachment into the reality of another landscape. It is a process that bears certain similarities to the three stages of the old initiation rituals:

separation, liminality, and reintegration.⁶ The purpose of these ancient customs was to bring transformation of the whole person—not just mind, but also heart and body. The initiation process enabled the individual to take leave of the old home, to accept a transitional stage of belonging nowhere, and to facilitate integration into a new social and cultural reality. The imagery of such rituals mirrors the age-old cyclical processes of life, death, and rebirth.

Whatever viewpoint one holds, immigrants need support in order to make use of their ingenuity and talents to find home in the host country. Subjecting them to discrimination only multiplies problems and makes integration more difficult. Obviously, if integration is to be successful it is extremely helpful if immigrants learn the language of their host country. Integration into a new society does not mean complete assimilation. Cultural differences and cultural traditions, especially language and religion, need to be sustained and respected. This does not mean that every aspect of immigrant culture gets reduced to the private, or the level of folklore. Only those values and norms that radically contradict the values and norms of the host country can be problematic. They can be tolerated as long as they are not practiced in defiance of the values of the host country. It is possible to have compatible interaction between different groups, even if they have incompatible value systems. When, however, incompatible values systems become operational, conflict is programmed.

Contemporary multicultural society cannot extend its jurisdiction to support clitoris removal, or arranged marriages without consent of the partners. These traditions, long practiced in the original homeland, contradict fundamental principles of a society that upholds gender equality and individual freedom as essential elements of cultural cohesion. The surrender of certain traditional values—at least when they are acted out in defiance of the law of the land—is part of the price immigrants have to pay if they wish to be integrated into the host country. Parental prohibition against mixed bathing or gender-inclusive school outings has been a matter of controversy in Switzerland. Nevertheless, enforcement or uncritical acceptance of this less harmful form of separatism has brought no satisfactory solution. A superficial form of integration might be achieved in a relatively short space of time, but integration or modification of longstanding values, as evident in religious traditions, requires a longer process of integration. The city of Basel had good experiences with making it obligatory for the children from non-Swiss cultures to learn their own language in school. Learning their own language empowered them and helped them to be more open to the Swiss dialect and the German language. Outer adaptation must go hand in hand with an inner work that weaves diverse threads into a new pattern. This is a difficult process of self-transformation that may extend over several generations.

The process of becoming a citizen of the world and yet retaining roots and a sense of belonging to the past or to one's local surroundings is certainly one that will occupy many generations to come. The whole issue of acculturation is immensely complex, involving "language, food habits, artistic traditions, bodily modifications and adornments, moral rules, religious allegiances."[7] Anna Duran's studies of acculturation show that the loss of one home and the gain of another may not be a question of one lifetime, but of generations. Acculturation causes the highest amount of stress, but without this kind of stress the immigrant ends up completely isolated. According to Duran, transition from one culture to another involves an ability to mourn the loss of the original homeland, to sustain exile from the past, to accept ambivalence so as not to repress the values of the original culture, and to avoid forced adaptation, which might lead to the loss of the ability to form any attachments whatsoever.[8] Acculturation can be a lifetime's work, for it affects the very ground of one's being. Often a patchwork and superficial integration may appear successful, but in some cases this creates a fragmentary existence at the cost of a deeper connection to soul, identity, and purpose in life. Like the old initiation rites, a transitional space involves an "in-between" period for an authentic change of attitude to take root. Acculturation is an art that has to be learned. This implies an ability to translate the interior language of soul, to grasp the manifold intentions of its archetypal grammar, so that the outsider may participate in a new collective identity in a free and meaningful way. Acculturation implies an art of constructing a context that allows an open cultural identity despite the loss and gain of home.

There can be no easy solution for the millions of homeless encountered in today's world. Homelessness can be experienced in many ways, according to the circumstances that create it. The distinction between homelessness as a loss of a concrete object and homelessness as loss of self is of great importance in deciding what kind of support people need. Loss of a sense of self can be confusing and pervasive, and requires specialized help. In the case of refugees, loss of self can be temporary and does not always follow the classical description of Post-Traumatic Stress Disorder.

The traumatized victims of war and rape, whose homes have been destroyed, will need professional care and understanding in order to achieve a renewed connection with themselves and their surroundings. They also need to be able to share their experiences with others who have had similar experiences. Professionals providing therapeutic care for refugees warn us not to pathologize them. They also caution against prolonged internment and isolation from family or social connections, which may cause depression. Placed in confinement, successful transition can become more difficult, triggering a retreat from the real world and idealization of the original home. A regressive restoration of values and norms of the original homeland can become a breeding ground of fundamentalism with its dangerous subgroups. Given a sufficient amount of support and freedom, most refugees will find all kinds of ways to adapt and achieve success in their new surroundings.

In the ever-changing world of the refugee, humans are seen less "as passive recipients of 'socialization' but as active creators of ideas and practices," so as to achieve goals in a host country.[9] Today, the internet and cellular phones enable refugees and migrants to establish a network of family and social communication with others from their home country within a short space of time. Political demonstrations, sharing food, seeing films, or listening to the music of the original homeland will fortify group solidarity. These activities can lead to withdrawal and the development of phobic alliances against the host country, or act as a home base that encourages acceptance of the new.[10] It is well known that women and youth whose lives have been restricted by patriarchal suppression and archaic family traditions welcome the liberal social and professional opportunities permitted by the constitutions of Western countries. Some migrants achieve an original and witty integration of their previous and current traditions, as expressed in the Scottish Sikh's turban made of tartan[11] or the words of an English municipal politician: "I am conservative, black, and British and I am proud of all three!"[12]

The tartan turban and the statement of the British politician may take on a symbolic significance for those who are less fortunate in achieving social integration. They draw attention to the symbol-creating capacity of the mind. A symbol of integration arising from the immigrant's unconscious may help other immigrants in facilitating a translation from the old to the new. Symbolic reality, with its expressive and representative functions, creates a potential space that can further a new and authentic attitude to the host environment. Expressive therapies with emphasis on imagination, play, and body can facilitate a process of restructuring an imaginal space between the old and new home. Symbolic reality, seen from a Jungian point of view, is not just a matter of interpreting culture, but is actively culture-making by "revivifying a feeling for culture and myth."[13] Jung has elaborated the psychological aspect of this process in his notion of the transcendent function, a term denoting the inherent creative potential of the human psyche to bridge worlds and to form new attitudes.

Many who specialize in work with refugees recommend a modified form of therapeutic care that can greatly facilitate and accelerate a process of integration. In *Therapeutic Care For Refugees*, edited by Renos Papadopoulos, several authors stress the importance of being witness to a wider context. The refugee's story first needs to be heard and validated. Refugees are invited to talk about their traditional, original, and familiar understandings of the world. They are encouraged to be active participants in clarifying the meaning of transition. Their inner "resilience" is to be respected and supported.[14] The use of narrative as a means of bridge building between the different worlds is to be employed. The context of loss of home with all its manifold dimensions has to be included in therapeutic care.[15] Workers in the field need to respect and understand the immigrant's inner psychological state of mind, besides the sociopolitical dimensions of the transitional period.

Papadopoulos understands that the pain of contemporary homelessness is not just about loss of the concrete object, of which refugees are aware, but is likely to include something beyond the refugees' understanding: a loss of self and the containment of multidimensional experiences of places and people that held a world together and made it meaningful. He likens home to a "substratum of identity which is structured as a mosaic and consists of a great number of smaller elements, which together form a coherent whole."[16] Besides the external dimensions, there is a second process of homecoming:

> The second moment is of a more internal and psychological nature, requiring more internal resources, stamina, containment, insightfulness and resilience. If the first is about arriving home, the second is about reconnecting with one's sense of self and accessing the dis-membered parts of one's personality.[17]

Similar to Jung's notion of the psyche as a container of multiple complexes, and Papadopoulos's mosaic identity, Salman Akhtar describes this second stage of homecoming as a "mourning-liberation process" resulting in a "reconsolidated hybrid identity and the view that the result of such a process is a contextually resilient confederation of self-representations."[18]

The above statements describe the significance of home in terms of identity and creativity. As one undergoes the pain of transitional periods of homecoming, one cannot assume any longer that there is just one home, one inherent identity. The narratives of the ever-shifting scenes of contemporary homecomings portray identity as multilayered and continually in a process of being invented. There may be moments when one feels partially dissociated. The process, however, requires an intrapsychic capacity to tolerate the tension between diverse identities and diverse homes, and to trust in the creative powers of the psyche to provide new symbols of integration. Jung's psychological understanding of the Self as the principle of unity, wholeness, and self-regulation; Papadopoulos's mosaic structure; or Akhtar's confederation of self-representations hint at a nonconscious matrix of the human mind that maintains a diversity of "identities" held together in a balanced equilibrium. As already stated, this balancing act is not a permanent state but a dynamic process that manifests in unexpected events when the conscious ego and the unconscious connect, as witnessed in Jung's notion of the transcendent function. If one can accept outer loss and move on, the old identity is likely to become more transparent and mature in embracing the new. Memories of one's old life become transformed, as they become critically reflected in the light of those transitional experiences that have diminished or enriched one's sense of self. If integration succeeds, the ability to take home wherever one goes emerges. You begin to realize that the diverse identities, accumulated in a lifetime, rest upon a deeper foundation, a transcendent "Self" that can only be grasped in moments when one feels carried by an underlying matrix of meaning transcending the conscious ego and finding expression in the hunger to belong.

The issues of homelessness, as in the case of the refugee or the migrant, affect us all. They have a symbolic significance extending beyond social and political events. Most of us reared in the affluent society of the West will find it difficult to understand the homeless, particularly those of us who have had the good fortune to start life in a home where people are well related with one another—especially in the early stages crucial to character formation. We will have to examine attitudes that take for granted that life is safe, secure, and meaningful in a world that is stable, and shelter is provided. We will have to ask ourselves how much of our "safe identity" is determined by an unconscious reaction to the lives of others who are unsafe, insecure, or homeless. We will have to probe hidden anxieties that create an impregnable dividing wall between the haves and have-nots. We can no longer deny that we are strangers to ourselves,[19] if we are to accept those homeless fragments of the soul that seem to know that there is no one final home in life on earth.

We can never underestimate the radical contingency of human existence. If we suffer the loss of one safe and meaningful world, we might not have the strength to create a new one. Then, like any homeless person, we will rely on the understanding and respectful eyes and voice of another to bear witness to the extent of that loss. Communications on these levels include visible and invisible presences, outer reality and intrapsychic dynamics, and a notion of identity as multilayered, ambiguous, and open-ended. In understanding the plight of the homeless, one needs to be aware of an underlying matrix of meaning, expressing itself in symbol, implicit memory, and the nighttime consciousness of dreams, to appreciate the inner resilience and creativity of those who find themselves in transient spaces. In relating to the other, one needs to embody a compassion that embraces the undeniable fact that we all belong to the same human family and are closer to one another than we often would like to believe.

NARRATIVE REALITY AND THE RECOVERY OF KINSHIP

I am convinced that if we are to construct cosmopolitan societies in which diverse populations of the global age can find a new home, we can only build on the older, deeper, and more enduring religious and mythic values that have nourished people over generations through attachment to family, community, nation, and the universe. Values are not the same as common interests. Interests are about what people want—such as food, work, security, or social welfare—or what they don't want. Values are embedded in the enduring attachments to a cultural heritage, and are encountered in judgments that have a religious, moral, or political significance. They possess a powerful narrative quality that is emotional and deeply rooted in collective memory. On the one hand, they can be divisive whenever they are taken for granted, not reflected on, and largely unconscious. On the other hand, they enrich the human connection when people recognize that their core values and traditional beliefs share a common foundation. The task of a cosmopolitan society is to make transparent the common ground of those values, despite their representation in differing narratives. The ethical values of service, respect, truthfulness, justice, and accountability are to be encountered in many of the worlds' religious traditions.

Narratives, those wonderful stories of the human heritage, grip the mind, heart, and body. A culture of reflexivity and communication cannot be successful if the language of the heart, peopled by all kinds of complexes, is excluded. Narratives, embracing old-fashioned notions of home and containing bonded memories of one's history of belonging, must now be prepared to enter a culture of exchange. The diverse narratives about home must be listened to and shared. Through imaginative narrative, one reaches deeper levels of soul attachments. They move the whole person and encourage neighbors, now living in ever-closer proximity, to respect difference, yet nevertheless be sources of inspiration for each other. Possessive bonding must be critically questioned as outlived attachments to persons, places, and ideas lose their relevance and dogmatic rigidity. Energy, inventiveness, and humor are part of a repertoire that allows the human story to recover its affinity for kinship and for those in-between spaces in which authentic relationship is established.

It has often been said that once a nation loses its story, it loses its identity. Narratives capture the soul of a nation. Such narratives can be a blessing or a curse, depending upon which side one is on. The conflicts in Ireland, Jerusalem, or Kosovo have been motivated by cherished narratives, mobilized by a collective memory that has molded national identity of a people over generations. Ireland's struggle for independence was shaped on the older enduring myth of the hero's sacrificial death in service to the goddess of the land. Jerusalem is upheld as Islam's third most holy site from a vision of Mohammed in which the prophet, accompanied by the angel Gabriel, ascends to heaven on a winged steed. Serbia justified its sovereignty over Kosovo by appealing to its heroic struggle against the Ottoman Turks in the battle of Kosovo, 1389, which ended in defeat and five centuries of Ottoman rule. Such narratives have promoted conflict and bloodshed, splitting families, societies, and nations. There are signs that the new narratives of today's global world traverse boundaries—they no longer simply repeat prescribed traditions. In a world of cross-cultural exchange, they may stimulate curiosity and encourage a bridge-building process that will continue to be woven for generations to come.

Yacob Arsano, writing about the Nile waters and the conflict of interests among adjoining nations, draws attention to the power of symbols and myths that are connected with the Nile. The narratives about the river have been a source of a people's identity. They contain reverence for a natural phenomenon that has regulated community life, endowing it with meaning and morality. Arsano recognizes the drawbacks and advantages of narrative reality. Its application and authority is local and limited when contrasted with international legal and political structures. Nevertheless, it is deeply internalized, much closer to the people, and, as part of their cultural heritage, held to be true. Arsano is convinced that traditional and local customs and beliefs must be taken into consideration if a sustainable peace and development are to be achieved in cross-border water management. Arsano outlines some of the stories, songs, and ritual performances long associated with the Nile. In Ethiopia, the Nile is believed to be "the father" of all rivers, and as such is held in great reverence, lending a spiritual identity and prestige to the local inhabitants. In both ancient Egypt and Ethiopia, it had been associated with gods of power, wealth, and healing—Ra, Ptah, and the Greek Prometheus. In Christian Ethiopia, various chants, blessings, purification rituals, and long processions celebrated on the banks of the Nile waters commemorate the baptism of Christ.[20] An approach to conflict resolution that is based solely on economic or political interests can be ineffectual in the face of older narratives, which have defined the identity and ways of life of local inhabitants.

Contemporary storytelling continues to occupy the peoples of the Nile's adjoining nations as they struggle to come to terms with each other. In the narratives surrounding the river one can detect themes illustrating divergence among the people who share the Nile waters. One story, told to an Egyptian just back from a visit to Ethiopia, describes the Ethiopian Nile as the source that created Egypt. He was told: "Egypt was born in Ethiopia, and from the red mountains of Ethiopia came the water, which is the stuff of our life and the silt that created the fertility of Egyptian soil."[21] This story was not appreciated in Egypt.

I was told another story by a participant who was present at a conference in Cairo concerning distribution of the Nile waters. It brought to consciousness the conflict among adjoining states concerning decisions about dams and the harnessing of the river. In accordance with traditional stories, the Ethiopian party described the Nile as a great fish, the head of which lies in Ethiopia. They concluded that, having the head in their territory, they were free to decide what was to be done with the Nile in their land. The Egyptians, using the same metaphor, countered by saying that the tail of the fish lay in Egypt, and the tail always decides what direction the fish will take. Both parties laughed, knowing well that the head and the tail will have to work in unison if the fish is to stay alive.

Narrative not only holds a nation together, but also bestows a sense of continuity and identity to a person's life. When someone tells the story of the homes he or she has lived in, they may reveal cherished secrets of a lifetime's struggle. The tales may be about success or failure, joy or despair. Despite the divisions and conflicts of a broken life, narrative binds what appears separate into a new whole. There is, for example, the story of Ramon, a man who came from North Africa. As a child, he saw his neighbor build a beautiful two-storied house, painted in bright colors. He felt ashamed of his father's mud hut. One day his neighbor told him that he should go to Europe, and then he too could build a nice house. Many of his friends in school heard similar stories and were planning to do the same. When Ramon became a man, he worked hard, saved, and borrowed money so he could pay the agent who organized that perilous journey. He became one of those tens of thousands of boat people heading for the promised land of Europe. He survived, and eventually arrived in Switzerland. Ramon had no difficulty in making contact with other immigrants from his native land. He found work and eventually could make several trips back home. He began to build his two-storied house.

Ramon was a handsome man; many white women were attracted to him. One became pregnant; they married and had a daughter. The marriage did not last. Ramon loved his daughter and worked hard to support her, even though he could only see her at odd weekends. Ramon continues to build his house in Africa, but his heart is with his daughter in Switzerland. In Africa he is a rich man; he is admired for his success. In Europe, his private life consists of the days spent with his daughter and close friends from Africa. Otherwise, he feels himself to be a stranger, unwanted and at times even hated. He feels he will never be accepted as a Swiss person, but he does enjoy the support of African groups living in Switzerland. He lives in two worlds. His life is broken. He does not know if he can ever put it together again. Ramon's life narrative is not yet completed. His story, however, acts as a symbol that holds his life together and gives it meaning. He might not always be aware of its meaning, but the one who hears his words and voice as he tells his tale cannot but be intensely moved by a story that is ongoing and exemplary.

Anna's story is different from Ramon's. This is a tale describing a transformation of transgenerational incompatibility between the original and the host home. It illustrates a process of linking of worlds, a process that might one day be taken up by Ramon's progeny. Anna's father was Italian and her mother Swiss. She was registered as an Italian national. Some years after her birth, Anna was given Swiss citizenship, together with her father. The family spoke the Swiss-German dialect. Coming from a well-integrated family, Anna did well in school. Once in a while, children would make derogatory remarks about Anna's dark complexion, but she managed to brush them off. What hurt her most was when teachers would say: "Restrain your temperament; Switzerland is not Italy!" Anna could not help sometimes feeling ashamed of her Italian heritage. She learned to be calm, moderate her emotions, and stop gesticulating with her hands. When the family visited Italy, Anna felt at home—the temperament that she tried so hard to repress simply burst out from every cell in her body, and to her surprise she found those around her acting in a similar way. Anna lived in two worlds. While still a young woman, she learned to speak Italian fluently and would often visit her relatives in Italy. By refueling in that way, Italy became substantiated as home. Anna accepted the fact that she had two homes, two identities. She did not try to unify them, but knew she was the same person who functioned in both. She could tolerate diverse worlds, despite moments of nostalgic longing for Italy when in Switzerland, and appreciation of Swiss competence when dealing with bureaucratic inefficiency in Italy.

Anna taught in a Swiss kindergarten. Her double identity became an asset to her profession, facilitating innovative social action. She was often given the task of helping young Italian children adapt to Swiss culture. One such child was Marietta. Marietta's parents were Italian. They could hardly speak Swiss-German. Both her elder siblings were in a Swiss school, and spoke Swiss-German with each other. Marietta would speak only Italian at home, but the moment she was outside of the house she refused to say anything whatsoever. She would walk to the kindergarten with her mother, but on arriving she would not move one step further. Her mother would have to change her shoes and carry her into the classroom. Anna and Marietta sat facing one another. Noticing the lively, inquisitive eyes of this otherwise motionless, speechless child, Anna felt kinship with Marietta. Those eyes were Italian, full of temperament!

Over the next few weeks, Anna devised several games for Marietta. They first played ball with each other. Anna pushed the ball in Marietta's direction; Marietta's mother moved her daughter's arms to roll the ball back to Anna. Whenever Anna would miss the ball, Marietta's eyes glistened with satisfaction. The more Anna missed the ball, the more Marietta got excited, until finally she hit the ball back without the mother's help. Next, Anna opened a picture book on farm animals. She would point to an animal and utter the correct Italian word, but when Anna called a "goat" a "cow," Marietta shook her head and vehemently pointed to the cow. Then Anna arranged memory games with the other children. Marietta won most of the games. Once her classmate, Danny, the previous winner, became so frustrated that he got up on a table and cried out, "I am the winner." And Marietta yelled: "No, I am!" From that day on, Marietta spoke Swiss-German.

Anna and Marietta's stories illustrate the diverse ways different worlds approximate to one another. Anna's parents prepared a firm foundation for their daughter to allow two cultures to exist side by side, without forcing Anna to favor one over the other. Marietta's parents came to Switzerland only for work. They had no interest in learning German, and wanted to return to their native Italy as soon as possible. Marietta was in the grip of a cultural complex. She identified and embodied her parents' split intentions. They had dismissed Switzerland and longed to return to their native Italy, and yet they expected their daughter to integrate into Swiss school culture. Anna had accepted the fact that she belonged to both cultures. Working with many Italian children and their parents, she had much opportunity to reflect on cultural diversity. By connecting with the healthy, playful, internal resources of Marietta, she could help the child build a bridge between Italian and Swiss cultures. Marietta benefited from this opportunity and overcame the split world of her parents. Within the context of Anna's kindergarten, Marietta's will to succeed enabled her to connect separate worlds and build a more inclusive identity. The meaning of Anna's life prospered as her lifelong attempt to hold different homes together became substantiated in witnessing the growth and development of children like Marietta. Anna's and little Marietta's exchange initiated a moment of cosmopolitan citizenship, a testimony to the self's capacity to bridge divergent worlds.

BRIDGE BUILDING AND HOMECOMING

Home narratives, whether collective or personal, can be divisive or creative, championing fundamentalism or welcoming reciprocation. The gods or goddesses, heroes or heroines of home narratives can be resorted to as an ultimate authority that decides on issues of war or peace—among cultures, nations, organizations, families, or individuals. Narratives are the way we make sense of the world, and sometimes make nonsense of other worlds for which we feel no affiliation. Conflicts may remain unresolved over generations, as witnessed in Olpak's struggle to piece together a family lineage and Arsano's narratives about the Nile waters. Home narratives of today concern bridge building—how to translate one cultural environment, one family inheritance, one natural landscape in terms of another.

Home can no longer be understood exclusively as an outer reality, as one particular family, house, or country. With the breakup of so many homes, most people today are forced to become conscious of home in other ways. The notion of home cannot be separated from personal biography, and is intrinsically related to identity, with all its manifold meanings. Home may be understood as an archetypal disposition of the soul—the cry of Eros, or the hunger to belong, which is rooted in the unconscious and equipped with a drive towards consciousness. As a symbolic experience it is both inherent and inventive. Once connected with environment in meaningful ways, home becomes a function of consciousness, an attitude of personality that expels indifference and approaches diversity with an open heart and mind. Within this perspective, one can embrace new worlds without loss of self, roots, and a sense of belonging. Despite all the tragedy of broken lands, broken people, and broken homes, humanity is becoming conscious of what home can truly be. Even if most of contemporary humanity at one time or another have had their lives broken, humans possess a remarkable resilience that enables them to adapt and survive. The challenges of today are making us aware of a capacity to change and make new worlds our very own. The process involves a subtle, lifelong work, the translation of one cultural heritage in terms of another, without loss of self. An attitude of conquest and subjugation prevents bridge building between diverse worlds. An imperial attitude to home fails to understand what home can be and what it means to be conscious, what it means to be human, and what it means to belong to the universe.

Not only are the refugees, immigrants, and migrant professionals with their families involved in this process, but considering the loss and gain of home expected in the average lifetime we all experience this issue in different ways. When we approach the problems of the millions of migrants of our times, we would gain more sympathy for their cause if we didn't divide the world up into the haves and have-nots, those who have homes and those who don't. We are all homeless; we are all searching for a new home. Somewhere in that in-between space of having or not having a home, we are searching for the very ground of our being: Where do we come from? Where are we going? We are all migrants, moving somewhere in that short span of life between birth and death—searching for survival. This involves a process of loss and readaptation, a process that keeps us alive to the ever-changing circumstances of inner and outer environments, a process that sensitizes us to the plight of the less-fortunate, a process that gives us hope for a better future.

CHAPTER 12

A Many-Storied House

The web of our life is of a mingled yarn, good and ill together.[1]
—William Shakespeare

A DREAM OF C. G. JUNG

This book has taken up a very old theme—a theme written, enacted, sung, dreamt, desired, loved, or hated by humankind at different times, in different placcs. Having gained and lost many homes, I have felt compelled to reflect on, understand, and articulate its significance. As each chapter unfolded, I became increasingly aware of home's multiform dimensions. Home expresses itself in preverbal, embodied, and natural instinct as well as the symbolic, conceptual, and linguistic dimensions of culture. Rooted in instinct, humans share similar behavior patterns with animals in the ways they create, love, and protect their territory. In addition, the human home consists of personal and deep attachments to family, school, nation, society, and culture. Home has a spiritual significance.

Home emerges into consciousness at the point of intersection of its horizontal and vertical axes—a midpoint between life and spirit, a space of transition, and an approximation of Jung's description of the Self as a many-storied house. One of Jung's early dreams, evocative of the vertical axis of home, suggests that the human psyche harbors a desire to embrace the entirety of evolution. The dream inspired him to envisage the human personality as a many-storied house, which is still in the process of being built. The top floor would symbolize the conscious personality, but as one descends, one discovers other stories containing relics of an historical consciousness. Already Jung's description of his 1912 dream invokes this kind of experience:

> It is as though we had to describe and explain a building whose upper storey was erected in the nineteenth century, the ground floor dates back to the sixteenth century, and careful examination of the masonry reveals that it was reconstructed from a tower built in the eleventh century. In the cellar we come upon Roman foundations, and under the cellar a choked-up cave with neolithic tools....That would be the picture of our psychic structure. We live on the upper storey and are only aware that the lower storey is slightly old-fashioned. As to what lies beneath the earth's surface, of that we remain totally unconscious.[2]

Whereas this dream views home from an inner, vertical perspective, one must not forget that Jung's development of that building involved a huge amount of work on the outer, horizontal plane, including many personal encounters, intensive research, travel, artistic expression, intricate masonry.

In the concluding pages of this book, I will review themes of the previous chapters, hopefully to grant them shelter in psyche's many-storied house. I shall begin with the ground floor. Here we encounter home as a physical, sensuous, and emotional reality in the intimacy of family relations, helpful or harmful for later development. From the ground floor we discover worlds outside of the parental home. We learn to create homes of our own, as we explore the invisible spaces between self and other. We may find home in a partnership, a family, a creed, a profession, or a social organization, as we build extensions to psyche's many-storied house to embrace the complexity of the world that surrounds us. When we move to the upper floors in search of meaning and spirituality, we may realize that the roots of identity reach down far below the cellar. Pursuing the threads of the self, woven by fate or destiny, we stumble into the lower foundations of the human psyche. We discover that all the levels and extensions of the psyche, all the identities we have created, have been held together by a collective history of which we are scarcely conscious. Our parents and teachers convey to us a set of cultural canons and beliefs that often determine our most fundamental attitudes to life, as we absorb the ideals of prophets, priests, or political leaders. The biblical exile from the Garden of Eden, the search for the Promised Land, the Wanderings of Ulysses—all bear witness to joy or grief over homes gained or lost. The Hebraic "Never forget" is an example of the power of a cultural memory that has bonded a people over thousands of years. Rooted in history, we gain assurance that the home we are building has solid foundations—crucial if we are to add one more story to a house that will survive the vicissitudes of fate. As this book comes to an end, I hope you may appreciate psyche's many-storied house as a symbol of the Self—embracing an indefinable totality, extending beyond the confines of our short life on earth.

EXPLORING THE GROUND FLOOR OF PSYCHE'S MANY-STORIED HOUSE

Why is the search for home so compelling? On the ground floor of psyche's many-storied house, we experience memories of home that bring to consciousness the specific, concrete, and intimate events of a lifetime. They hit us on the sensory level: an image, a smell, a sound, or the taste of a favorite food. These are not just fleeting images, sounds, or tastes, but are embedded in special circumstances that constantly repeated themselves and caused us to grow accustomed to them, thus binding us to our personal, family, and social history. We remember a world that we trusted and in which we felt secure. Christian von Krockow feels we never forget our childhood home because it was a world that remained always the same.[3] Frederick Buechner recalls that there was one childhood home, which would not pass into oblivion.[4] For him, the place and the people of that one home maintained a sense of permanence, a sense that they would keep going on into the future while others came and went. Eva Hoffman describes the lost home of her childhood in Poland.[5] She remembers the hum of the trams in Cracow, and the feeling that home was a world in which everything was unchanging and predictable. She knew that her home in Poland was no paradise, but in exile it would have been, for her, if she had not succeeded in her struggle to find home in the New World. Yet she refers back to those early experiences as expressing the very core of herself—experiences of a whole world that preserved continuity and protected from fragmentation:

> How absurd our childish attachments are, how small and
> without significance. Why did that one, particular willow tree
> arouse in me a sense of beauty almost too acute for pleasure, why
> did I want to throw myself on the grassy hill with an upwelling
> of joy that seemed overwhelming, oceanic, absolute? Because
> they were the first things, the incomparable things, the only
> things. It's by adhering to the contours of a few childhood ob-
> jects that the substance of our selves—the molten force we're
> made of—molds and shapes itself. We are not yet divided.[6]

Memories of home, and homesickness, are by no means innate inti-
mations of a paradise lost. They originate where the horizontal and vertical planes of matter and mind intersect, in experiences of the external
world that were personal but imbued with cultural and symbolic significance. Presumably, at some point these experiences became internalized,
and gained in verticality. They draw our attention to the history of our
deeper self as recorded through the narrative power of memory. Our
whole life seems to be condensed into such moments of feeling at home
with someone or in some place. They are experiences of wholeness,
when our internal feeling of wholeness was matched by an external
world felt as whole.

The need to be at home in the world is certainly influenced by those
early childhood memories that make up the substance of home and
homesickness. In some cases, the natural ability to attach oneself to some
place, person, or thing may have become so impaired that a person is incapable of bonding in any way whatsoever, as is observed in instances of
early abandonment. On the other hand, with the new freedom of our
times, the attachment instinct can manifest in unlimited ways—not just
in attachment to one family, one school, one village, or one church, but to
many different kinds of relationships, schools, professions, dwelling places,
cultures, and religions—so much so that there is hardly enough time to feel
at home in any one of them. Despite these unlimited possibilities, attachment does not develop as a matter of course to anything and everything.
According to Bowlby, attachment is selective. As an inner disposition to
form inner, enduring attachments, it manifests in children as a "clear hier-
archy of preferences…with a number of highly specific features, which
include representational models of the self and attachment figures."[7]

Attachment is a living phenomenon. It is an expression within each
individual of the hunger to belong that is striving for containment, con-

nectedness, and continuity. In deep attachments we may reexperience the disappointments and expectations of earlier relationships, which mirror a history of how we felt or how we wanted to feel. Attachment unleashes archetypal energies, which may attract and engage, or sometimes even repel. It makes people and things come alive with tremendous intensity, and thus gives unique meaning and purpose to a relationship. The energetic force of an archetype might first appear as a personal issue, but on deeper levels we discover that it has been formed over generations, archived in the cellars of psyche's many-storied house.

Attachment to home is permeated with ambivalence and paradox. On the one hand, it may chain us to the past; on the other hand, it motivates us to appropriate new landscapes. In the past, home was primarily embedded in collective traditions; today, many have no alternative but to gain a new appreciation of the older ways through an individual quest. This does not mean we can be open to everything, as advocated by some self-realization groups. Considering the many ideologies available in today's intellectual markets, we hardly have the capacity to integrate any one of them. Christopher Lasch draws attention to levels below the surface of psyche's many-storied house:

> To live for the moment is the prevailing passion—to live for yourself, not for your predecessors or posterity. We are fast losing the sense of historical continuity, the sense of belonging to a succession of generations originating in the past and stretching into the future.[8]

There are few experiences that we can integrate by claiming: "This belongs to me; this is part of my core identity and history." Meaning is like a language that takes a lifetime to learn. This language evolves in the layers of soil from which we have originated, and includes both mother and father tongues. The archetypal energy, images, and associations coming from this depth sensitize us to cultural history, kinship with our surroundings, and fellowship with other human beings. Each individual is a microcosm of evolution and history—a living, evolving interior language. This view approximates to Hans Georg Gadamer's consciousness of effective history (*wirkungsgeschichtliches Bewusstsein*), which involves "the recognition that we are part of a larger effective history that happens to us beyond our willing and doing more than it is guided by our conscious direction."[9] Home manifests as a creative capacity of human consciousness, rooted in historical antecedents. It reveals a symbolic ability to discover identity in new objects and relationships, which partly reflect experiences of older attachments that have since served their purpose.

Living within an evolving, historical consciousness, each person can rely on a foundation to appropriate new material in an authentic way. We do not choose our history, and we can only partially invent identity. Self-realization becomes authentic within an ego-Self axis, within the tension between the conditions of the past, the experiences of the present, and the possibilities of the future. Evolution and history are preserved within the psyche's many-storied house, which can be compared to a storehouse of kinship connections, sustaining us and reminding us that we are part of a larger continuity. Living in the tension between the familiar and the strange, we find ways of appropriating new experiences. Appropriation—implying making something one's own in an authentic way—is not to be understood as an act of possession or as an achievement of the solitary ego, but as an expression of kinship—not assumed, but re-created according to life's changing circumstances. In this process, different people and objects are brought into a relationship of belonging to one another, within a particular historical context.[10]

Here, self-knowledge and knowledge of one's intimate history are essential to contain the energy and potential of human relationships, see through projections, and recognize who we truly are. It has become increasingly evident that it is easier for the adult person to become aware of the significance of these archetypal patterns if he or she has experienced in infancy a holding environment that matched an emerging awareness of self-continuity, which Daniel Stern identifies as one of the four "invariants" of the core self.[11] And it is easier to maintain a sense of containment and continuity (not as a permanent state, but as one of dynamic equilibrium) if one can protect oneself from the shallow influences of a lifestyle that prevents one from distinguishing superficial or pathogenic forms of attachment behavior from those enduring attachments that mirror who one truly feels oneself to be. With this foundation secured, memories of the time you experienced the world as whole become part of your identity and history. Home may be understood as representing the possibility of a return to the core self—a dynamic process grasped through symbolic experiences that evoke hope, security, and continuity so that you can survive those transitional processes to make new landscapes your very own.[12]

The Wider Context of Psyche's Many-Storied House

The stories of the uprooted peoples of our fast-moving times have made home a key issue that compels us to reflect anew on human destiny. Today, we are likely to encounter dramatic tales among those who have suffered loss of home and are continually on the move. Faced with the traumatic predicaments of the homeless, we may begin to question fundamental assumptions that we have hitherto taken for granted. What holds our worlds together, what makes them meaningful, and what constitutes identity? When we are deprived of a home, the search for home and its significance becomes a lifelong quest. Home is not just about a specific place, person, or profession, but the search for home raises fundamental questions: Who am I? Where do I come from? Where am I going? We might create several identities in the course of a lifetime, but do we know the threads that hold them together?

Jung's notion of a self being both transcendent and immanent provides an indispensible answer to such questions. The Self in Jungian psychology is more like an event than a state. It is where we are most intimately ourselves, yet we can only catch sight of it in dreams, fantasies, memories, and deep relationships. Its intention is kinship with the entire universe, a goal that we cannot fully realize, but perhaps anticipate in moments of trial or inspiration, unexpected coincidences, and deeds of love. We never fully understand the Self, we can never fully identify with it, but encountering it in the soul's hunger to belong we can describe it through symbol, metaphor, or narrative. We may discover it as the source of various identities we have created, as the one who maintains equilibrium between them, and as the one who inspires the ego to weave the threads of fate and destiny into new narrative patterns. The Self is a many-storied house, whose origins lie in the mists of antiquity and whose upper levels are still in the process of being built.

As we move out from the ground floor, we discover psyche's many-storied house is situated in a wider context. Not only does it have a vertical axis; its sustenance and horizontal significance depends on other psyches and other homes. Home is not just an inner reality, but is created between people. As we continue to explore the soul's history of attachments, we might one day notice that we don't possess them as objects. Our narrative identity emerges into consciousness in and through relationships with others, whether these others are real people outside or unknown figures within. Many questions will emerge, as one sees without and looks within. It is crucial to understand that identity is not something encapsulated within a person, nor should it be conditioned solely by outer circumstances. The old inner/outer split is only too likely to favor alienation by casting away those unwanted parts of the self onto the stranger through the mechanisms of projection, displacement, or scapegoating. Identity not only has an archetypal core, which Jung understood to be an inner disposition for wholeness, regulating one's mental and emotional life. Identity is a social reality, formed between, rather than within persons.

Home also emerges into consciousness in the reciprocal interaction between the human and nonhuman environment. Why can't we restore and invest living symbolic forms in the objects of our surroundings? Material objects do not have to be reduced to signs devoid of meaning in a world that has become purely functional. Why can't the objects created by the human hand gain once more an excess meaning, creating a world that invites play and imagination? We do not have to be ashamed of myth-creating languages, which may not achieve the clarity of scientific discourse, but can inspire people to create objects of beauty. Inspired by soul images, the objects of the world become open-ended, wombs of inexhaustible possibility, leaving space for imagination and symbolic form. The sounds and symmetries of this unfinished language can be compared to the polymorphous linguistic landscape of a James Joyce, the purposefully incomplete paintings of a Cézanne, the metaphysical voids in a Giacometti sculpture, the daring asymmetry of Frank Gehry's deconstructive aesthetic. With this language, we may see and hear again the mysterious and beautiful intentionality of all natural phenomena, including the human—a vision that now can be enriched with knowledge of its material complexity. We can inspire architects to invest our buildings with metaphysical intention that would include the technical and functional achievements of our times. We can support political, social, and educational institutions that are guided by individuals whose norms and values are not just conditioned by power, production, or profit, but account for the indefinable potentiality in every human to live a symbolic life. The creative imagery that lies dormant in the cellars of psyche's many-storied house invites us to discover the world as an interim realm of multiple meanings. Exploring those in-between spaces, we learn to appreciate the mysterious threads that weave "polis" and "cosmos" into new patterns, threads that anticipate an innovative understanding of citizenship.

Opening the doors and windows of psyche's many-storied house, I have tried to elucidate the sounds and symmetries of belonging to nature, family, community, nation, and culture. As this book draws to an end, I hope more to raise questions than provide answers. So I continue to ask questions to you, dear reader. Can you still live a symbolic life? Do you see those dark regions of your being reflected in the mysteries of nature? Do you still feel gratitude when you behold the golden radiance of the rising and setting sun? Do you still appreciate the soft, gentle light of the moon, shining in the darkness of your night? Have you enjoyed the springtime flowers of your youth and the autumn fruits of your maturity? When you wash yourself in fresh waters, do you feel renewed and ready to start a new day?

Do you still look back on your childhood and remember those special moments when everything seemed to fit together, and you thought they would last forever? Do you still love your parents and siblings? Are you grateful for what they gave you? Or do you still harbor bitter memories? Have you continued to struggle with those dark moments of abandonment, abuse, or betrayal? Have you sought help? Can your soul breathe again, throw off the shackles of the past, and bring to fruition dreams of a world you never had? Have you found new friends, playmates, and teachers?

Have you been satisfied in your adult life? Have you found your true love and created a new home? Have you overcome the pain of rejection? Have you helped your children find their future? Have you served them well? Have you discovered your place in a profession, community, or nation? Has your being blossomed in sharing your life with companions, colleagues, and fellow citizens? Have you seen unwanted parts of yourself in enemies, rivals, or foreigners? Have you built a palace and forgotten those who live in boxes? Or have you chosen to be alone, contemplating the stars, connecting with all that is unseen? Have you been able to share your secrets with others and let them see the shine of the stars in your eyes?

I began this book describing my own home. Home has become an experience, born from a sense of belonging to family of origin, matured through the family I created, devastated in leaving that family, reborn in encounters that helped me find space for those exiled parts of the self that never had been appropriately housed. Home has been a profession. In the work with clients, I have been challenged, humbled, and inspired. Crucial to the work is the support and criticism of colleagues. In 2004, many colleagues in Zürich suffered the loss of their professional home, the venerable C. G. Jung Institute of Zürich. Thanks to the unsparing efforts of several colleagues, a new home, ISAP (International School of Analytical Psychology, Zurich), came into being. My home would never have been possible without others: parents, a sibling, family, wife, children, a mystic, friends, clients, and colleagues. The list is long, and it would also include nature, animals, plants, and objects, and all the events that I have loved, and sometimes hated. As I am aging, I believe I am beginning to gather them all into a vessel to take with me on a journey into unknown territory. By enduring the trials of my personal and professional life, I have added one more story to a house—its origins and future I can only dimly perceive in the penumbra of the dawn and dusk of life.

Home remains a paradox, a word that everyone understands in different ways, depending on one's life story. Seen from a horizontal perspective, home is formed in and through relationships. Identities have emerged from attachments to the diverse homes we have created and interiorized in that space between self and other, between inner and outer reality. The notion and experience of home serves as a containing vessel that preserves a sense of continuity as we find ourselves thrown into a world that can be alien and unpredictable. Home is also about boundaries, the windows and walls of the realms of privacy, which allow one to gain perspective on the world outside. Home, as an expression of the Self, represents the way we hold worlds together, the way we can relate to others, and the way we can protect and care for the living universe.

Seen from a vertical perspective, home reveals a quest for selfhood, which transcends the fleeting experiences of time and embraces a totality not identical with the conscious ego. In the beginning of life, those of us who have had good homes presumed that they would never change. At the end of life, many hope they will visit a home that will last forever. That is an ideal of the spirit, which is continually subject to the seasons and the cyclic patterns of life, death, and rebirth. Most of us gain or lose homes as we proceed through life. Despite loss or gain, something in us seems never to give up the hope that we belong to somebody, some event, or something, as we continue to build psyche's many-storied house. Home has a spiritual significance that is not confined to a particular confession, as witnessed in the transforming influence of Ruggero's olive field, San's three homes, Alara's restoration of an Islamic garden, or my own Christian heritage. Home becomes a conscious reality in those moments when we take in worlds and make them our own—not just as a possession, more as gifts that require respect and gratitude, gifts from a source unknown.

As I was attempting to bring this work to its end, I felt sure that my soul would have some final comment to make. One dream seemed to express that comment more than others.

> I found myself back at the railway station near my childhood home. Beside the station I saw a new house. The back part was made with red brick. My attention was drawn to the front of the house, with large windows. I could see it was constructed from rough-hewn stones of many different colors.

After I awoke, I thought: "O God, I am back in childhood!" I did not want to look at the dream, for fear I would discover that all the work I had done on the manuscript exhibited a massive regression. Some days later, while walking on the beaches of Patmos, a beautiful stone of different colors caught my eye. All at once, the dream flashed across my mind, and I "knew" what it was trying to say. The railway station, built on the seacoast, was my opening to worlds beyond the horizon of my family of origin. The house was my book on home. The brickwork symbolized the thoughts and ideas of others who had influenced me, and contributed to its making. The rough-hewn stones indicated that the work was connected with my identity. Part of it had to encompass personal experiences that I have endured, enjoyed, or suffered throughout my time on earth. Whatever can be said about these experiences, they are not perfect—roughly hewn, but possessing a colorful beauty. They have become an intrinsic part of who I am. I have built a house from the materials of the earth. It is a house that contains, but is also open to the world and to the spirit. Hopefully it can be an object of delight and contemplation, not just for me, but also for all who have crossed its threshold, so that you, dear reader, may appreciate your own home in new and creative ways.

Permissions

"Mise Eire," in *New Collected Poems*, by Eavan Boland, © Eavan Boland 2005, reprinted with permission of Carcanet and W. W. Norton & Company, Inc.

Citizenship in a Global Age: Society, Culture, Politics, by Gerard Delanty, © Gerard Delanty 2000, reprinted with permission of Open University Press.

The Brothers Karamazov, by Fyodor Dostoyevsky, translated by David McDuff, © David McDuff 1993, reprinted with permission of Penguin UK.

"The Haulier's Wife Meets Jesus on the Road Near Moone," by Paul Durcan, in *Life Is a Dream*, published by Harvill Secker, 2009, © Paul Durcan, 2009, reprinted with permission of the author.

Teaching a Stone to Talk: Expeditions and Encounters, by Annie Dillard, reprinted by permission (USA, Canada, etc.) of HarperCollins Publishers. Reprinted (world) with the permission of Russell & Volkening as agents of the author, ©1982 by Annie Dillard.

The Sacred and Profane: The Nature of Religion, by Mircea Eliade, © 1957 by Rowolt Taschenbuch Verlag Gmbh, English translation © 1959 and renewed 1987 by Houghton Mifflin Harcourt Publishing Company. Reprinted with permission of the publisher.

"Thomas," in *The Western Isle, or Great Blasket*, by Robin Flower, ©1996, The Clarendon Press, reprinted with permission of Oxford University Press.

"The Tollund Man," in *Open Ground, Poems 1966-1996*, London: Faber and Faber, Ltd, © Seamus Heaney, reprinted with permission of the author.

"A Great Man in Africa," in *The Independent Review* (Australian Newspaper, 31 October 2002), © Seamus Heaney, reprinted with permission of the author.

The Collected Poems of John Hewitt, by John Hewitt, ed. Frank Ormsby (Blackstaff Press, 1991), reproduced with permission of Blackstaff Press on behalf of the Estate of John Hewitt, © 1928-1986.

Lost in Translation, by Eva Hoffman, © 1989 by Eva Hoffman. Reprinted with permission of Dutton, a division of Penguin Group/(USA) Inc.

Memories, Dreams, Reflections, by C. G. Jung, edited by Aniela Jaffé, translated by Richard and Clare Winston, translation © 1961, 1962, 1963, and

Notes

PART I: HOME: WOMB OF MANY STORIES

1. INTRODUCTION

1. Renos Papadopoulos, *Therapeutic Care for Refugees: No Place Like Home* (London: Karnac, 2007), p. 17.

2. Georg Kreisler, "Ich kann sehr gut ohne Heimat leben," *Tages Anzeiger,* December 5, 2005, http://www.tages anzeiger.ch/service/archaiv/.

3. Robin Flower, *The Western Island, or the Great Blasket* (Oxford: Clarendon, 1973), p. 14.

4. Jhumpa Lahiri, *The Namesake* (London: Harper Perennial, 2004), p. 138.

5. Witold Rybczynski, *Home, A Short History of an Idea* (New York: Penguin, 1986), p. 18.

6. *Ibid.*, p. 48.

7. *Ibid.*, p. 35.

8. *Ibid.,* p. 217.

9. Roger D. Abrahams, "Foreword," in *The Ritual Process: Structure and Anti-Structure*, Victor Turner (New York: Aldin De Gruyter, 1995 [1969]), p. vii.

10. John Hill, "Home—The Making or Breaking of the Heart," in *Intimacy: Venturing the Uncertainties of the Heart*, ed. Isabelle Meier, Stacy Wirth, and John Hill, Jungian Odyssey Series, vol. 1 (New Orleans: Spring Journal Books, 2009), pp. 44-45.

11. Gaston Bachelard, *The Poetics of Space* (Boston: Beacon, 1969 [1958]), pp. 25-26.

12. John O'Donohue, *Eternal Echoes: Exploring our Hunger to Belong* (London: Bantam, 2000), pp. 164-165.

2. MY OWN HOME

1. William Butler Yeats, "Sailing to Byzantium," *Collected Poems* (Basingstoke, UK: Papermac, 1982 [1933]), p. 217.

2. John Hill, "Odysseys and Standing Stones: A Life between Worlds," in Rob-

ert and Janis Henderson, *Living with Jung: Enterviews with Jungian Analysts*, vol. 3 (New Orleans: Spring Journal Books, 2010).

3. Sean O'Faolain, *The Irish* (Harmondsworth, Middlesex: Pelican, 1969 [1947]), p. 53.

4. Maurice Merleau-Ponty, *The Phenomenology of Perception* (London: Routledge and Keegan Paul, 1974 [1962]), pp. 92-96.

5. C. G. Jung, *Psychology and Religion,* vol. 11 of *The Collected Works of C. G. Jung,* trans. R. F. C. Hull (Princeton, NJ: Princeton University Press, 1969 [1938]), § 167.

6. Gebhard Frei, *Beurteilung der Aufzeichnungen von Joa Bolendas*, p. 3, unpublished.

7. Robert Sardello, "The Visions of Joa Bolendas," in *So That You May Be One* (New York: Lindisfarne, 1997), p. 23.

8. Jürgen Moltmann, *The Source of Life: The Holy Spirit and the Theology of Life* (Minneapolis: Fortress, 1997), pp. 33-34.

9. Alwyn Rees and Brinley Rees, *Celtic Heritage: Ancient Tradition in Ireland and Wales* (London: Thames and Hudson, 1961), p. 276.

10. Arthur Schopenhauer, *Philosophical Essays*, trans. T. Bailey Saunders (New York: Cosimo, 2007 [1894]), p. 102.

Part II: Home: Birthplace of Culture

3. Preserving a Cultural Context

1. John Ruskin, *Selections from the Writings of John Ruskin* (London: George Allen, 1894), p. 9.

2. Gerard Delanty, *Citizenship in a Global Age: Society, Culture, Politics* (Buckingham, UK: Open University Press, 2002 [2000]), p. 82.

3. Advertisement in *Der Spiegel,* 20 November 2000.

4. Susanne Langer, *Philosophy in a New Key* (Cambridge, MA: Harvard University Press, 1996 [1942]), pp. 278, 290.

5. Allan Schore, *Affect Regulation* (New York: W. W. Norton, 2003), p. xvi.

6. Maurice Merleau-Ponty, *The Visible and the Invisible* (Evanston, IL: Northwestern University Press, 2000 [1964]), pp. 125, 194, 155.

7. Seamus Heaney, "A Great Man in Africa," in *The Independent Review* (Australian newspaper, 31 October 2002), online at http://www.independent .co.uk/arts-entertainment/films/reviews/aus.

8. David Abram, *The Spell of the Sensuous* (New York: Vintage, 1996), pp. 85-86.

9. Martin Heidegger, *Being and Time,* trans. John Macquarrie and Edward Robinson (New York: Harper & Row, 1962), p. 401.

10. Anthony Stevens, *Evolutionary Psychiatry: A New Beginning* (London/ New York: Routledge, 1996), pp. 15-17.

11. Paul Ricoeur, *The Symbolism of Evil* (Boston: Beacon, 1969), p. 5.

12. *Ibid.,* p. 15.

13. Wole Soyinka, *Myth, Literature and the African World* (Cambridge, UK: Cambridge University Press, Canto Edition, 1990), p. 4.

14. Eva Hoffman, *Lost in Translation: A Life in a New Language* (New York: Penguin, 1990), p. 108.

15. Mircea Eliade, *The Sacred and the Profane: The Nature of Religion* (New York: Harcourt, Brace and World, 1959), p. 20.

16. *Ibid.*, p. 45.

17. *Ibid.*, p. 33.

18. *Ibid.*, p. 29.

19. Jane Morais, *Homesickness: Loss of Sacred Place* (unpublished diploma thesis of the C. G. Jung Institute, Zürich, 1986).

20. Friedrich Nietzsche, *The Birth of Tragedy* (New York: Vintage, 1957), p. 136.

21. Eliade, *The Sacred and the Profane*, p. 57.

22. *Ibid.*, pp. 56-57.

23. Rybczynski, *Home, A Short History of an Idea,* p. 202.

24. Friedrich Nietzsche, *Human, All Too Human* (London: Penguin, 1984 [1878]), p. 6.

25. Clare Cooper Marcus, *The House as a Mirror of Self* (Berkeley, CA: Conari, 1995/1997), p. 8.

26. Rybczynski, *Home, A Short History of an Idea*, p. 210.

27. Alain de Botton, *The Architecture of Happiness* (New York: Vintage International, 2006), p. 62.

28. James Joyce, *Ulysses* (New York: Modern Library, 1992 [1922]), p. 415.

4. TRANSIENT SPACES: BETWEEN THE LANGUAGES OF CONTAINMENT AND REFLECTION

1. John O'Donohue, *Eternal Echoes*, p. xvii.

2. C. G. Jung, "Mind and Earth," in *Civilization in Transition*, vol. 10 of *The Collected Works of C. G. Jung*, trans. R. F. C. Hull (Princeton, NJ: Princeton University Press, 1970 [1931]), §103.

3. Yuichi Kitaguchi, *Über Weibliche Beschneidung* (unpublished symbol paper, C. G. Jung Institute, Zürich, 2001), p. 3.

4. Norbert Elias, *The Civilizing Process* (Oxford: Blackwell, 2000 [1939]), p. 59.

5. Thomas Singer and Samuel Kimbles, eds., *The Cultural Complex* (Hove and New York: Brunner Routledge, 2004), p. 21.

6. Rollo May, *The Cry for Myth* (New York: W. W. Norton, 1991), p. 45.

7. Isaiah Berlin, *The Roots of Romanticism* (Princeton, NJ: Princeton University Press,1999 [1965]), p. 127.

8. *Ibid.*, p. 146.

9. Ernst Cassirer, *The Philosophy of Symbolic Forms*, vol. 3 (New Haven and London: Yale University Press, 1985 [1957]), p. 424.

10. Ernst Cassirer, *Language and Myth* (New York: Dover, 1953 [1946]), p. 33.

11. *Ibid.*, p. 32.

12. Cassirer, *The Philosophy of Symbolic Forms*, vol. 3, p. 284.

13. C. G. Jung, *Psychology and Alchemy,* vol. 12 of *The Collected Works of C. G. Jung,* trans. R. F. C. Hull (Princeton, NJ: Princeton University Press, 1970 [1953]), § 88.

14. Jan Assmann, *Religion and Cultural Memory*, trans. Rodney Livingstone (Stanford, CA: Stanford University Press, 2006), p.17.

15. *Ibid.*, p. 5.

16. Charles Taylor, *The Sources of the Self* (Cambridge, MA: Harvard University Press, 1989), p. 144.

17. *Ibid.*, p. 68.

18. Andy Fisher, *Radical Ecopsychology: Psychology in the Service of Life* (Albany, NY: State University of New York, 2002), p. 130.

19. Swiss National Radio, "Abholzung ist der grösste Klimakiller," from DRS 2, *Kontext*, 17 November 2009, online at http://pod.drs.ch/mp3/kontext/kontext_200911171000_10105999.mps. For written confirmation see also: Julius Ary Mollet, "Educational Investment in Conflict Areas of Indonesia: The Case of West Papua Province," in *International Education Journal* 8/2 (ISSN 1443-1475, Shannon Research Press, 2007, http://iej.com.au), pp. 155-166.

20. David Tacey, *Edge of the Sacred: Jung, Psyche, Earth* (Einsiedeln, Switzerland: Daimon Verlag, 2009), p. 25.

21. Cassirer, *Language and Myth*, p. 99.

22. Ernst Cassirer, *The Philosophy of Symbolic Forms*, vol. 4 (New Haven and London: Yale University Press, 1996), p. 18.

23. Susanne Langer, *Feeling and Form: A Theory of Art* (London: Routledge & Keegan Paul, 1963 [1953]), p. 378.

24. Langer, *Philosophy in a New Key*, p. 286.

25. Cassirer, *The Philosophy of Symbolic Forms*, vol. 4, p. 16.

26. Margaret Wilkinson, *Coming into Mind* (London: Routledge, 2006), p. 46.

27. Walter Ong, *Orality and Literacy: The Technologizing of the Word* (London: Routledge, 1982), pp. 111-112.

28. John Hill, "Changing Images of God: An Anticipatory Appraisal of the Jung/White Encounter," in *Cultures and Identities in Transition: Jungian Perspectives* (London and New York: Routledge, 2010), p. 165.

Part III: Home: Temenos of the Soul's Lineage

5. DEVELOPMENTAL PERSPECTIVES

1. Annie Dillard, "Sojourners," *Between Worlds*, ed. Maggie Goh & Craig Stephenson (Oakville, Ontario: Rubicon, 1989), p. 20.

2. Renos Papadopoulos, *Therapeutic Care for Refugees: No Place Like Home* (London: Karnac, 2007), p. 19.

3. Alice Miller, *The Drama of the Gifted Child* (London: Faber, 1983), pp. 24-37.

4. Kathrin Asper, *The Abandoned Child Within: On Losing and Regaining Self-Worth* (New York: Fromm International Publishing Corporation, 1993), p. 66.

5. John Bowlby, *A Secure Base* (London: Routledge, 1988), p. 27.

6. Anthony Stevens, *Archetype: A Natural History of the Self* (London: Routledge & Keegan Paul, 1982), pp. 11-12.

7. Joseph Lichtenberg, *Psychoanalysis and Infant Research* (Hillsdale, NJ: Analytic Press, 1983), p. 6.

8. Daniel Stern, *The Interpersonal World of the Infant: A View from Psychoanalysis and Developmental Psychology* (New York: Basic Books, 1985), p. 90.

9. Donald Winnicott, *The Maturational Processes and the Facilitating Environment* (London: Hogarth, 1987 [1965]), p. 43.

10. Donald Winnicott, *Playing and Reality* (London: Penguin, 1988 [1971]), pp. 3-5.

11. *Ibid.*, p. 128.

12. Michael Balint, *The Basic Fault* (London & New York: Routledge, 1989 [1968]), p. 67.

13. Ad Vingerhoets, "The Homesickness Concept: Questions and Doubts," in *Psychological Aspects of Geographical Moves: Homesickness and Acculturation Stress*, ed. Miranda A. L. Van Tilburg and Ad Vingerhoets (Tilburg: Tilburg University Press, 1997), p. 5.

14. Allan Schore, *Affect Regulation*, p. xvi.

15. *Ibid.*, p. 13.

16. *Ibid.*, p. xv.

17. Jean Knox, *Archetype, Attachment, Analysis* (Hove and New York: Brunner-Routledge, 2003), p. 139.

18. Margaret Mahler, Fred Pine, and Anni Bergman, *The Psychological Birth of the Human Infant* (London: Maresfield Library, 1985), pp. 109-111.

19. Marshall D. Schechter and Doris Bertocci, "The Meaning of the Search," in *The Psychology of Adoption,* ed. David M. Brodzinsky and Marshall D. Schechter (New York/Oxford: Oxford University Press, 1990), p. 69.

20. James Hillman with Laura Pozzo, *Inter Views* (Dallas: Spring Publications, 1983), p. 129.

21. Grimm, "Mother Holle," No. 24 in *Grimm's Tales for Young and Old*, trans. Ralph Manheim (London: Victor Gollancz, 1979), p. 94.

22. David Tacey, *Edge of the Sacred: Jung, Psyche, Earth* (Einsiedeln, Switzerland: Daimon Verlag, 2009), p. 10.

23. Alice Howell, *The Beejum Book* (Great Barrington, MA: Bell Pond Books, 2002), p. 308.

24. Harold F. Searles, *The Non Human Environment* (New York: International Universities Press, 1979 [1960]), p. 7.

25. Thomas Moore, *The Re-Enchantment of Everyday Life* (New York: Harper Perennial, 1997), p. 49.

26. Mario Erdheim, "Spätadoleszenz und Kultur," in *Phantasie und Realität in der Spätadolezenz* (Opladen: Westdeutscher Verlag, 1993), p. 134, my translation.

27. Edward Said, *Out of Place* (New York: Vintage, 2000), p. 165.

28. Eva Hoffman, *Lost in Translation*, p. 82.

6. Homecoming: A Metaphor in Therapy

1. Rainer Maria Rilke, "The Ninth Elegy," in *Rilke: Selected Poems,* trans. J. B. Lieshman (London: Penguin, 1988 [1968]), pp. 63-64.

2. Allan Schore, *Affect Regulation*, p. xvi.

3. Alfred North Whitehead, *Process and Reality: An Essay in Cosmology* (New York: Harper Torchbooks, 1960 [1929]), p. 133.

4. John A. Vella, *Aristotle, A Guide for the Perplexed* (New York: Continuum, 2008), p. 93.

5. C. G. Jung, *Memories, Dreams, Reflections,* ed. Aniela Jaffé (New York: Vintage, 1963), pp. 33-36.

6. Charles Rycroft, *The Innocence of Dreams* (London: Hogarth, 1991 [1979]), p. 4.

7. *Ibid.,* p. 53.

8. Inge Strauch and Barbara Meier, *In Search of Dreams: Results of Experimental Dream Research* (Albany, NY: State University of New York Press, 1996), p. 164.

9. Daniel Schacter, *Searching for Memory: The Brain, the Mind, and the Past* (New York: Basic Books, 1996), p. 70.

10. *Ibid.,* p. 5.

11. Paul Ricoeur, *Figuring the Sacred: Religion, Narrative and Imagination* (Minneapolis: Fortress, 1995), pp. 308-309.

12. Allan Hobson, *Dreaming: A Very Short Introduction* (Oxford: Oxford University Press, 2002), p. 68.

13. Steph Lawler, *Identity: Sociological Perspectives* (Cambridge: Polity Press, 2008), p. 8; Daniel Stern, *The Interpersonal World of the Infant*, p. 27; Louis Zinkin, "Your Self: Did you find it or did you make it?" *Journal of Analytical Psychology* 53/3 (2008), p. 389.

14. Joseph Lichtenberg, *Psychoanalysis and Infant Research* (Hillsdale, NJ: Analytic Press, 1983), p. 226.

15. Heinrich Racker, *Transference and Countertransference* (London: Karnac, 1988 [1968]), p. 151.

16. Donald Winnicott, *The Maturational Processes and the Facilitating Environment* (London: Hogarth, 1987 [1965]), p. 185.

17. Donald Winnicott, *Playing and Reality* (London: Penguin, 1988 [1971]), p. 126.

18. Cited in Renos Papadopoulos, *Therapeutic Care for Refugees: No Place Like Home* (London: Karnac, 2007), p. 23.

19. Diane Bell, *Daughters of the Dreaming* (Sydney: Allen and Unwin, 1990 [1983]), p. 25.

20. C. G. Jung, "The Psychology of the Transference," in *The Practice of Psychotherapy*, vol. 16 of *The Collected Works of C. G. Jung*, trans. R. F. C. Hull (Princeton, NJ: Princeton University Press, 1966 [1946]), § 445.

21. Fred Plaut, *Analysis Analysed* (London and New York: Routledge, 1993), pp. 25-33.

7. Homes of Fate, Homes of Destiny:
Individuation and the Transcendent Function

1. Thomas Mann, *Joseph and his Brothers* (Harmondsworth, UK: Penguin Modern Classics, 1978 [1933]), p. 281.

2. Fyodor Dostoyevsky, *The Brothers Karamazov* (London: Penguin, 1993 [1880]), p. 265.

3. Oscar Wilde, quoted in Richard Ellmann, *Oscar Wilde* (London: Penguin, 1988), p. 3.

4. Jürgen Moltmann, *The Source of Life: The Holy Spirit and the Theology of Life*, p. 33.

5. Lin Yutang, 1943, quoted in Paul B. Baltes, Max Planck Institute for Human Development, Berlin, book in preparation, p. 50. Google: 2004. http://library.mpib-berlin.mpg.de/ft/pb/PB_Wisdom_2004.pdf.

6. C. G. Jung, *Freud and Psychoanalysis,* vol. 4 of *The Collected Works of C. G. Jung*, trans. R. F. C. Hull (Princeton, NJ: Princeton University Press, 1970 [1909]), § 727.

7. Jolande Jacobi, *Complex, Archetype, Symbol* (Princeton, NJ: Princeton University Press, 1959), pp. 33-34.

8. C. G. Jung, *Symbols of Transformation,* vol. 5 of *The Collected Works of C. G.*

Jung, trans. R. F. C. Hull (Princeton, NJ: Princeton University Press, 1970 [1967]), § 467.

9. Cassirer, *Language and Myth*, p. 33.

10. F. M. Cornford, *From Religion to Philosophy: A Study in the Origins of Western Speculation* (Princeton, NJ: Princeton University Press, 1991 [1912]), p. 261.

11. James Hillman, *The Soul's Code: In Search of Character and Calling* (London: Bantam, 1997), pp. 194-196.

12. Vincent deMoura, *Destiny and Personal Myth* (Zürich: unpublished thesis, C. G. Jung institute, 1995), p. 5.

13. Christopher Bollas, *Forces of Destiny: Psychoanalysis and Human Idiom* (London: Free Association Books, 1989), p. 131.

14. *Ibid.*, p. 32.

15. *Ibid.*, p. 33.

16. Assmann, *Religion and Cultural Memory*, p. 9.

17. John Hill, "Amplification: Unveiling Emergent Patterns of Meaning," in *Jungian Psychoanalysis*, ed. Murray Stein (La Salle and London: Open Court, 2010), forthcoming.

18. C. G. Jung, *Memories, Dreams, Reflections*, p. 48.

19. Deirdre Bair, *Jung: A Biography* (Boston, London: Little, Brown, 2003), pp. 15-18.

20. *Ibid.*, p. 19.

21. Susan Rowland, *Jung: A Feminist Revision* (Cambridge, UK: Polity, 2002), p. 15.

22. Bair, *Jung*, p. 19.

23. *Ibid.*, p. 31.

24. C. G. Jung, *Memories, Dreams, Reflections*, p. 203.

25. *Ibid.*, p. 205.

26. *Ibid.*, pp. 223-237.

27. *Ibid.*, p. 225.

28. Roger Brooke, *Pathways into the Jungian World: Phenomenology and Analytical Psychology* (London and New York: Routledge, 2000), pp. 20-21.

29. C. G. Jung, *Memories, Dreams, Reflections*, p. 269.

30. Brooke, *Pathways into the Jungian World*, p. 14.

31. C. G. Jung, *Memories, Dreams, Reflections*, p. 359.

32. *Ibid.*, p. 291.

33. C. G. Jung, "The Transcendent Function," in *The Structure and Dynamics of the Psyche*, vol. 8 of *The Collected Works of C. G. Jung*, trans. R. F. C. Hull (Princeton, NJ: Princeton University Press, 1969 [1916]), § 131-193.

34. *Ibid.*, Prefatory Note, p. 67.

35. Jung, "The Transcendent Function," *CW* 8, § 170.

36. John Hill, *Transcending the Opposites: A Study in Psychology and Ethics* (unpublished M.A. dissertation, Washington D.C: The Catholic University of America, 1970), pp. 77-78.

37. C. G. Jung, *Memories, Dreams, Reflections*, p. 358.

38. Martin Heidegger, *Poetry, Language, Thought* (New York: Harper & Row, 1971), p. 161.

Part IV: Home: An Odyssey through Many Lands

8. Lost Homes, Lost Nations

1. T. C. McLuhan, *Touch the Earth: A Self-Portrait of Indian Existence* (New York: Pocket Books, 1972), p. 99.

2. Marie-Louise von Franz, *Die Visionen des Niklaus von Flüe* (Zürich: Daimon Verlag, 1980), p. 36.

3. *The Popular Encyclopedia*, vol. 4 (London: Blackie and Son, 1859), p. 738.

4. Johann Heinrich Zedler, *Grosses Universal Lexikon*, Band 12 (Halle & Leipzig: Verlag Johann Heinrich Zedlers, 1735), pp. 1190-1191.

5. Johann Jakob Scheuchzer, "Von dem Heimwehe," in *Seltsamen Naturgeschichten des Schweizer-Lands wochentliche Erzehlung* (1705), quoted by Christian Schmid-Cadalbert, "Die unaussprechliche Begierde nach der Heimat: Als Heimweh noch krank machte," radio interview by Martin Heule, Montagsstudio DRS2, March 2, 1992, my translation.

6. *Ibid.* See also, Johann Jakob Scheuchzer, *Natur-Historie des Schweitzerlandes* (Zürich: In der Bodmerischen Truckerey, 1716), p. 32, my translation.

7. *Ibid.*, p. 12, my translation.

8. Johann Christoph Adelung, *Grammatische Kritisches Wörterbuch der Hochdeutschen Mundart, Band II* (Leipzig: Johann Gottlob Breitkopf & Sohn, 1796), p. 1084.

9. Johann Gottfried Ebel, *Schilderung der Gebirgsvölker der Schweiz* (Leipzig: Wolfischen Buchhandlung, 1798), 416, my translation.

10. *Ibid.*, p. 419, my translation.

11. *Ibid.*, p. 421, my translation.

12. "Ranz des vaches," *The New Grove Dictionary of Music and Musicians*, vol. 20, ed. Stanley Sadie, 2nd ed. (London: Macmillan, 2001 [1878]), p. 826.

13. Ad Vingerhoets, "The Homesickness Concept: Questions and Doubts," p. 6.

14. Fyodor Dostoyevsky, *The Brothers Karamazov* (London: Penguin, 1993 [1880]), p. 371.

15. Alex Haley, *Roots: The Saga of an American Family* (New York: Dell, 1977), p. 82.

16. *Ibid.*, p. 72.

17. Jhumpa Lahiri, *The Namesake*, p. 287.

18. Enrique Yepes, "To Be at Home: Reflections on the Concept of Home in Personal and Collective Transformation," Speech at the Karofski Encore Lecture, at Bowdoin College, 31 August 2001.

19. Miranda A. L. Van Tilburg, "The Psychological Context of Homesickness," in Van Tilburg and Vingerhoets, *Psychological Aspects of Geographical Moves*, pp. 36-37.

20. *Ibid.*, pp. 42-47.

21. Christopher Thurber, "Children's Coping with Homesickness: Phenomenology and Intervention," in Van Tilburg and Vingerhoets, *Psychological Aspects of Geographical Moves*, p. 140.

22. Salman Akhtar, *Immigration and Identity: Turmoil, Treatment, and Transformation* (Lanham, New York and Oxford: Jason Aronson, 2004), pp. 6-7.

23. Elie Wiesel, *Night* (New York: Hill and Wang, 2006 [1960]), p. 110.

24. H. G. Wells, *The Outline of History*, vol. 2 (Garden City, NY: Garden City, 1949), pp. 991-995.

25. Eric Hobsbawm, *Nations and Nationalism since 1780* (Cambridge: Cambridge University Press, 1990), pp. 11-18.

26. Erich Fromm, *The Anatomy of Human Destructiveness* (London: Penguin, 1984), pp. 493-522.

27. William L. Shirer, *The Rise and Fall of the Third Reich* (New York: Simon and Schuster, 1960), p. 932.

28. Delanty, *Citizenship in a Global Age*, p. 92.

29. Adolf Guggenbühl, "Die Nationale Phantasie," in *Gorgo: Zeitschrift für Archetypische Psychologie und Bildhaftes Denken* (Zürich: Schweizer Spiegel Verlag, Raben-Reihe, 1991), p. 10, my translation.

30. Salman Akhtar, *Immigation and Identity*, p. 24.

31. Elena Liotta, *On Soul and Earth: The Psychic Value of Place* (Hove, United Kingdom: Routledge, 2009), p. 15.

32. T. C. McLuhan, "Chief Plenty-Coups' Farewell Address," in *Touch the Earth: A Self-Portrait of Indian Existence* (New York: Pocket Books, 1972), p. 136.

33. Fools Crow, Lakota Nation, www.wikipedia.org/wiki/Frank_Fools_Crow.

34. John Updike, *Rabbit, Run* (London and New York: Penguin, 2006 [1961]), p. 91.

35. *Ibid.*, p. 79.

36. Robert Frost, "Death of a Hired Man," in *Selected Poems of Robert Frost* (New York: Holt, Rinehart and Winston, 1963), p. 25.

37. *Ibid.*, p. 28.

38. Barack Obama, *Dreams from my Father* (New York: Three Rivers Press, 2004 [1995]), p. 45.

39. *Ibid.*, p. 17.

40. *Ibid.*, p. 37.

41. *Ibid.*, p. 25.

42. Salman Rushdie, *Imaginary Homelands: Essays and Criticism 1981-1991* (London: Granta, 1992 [1981]), p. 21.

43. Rilke, "The Ninth Elegy," in *Rilke Selected Poems*, p. 65.

9. IRELAND: CONTEMPLATING A NATION FROM A PLACE OF EXILE

1. Declan Kiberd, *Inventing Ireland* (London: Vintage, 1996), p. 1.

2. C. G. Jung, *Symbols of Transformation*, p. xxiv.

3. Andrew Samuels, *The Political Psyche* (London and New York: Routledge, 1993), p. 332.

4. Eric Hobsbawm, *Nations and Nationalism since 1780*, p. 8.

5. Tom Cross and Clark Slover, *Ancient Irish Tales* (Dublin: Allen Figgis, 1969 [1936]), pp. 508-513.

6. J. Weisweiler, *Heimat und Herrschaft* (Halle: Schriften der Deutschen Gesellschaft für Keltische Studien, 1943), p. 118.

7. Alwyn Rees and Brinley Rees, *The Celtic Heritage* (London: Thames and Hudson, 1961), chaps. 4 and 5.

8. *Ibid.*, pp. 119-128.

9. *Ibid.*, p. 96.

10. Proinsias MacCana, *Celtic Myth* (London and New York: Hamlyn, 1970), p. 120.

11. Proinsias MacCana, "Notes on the Early Irish Concept of Unity," in *The Crane Bag* 2/1–2 (1978), pp. 65-66.

12. Egan O'Rahilly, "Brightness of the Bright," in *The Penguin Book of Irish Verse*, ed. Brendan Kennelly (Harmondsworth, Middlesex: Penguin, 1970), p.72.

13. William Butler Yeats, *Cathleen ni Houlahan*, in *Selected Plays*, ed. Norman Jeffares (London: Pan Books, 1964), p. 245.

14. Patrick Pearse, "I am Ireland," in *The Penguin Book of Irish Verse*, ed. Brenden Kennelly (Harmondsworth, Middlesex: Penguin, 1970), p. 295.

15. Richard Kearney, "Beyond Art and Politics," in *The Crane Bag* 1/1 (1977), p. 12.

16. Sean O'Casey, *The Plough and the Stars* (London: Macmillan, St Martins Press, 1978 [1926]), p. 185.

17. James Joyce, *Ulysses* (New York: Modern Library, 1992 [1914]), p. 595.

18. *Ibid.*, p. 591.

19. James Joyce, *A Portrait of the Artist as a Young Man* (Middlesex, UK: Penguin, 1960 [1916]), p. 247.

20. Richard Kearney, "Faith and Fatherland," in *The Crane Bag* 8/1, p. 55.

21. *Ibid.*, p. 65.

22. *Ibid.*

23. Eavan Boland, "Mise Eire," in *Collected Poems* (Manchester: Carcanet, 1995), p. 102.

24. Sabina Müller, *Through the Mythographer's Eye* (Tübingen: Narr Franke Verlag, 2007), p. 78.

25. Paul Durcan, "The Haulier's Wife Meets Jesus on the Road Near Moone," in *Life is a Dream: 40 Years Reading Poems, 1967-2007* (London: Harvill Secker, 2009 [1985]), p. 117.

26. Müller, *Through the Mythographer's Eye,* p. 49.

27. Seamus Heaney, "The Tolund Man," in *Opened Ground: Poems 1966-1996* (London: Faber and Faber, 1998), p. 65.

28. *Ibid.*, p. 65.

29. John Hewitt, "Ireland," in *The Collected Poems of John Hewitt* (Belfast: Blackstaff, 1992), p. 58.

30. *Ibid.,* pp. 400-416.

31. Thomas Singer and Samuel Kimbles, eds., *The Cultural Complex* (Hove and New York: Brunner Routledge, 2004), p. 21.

Part V: Home: Responsibility in Unsettled Times

10. AT HOME IN A GLOBAL SOCIETY?

1. Edward Said, "Reflections on Exile," in *Reflections on Exile and Other Essays* (Cambridge: Harvard University Press, 2002 [1984]), p. 86.

2. Edward Said, *The Question of Palestine* (New York: Vintage, 1992 [1979]), p. 116.

3. Khalid Koser, *International Migration, A Very Short Introduction* (Oxford: Oxford University Press, 2007), p. 17.

4. UNCR Annual Report shows 412 million people uprooted: http:77www.unhcr.org/4a2fd52412d.html.

5. Richard Sennett, *The Corrosion of Character: The Personal Consequences of Work in the New Capitalism* (New York and London: W. W. Norton, 1998), p. 24.

6. *Ibid.*, p. 31.

7. Susanne Langer, *Philosophy in a New Key*, pp. 291-292.

8. Richard Sennett, *The Craftsman* (London: Penguin, 2008), p. 9.

9. Kiberd, *Inventing Ireland*; Said, *Out of Place*; Lawler, *Identity.*

10. Lawler, *Identity*, p. 8.

11. Andrew Samuels, Bani Shorter, and Fred Plaut, *A Critical Dictionary of Jungian Analysis* (London and New York: Routledge & Kegan Paul, 1986), p. 34.

12. Rosemary Gordon, *Dying and Creating: A Search for Meaning* (London and New York: Karnac, 2000 [1978]), p. 33.

13. Gellert Tamas, *De apatiska: Om makt, myter och manipulation* (Stockholm: Natur & Kultur, 2009). Personal communication from Gunilla Midboe, Sweden.

14. Hans-Joachim Hoffman-Nowotny, *Chancen und Risiken Multikultureller Einwanderungsgesellchaften* (Bern: Conseil suisse de la Science, 1992), pp. 37-38.

15. Anthony Stevens, *Archetype: A Natural History of the Self* (London: Routledge & Kegan Paul, 1982), p. 230.

16. Margaret Little, *Transference Neurosis and Transference Psychosis* (Northvale, NJ: Jason Aronson, 1993), p. 138.

17. Jürgen Habermas, "Glauben und Wissen," Deutschen Buchhandels Preis, *Frankfurter Allgemeine Zeitung,* 15 October 2001. My translation.

18. Leonardo Boff, "Vergesst nicht, Europäerinnen und Europäer," *Tages Anzeiger,* 31 August 1992, http://www.tages anzeiger.ch/service/archaiv/.

19. Wolfgang Giegerich, "Islamic Terrorism," in *Jungian Reflections on September 11*, ed. Luigi Zoja and Donald Williams (Einsiedeln: Daimon Verlag, 2002), p. 76.

20. Richard Sennett, *The Corrosion of Character*, p. 143.

21. Personal communication, Simon Mason, CSS Centre, Zürich.

22. Delanty, *Citizenship in a Global Age*, pp. 2, 19-22.

23. *Ibid.*, pp. 73-78.

24. *Ibid.*, p. 25.

25. *Ibid.*, pp. 139-140.

26. *Ibid.*, p. 142.

27. Edward Said, "The Clash of Ignorance," in *Z Magazine,* September 2001, quoted in Richard Kearney, *Strangers, Gods and Monsters: Interpreting Otherness* (Oxford and New York: Routledge, 2003), p. 262.

28. Richard Kearney, Boston College, College of Arts and Sciences: www.guestbookproject.com. See also: Kearney, *Strangers, Gods and Monsters.*

29. Delanty, *Citizenship in a Global Age,* p. 144.

30. *Ibid.,* p.145.

31. Andrew Samuels, *Politics on the Couch: Citizenship and the Internal Life* (New York: Karnac, 2001), pp. 4-5.

32. Samuels, *The Political Psyche*, p. xi.

33. Bollas, *Forces of Destiny*, pp. 23-25.

34. Turner, *The Ritual Process*, pp. 94-96.

35. *Ibid.*, p. 129.

36. Delanty, *Citizenship in a Global Age,* p. 145.

37. C. G. Jung, "Archetypes of the Collective Unconscious," in vol. 9/1 of *The*

Collected Works of C. G. Jung, trans. R. F. C. Hull (Princeton, NJ: Princeton University Press, 1969 [1954]), § 46.

38. Michael Appleton, Patrick Magee, Joanna Berry, "Facing the Enemy," in *Spring* 81 (2009), p. 217.

39. Julia Kristeva, *Strangers to Ourselves* (New York: Columbia University Press, 1991), p. 191.

11. TRAVERSING CULTURAL BOUNDARIES

1. Jung, *Memories, Dreams, Reflections*, p. 355.

2. Christiane Schlötzer, "Zur Strafe landete der Grossvater im Käfig," *Tages Anzeiger*, 10 March 2006. My translation.

3. Hans-Joachim Hoffman-Nowotny, *Chancen und Risiken Multikultureller Einwanderungsgesellschaften*, my translation, pp. 10-11.

4. Heinz Stefan Herzka, "Die Neue Identität," in Eva Burkard and Geny Russo, *global_kids.ch* (Zürich: Limmat Verlag, 2004), p. 169. My translation.

5. Burkard and Russo, *global_kids.ch*, p. 142. My translation.

6. Arnold van Gennep, *The Rites of Passage* (Chicago: University of Chicago Press, 1975 [1960]), p.11.

7. Peter Loizos, "Misconceiving Refugees?" in Papadopoulos, *Therapeutic Care for Refugees*, p. 51.

8. Anna Duran, "Cross Cultural Problems," lecture at Columbia University, Spring 1981, quoted in Jane Morais, *Homesickness, Loss of Sacred Place*, p. 28.

9. Loizos, "Misconceiving Refugees?" p. 42.

10. Akhtar, *Immigration and Identity*, p. 87.

11. Adolf Guggenbühl, "Die Nationale Phantasie," p. 21.

12. Hoffman-Nowotny, *Chancen und Risiken*, p. 20.

13. C. G. Jung, "Letter to Freud, 11 February 1910," in *The Freud/Jung Letters: The Correspondence between Sigmund Freud and C. G. Jung*, trans. William McGuire (London: Penguin, 1991 [1974]), p. 176.

14. Chris Glenn, "We have to Blame Ourselves—Refugees and the Politics of Systemic Practice," in Papadopoulos, *Therapeutic Care for Refugees*, p. 184.

15. Renos Papadopoulos and Violeta Hulme, "Transient Familiar Others: Uninvited Persons in Psychotherapy with Refugees," in Papadopoulos, *Therapeutic Care for Refugees*, p. 155.

16. Renos Papadopoulos, "Refugees, Home and Trauma," in Papadopoulos, *Therapeutic Care for Refugees*, p. 17.

17. *Ibid.*, p. 15.

18. Akhtar, *Immigration and Identity*, p. 106.

19. Kristeva, *Strangers to Ourselves*, p. 192.

20. Yacob Arsano, *Ethiopia and the Nile: Dilemmas of National and Regional*

Hydropolitics (Zürich: Center of Security Studies, Swiss Federal Institute of Technology, 2004), pp. 3-4.

21. *Ibid.*, p. 5.

12. A MANY-STORIED HOUSE

1. William Shakespeare, *All's Well That Ends Well*, IV: iii.

2. C. G. Jung, "Mind and Earth," in *Civilization in Transition*, vol. 10 of *The Collected Works of C. G. Jung*, trans. R. F. C. Hull (Princeton, NJ: Princeton University Press, 1970 [1931]), § 54.

3. Christian Graf von Krockow, *Heimat* (Munich: DTV, 1992), pp. 8-10.

4. Frederick Buechner, *The Longing for Home: Recollections and Reflections* (San Francisco: HarperSanFrancisco, 1996), p. 11.

5. Hoffman, *Lost in Translation*, pp. 5-6.

6. *Ibid.*, p. 74.

7. John Bowlby, *A Secure Base* (London: Routledge, 1988), pp. 28-29.

8. Christopher Lasch, *The Age of Narcissism: American Life in an Age of Diminishing Expectations* (New York: Warner, 1979), p. 30.

9. Jerald Wallulis, *The Hermeneutics of Life History* (Evanston, IL: Northwestern University Press, 1990), p. 5.

10. *Ibid.*, pp. 15-30.

11. Stern, *The Interpersonal World of the Infant*, pp. 77ff, 100.

12. John Hill, "At Home in the World," *Journal of Analytical Psychology* 14/4 (1996), p. 585.

Index

Lightning Source UK Ltd.
Milton Keynes UK
UKOW06f2111131015

260452UK00011B/203/P